TWO CENTURIES OF NEW MILFORD, CONNECTICUT

One thousand copies of this book have been printed from type and the type distributed.

ROGER SHERMAN
From a painting by Ralph Earle, now the possession of Mr. Charles Atwood White of New Haven

TWO CENTURIES OF
NEW MILFORD
CONNECTICUT

AN ACCOUNT OF THE BI-CENTENNIAL CELEBRATION
OF THE FOUNDING OF THE TOWN HELD JUNE
15, 16, 17 AND 18, 1907, WITH A NUMBER
OF HISTORICAL ARTICLES AND
REMINISCENCES

PREPARED UNDER THE DIRECTION OF THE HISTORICAL
COMMITTEE BY VARIOUS CITIZENS OF NEW MILFORD AND
BY THE EDITORIAL DEPARTMENT OF THE GRAFTON PRESS

JANAWAY PUBLISHING
Santa Maria, California

Notice

In many older books, foxing (or discoloration) occurs and, in some instances, print lightens with wear and age. Reprinted books, such as this, often duplicate these flaws, notwithstanding efforts to reduce or eliminate them. The pages of this reprint have been digitally enhanced and, where possible, the flaws eliminated in order to provide clarity of content and a pleasant reading experience.

Two centuries of New Milford, Connecticut: An account of the bi-centennial celebration of the founding of the town held June 15, 16, 17, and 18, 1907, with a number of historical articles and reminiscences

Copyright © 1907, by The Grafton Press

Originally published:
New York
1907

Reprinted by:

Janaway Publishing, Inc.
732 Kelsey Ct.
Santa Maria, California 93454
(805) 925-1038
www.JanawayGenealogy.com

2016

ISBN: 978-1-59641-382-5

Made in the United States of America

CONTENTS

PART I

THE PAST AND PRESENT

PAGE

INTRODUCTION. By MINOT S. GIDDINGS. 3
    The first settlers of New Milford. Zachariah Ferriss sued for trespass. John Reed and his career. Organizing a township. Organizing a church and calling a minister. The sturdy character of the Fathers. Noted men. Roger Sherman. The splendid heritage of New Milford.

GLIMPSES OF OLD NEW MILFORD HISTORY. By CHARLOTTE BALDWIN BENNETT 8
    The site of New Milford two hundred years ago. The character and career of John Noble. The Boardman well. The first minister and the first meetinghouse. The union of town and church. "Seating and dignifying the meetinghouse." People called to church by a drum. The tithing-man. The Sabbath-day house. Importance of the minister. The first Episcopal services. The Separatists. The Baptists. The Methodists. The Quakers. The different church edifices. Church music. The schools. The singing schools. The early wars. A romance of the Revolution. Illustrious visitors. Social life after the war. Anecdote of Parson Taylor. Transportation. Main street nearly a century ago. Beautifying "The Green." The village doctor. Slavery. The "Underground Railroad." The Civil War. The fire of 1902.

THE OWNERS OF NEW MILFORD. By GEN. HENRY STUART TURRILL 22
    Proprietors to the amount of £1, 4s. Proprietors to the amount of 12s.

TWO HUNDRED YEARS AGO (POEM). By SARAH SANFORD BLACK 24

THE TWO ABIGAILS. By GEN. HENRY STUART TURRILL 26
    Caleb Terrill settles in New Milford. Major Turrill. Marriage of Caleb Terrill and Abigail Bassett in Stratford. Caleb and Abigail visit Caleb's family at Milford. They mount the "Great River." Halt at "the Cove." The home on Second Hill. The wonderful life of Abigail. The career of Abigail Ufford.

Contents

PAGE

NEW MILFORD IN THE WARS. By Gen. Henry
Stuart Turrill 31

Military inactivity of the first fifty years. The first company in New Milford. Arduousness of the train-band service. The Second Company. Tenth Company of Col. David Wooster's Third Regiment of Connecticut Levy. Other Companies. The Eleventh Company of the Fourth Regiment. The Tenth Company of the Second Regiment. Captain Joseph Canfield's Company. The good understanding with the Indians. The most prominent names in military affairs. The first company mentioned in connection with the Revolution. Its history indefinite. Captain Isaac Bostwick's Company. The Nineteenth Regiment of Connecticult Line. Part played in the movements about New York. At Spuyten Duyvil Creek. Tradition of a sergeant's guard under the command of David Buell. The capture of Fort Washington. New Milford men made prisoners of war. Confined in a barn. The Old Sugar House Prison. Prison hardships. Roger Blaisdell's pork barrel. The prison-ship *Dutton*. Arrival of the surviving prisoners in New Milford. Captain Bostwick's company about Philadelphia. The Danbury alarm. Captain Daniel Pendleton's company. The stay-at-homes. The leading families in the Revolution. Engagements in which New Milford men participated. New Milford soldiers refreshed by Deacon Gaylord. New Milford men at Stony Point. The old age of David Buell. Reunions of old soldiers at the home of John Turrill. The adventures of Stephen Turrill.

The Colonial Wars 45

New Milford men in the Colonial Wars as given in the Connecticut Historical Society rolls.

The Revolution 49

Muster roll of a company said to have been raised in New Milford and to have formed a part of Colonel Andrew Ward's Regiment of Connecticut Militia. Roll of Captain Isaac Bostwick's company, Seventh Company, Sixth Regiment, of Connecticut Line. Men who crossed the Delaware with Captain Isaac Bostwick and were in the battles of Trenton and Princeton. Officers and men from New Milford who served in the Sixth Company of the Fourth Regiment of Connecticut Line. New Milford men who served in Lieutenant-Colonel Josiah Starr's Regiment, Connecticut Line. New Milford men who were in Lieutenant-Colonel Samuel Canfield's Regiment of Connecticut Militia at West Point in 1781. New Milford men who served in Connecticut Regiment of Pioneers. New Milford men who served in Col. Moses Hazen's Regiment, Connecticut Militia. New Milford men who served in the Fifth Troop, Shelden's Dragoons. New Milford men who served in Second Regiment, Connecticult Line. Company of forty volunteers. New Milford men in Captain Charles Smith's company. General David Waterbury's State Regiment. Lieutenant John Phelp's Troop of Horse. New Milford men in Sixth Company, Fourth Regiment, Continental Line. New Milford Men in Captain Kimberley's Company, Second Regiment, Contintal Line. New Milford men who served under Lieutenant-Colonel Canfield in the Tryon invasion. New Milford members of the Society of the Cincinnati.

THE WAR OF 1812 53

THE MEXICAN WAR 53

THE CIVIL WAR 54
List of men from New Milford who had service in the Civil War. Recapitulation.

THE SPANISH-AMERICAN WAR 66

RECOLLECTIONS OF OLD NEW MILFORD HOMES.
By ALICE MERWIN BOSTWICK 67
The pre-Revolutionary houses. The great chimney. The good cooking of the early days. The hard work. The quilting bee. The shoemaker. The schoolmaster. Homeless wanderers. Indians from the Reservation. The calls of the parson. Visiting. Sunday. First Day. Thanksgiving. The long winters. Comparison of the life then and now.

UNCHARTERED INSTITUTIONS. By FREDERIC KNAPP 75
The general "sitting-down" place. Levi Knapp's store. Its influence. Remarkable longevity of its habitués.

TRAINING DAYS IN THE 'FORTIES, AS TOLD BY AN OLD BOY. By FREDERIC KNAPP . . . 78
Emerson's appreciation of boys. Training day *the* day of the year. Off for a good time. On the parade-ground. At the tavern. The evolutions of the train-band. The lessons taught.

REMARKABLE LONGEVITY OF NEW MILFORD CITIZENS. By MINOT S. GIDDINGS 81

ACTIVITIES OF NEW MILFORD IN LATER YEARS
Original extent of New Milford. Well watered and fertilized. Beauty of the landscape. Growth of the town. The production of milk and butter. Account of the tobacco industry, by Vincent B. Sterling. The hatting industry. The button industry. The furniture industry. The manufacture of machinery. Paper making. Grist mills and saw mills. The iron industry. Cloth making. Operations in wood and lumber. Quarrying and burning lime rock. The electric light plant. The New Milford Power Company.

viii CONTENTS

    Pottery making. Account of the Bridgeport Wood Finishing Company by George B. Calhoun. Education in New Milford. The early schools. The Housatonic Institute. Adelphi Institute. The Center School. The first kindergarten. The Ingleside School. The New Milford churches. The Memorial Hall and Library. The New Milford newspapers. The New Milford Brass Band. Roger Sherman Hall. The banks. The Agricultural Society. The water supply. The fire department. The fires of New Milford. The fire of 1902. Recovering from the fire of 1902. Recent growth and improvements.

THE STORY OF NEW MILFORD TOLD IN CHRONOLOGICAL EPITOME. By RUSSELL B. NOBLE and MINOT S. GIDDINGS 98

RECORD OF THE PUBLIC SERVICES OF ROGER SHERMAN. By HON. EBENEZER J. HILL . . . 115

PART II
THE BI-CENTENNIAL EXERCISES

INCEPTION AND ORGANIZATION . . . . . .

    Call for a meeting in the New Milford Gazette. The meeting. Preamble and resolution adopted. Further action of the meeting. Meeting of the General Committee of Arrangements on July 6, 1906. Action of this meeting. Officers. Sub-committees. Duties of sub-committees. Assessments. Other sub-committees. Names of the officers and members of the General Committee of Arrangements. The members of the special committees. The work accomplished by the various committees. The Finance Committee. The Executive Committee. The Committee on Exercises. The appointment of district committees. Names of the members of the district committees. The Committee on Refreshments. The Committee on Decorations. The Committee on Publicity. The Committee of Invitation, Reception and Entertainment. The Committee on Religious Observances. The Committee of Public Safety. The Historical Committee. The Loan Exhibit Committee. The Committee on Colonial Features. The Committee on Colonial Reception. The Committee on Vocal Music. Rest houses. Committee of Public Health and Comfort. Marshal's aides. Faithfulness and efficiency of the committees.

THE OPENING EXERCISES 136

    The weather. Beauty of the decorations on "The Green." The Doxology rendered by the chimes of all Saints'. The Invocation. Address of welcome by Charles N. Hall. The flag-raising.

THE LOAN EXHIBITION 140
    Richness of the collection. Source of joy to the aged and a means of instruction for the young. An exemplification of public spirit. Possibility of a permanent museum. A complete list of the exhibits.

THE OLD HOME GATHERING 170
    Address of welcome by W. Frank Kinney. The exercises. Poem by Mary Murdoch Mason. Cablegram from Frank Hine. Letter from Henry S. Mygatt.

OUR FOREFATHERS (POEM). By CHARLES N. HALL 175

THE SUNDAY EXERCISES 176
    Preaching appropriate to the occasion. Sermon of Rev. Frank A. Johnson in the First Congregational Church. Hymn by Charlotte Baldwin Bennett. Sermon by Rev. Samuel Hart, D. D., in St. John's Episcopal Church. Sermon by Rev. S. D. Woods in the Baptist Church. Sermon by Rev. H. K. Smith in the Methodist Episcopal Church. Sermon by Rev. Orville Van Keuren in the Gaylordsville Methodist Episcopal Church. Sermon by Rev. E. Z. Ellis in the Advent Christian Church. Sermon by Father Ryan in the Catholic Church. The Union meeting. Address by Rev. Frederick A. Wright of New York. The evening services. The services at All Saints' Memorial Church. Sermon by Rev. Charles J. Ryder, D. D., of New York in the First Congregational Church. Sermon by Rev. George S. Bennitt, D. D., in St. John's Church.

THE AUTOMOBILE PARADE 227
    A bold experiment. Unqualified success. The owners of the cars. The prize winners. The decorations of the various cars.

THE HISTORICAL MEETING 228
    Greeting by Frederic M. Williams. Address by Dr. Samupel Hart. Introduction of Chief Justice Baldwin by Mr. Williams. Address on "Roger Sherman" by Chief Justice Baldwin. Introduction of Hon. Daniel Davenport. Mr. Davenport's address.

THE COLONIAL RECEPTION 275
    The arrival of Governor Woodruff. The dinner at Ingleside School. Arrival of the gubernatorial party at Roger Sherman Hall. List of persons who assisted in receiving. The ordering of the reception. Brilliancy of the spectacle. The dancing. Governor Woodruff entertained by various organizations.

Contents

GOVERNOR'S DAY **277**
    Temporary population of New Milford. The weather. The Civic and Military Parade. Formation of Parade. Its distinguishing and memorable features. The school floats. The Colonial floats. The industrial floats. The review. The last formal exercises on "The Green." Introduction of Rev. Timothy J. Lee by Charles M. Beach. Remarks of Mr. Lee. Introduction of Governor Woodruff. Address of Governor Woodruff. Presentation of Rev. Watson L. Phillips, D. D. Eulogy of the Foot Guard by Dr. Phillips. Presentation of Hon. E. J. Hill. Address of Congressman Hill. Remarks by Rev. Marmaduke Hare. Concluding remarks by Mr. Beach. The fireworks.

THE AFTERMATH **295**
    Retrospect in the New Milford *Gazette*. Letter from Governor Woodruff to Charles M. Beach. Letter from J. Moss Ives to H. Le Roy Randall.

ILLUSTRATIONS

Roger Sherman; reproduced from a painting . . *Frontispiece*

                                                            FACING PAGE

Minot S. Giddings; Dr. George H. Wright; the Knapp Residence 4
Elijah Boardman 6
Congregational Church, with Residences of Rev. Nathaniel Taylor and Nathaniel Taylor, Jr. 14
Jehiel Williams, M. D. 18
Sally Northrop; David Curtis Sanford; Henry Seymour Sanford; William Dimon Black 20
The First Well in the Town of New Milford 24
Falls Bridge and the Gorge 28
Henry Stuart Turrill 44
Charles D. Blinn 54
Levi Sydney Knapp 74
Alanson N. Canfield 76
William J. Starr 80
New Milford Hat Company 84
Honorable Isaac Baldwin Bristol 86
United Bank Building 88
Manufacturing Plant of the Bridgeport Wood Finishing Company 90
Views of Ingleside School, Post-graduate Department; Ingleside Bungalow; Foundation House 92
Andrew B. Mygatt 94
New Milford after the Fire 96
Captain Garry Brooks 102
Rev. Noah Porter, D. D., LL. D. 110
John Prime Treadwell 112
Henry S. Mygatt 120
Seymour S. Green; Stephen C. Beach; Andrew G. Barnes; Francis E. Baldwin 124
H. Leroy Randall; W. F. Kinney; Frederick E. Starr; Charles P. Bentley 128

xii   ILLUSTRATIONS

	FACING PAGE
Edwin G. Clemence; Miss Adaline L. Buck; Charles J. Ryder, D. D.; Henry Donnelly	132
Charles N. Hall; Charles M. Beach	136
Roger Sherman Hall and Church Street	170
Some New Milford Churches. Methodist Episcopal; Baptist, Northville; Methodist, Gaylordsville; Saint Francis Xavier	176
Saint John's Church	182
Advent Christian Church	196
New Milford Pastors. Rev. Frank B. Draper; Rev. Timothy J. Lee; Rev. Harris K. Smith; Rev. Marmaduke Hare; Rev. Frank A. Johnson; Rev. John F. Plumb; Rev. Father John J. Burke; Rev. Solomon D. Woods; Rev. Stephen Heacock	202
Memorial Building and Public Library; All Saints' Memorial Church	208
Hon. Simeon E. Baldwin	232
Egbert Marsh; Hon. Daniel Davenport	254
Governor Woodruff, Staff and Guard, in front of Roger Sherman Hall	276
Samuel R. Hill; Samuel Randolph Hill, Jr.	278
Main Street from the North	280
Main Street from the South	282
Honorable Rollin S. Woodruff	286

PART I
THE PAST AND PRESENT

INTRODUCTION

Two hundred years ago, in the summer of 1707, the pioneer John Noble, with his little daughter, made his way through the wilderness from Westfield, Mass., and set up his rude cabin in the beautiful valley of Weantinock, on the west side of " Stratford " River, under the shadow of Fort Hill, near neighbor to the Indians, with whom he became very friendly. He trusted their friendship so much that he left his daughter in their care while he went on a journey, following the Indian trail through the wilderness to Albany, to pilot some gentlemen; and, on his return, he found her well taken care of.

He subsequently built a log house on the east side of the river on land now occupied by the residence of Levi P. Giddings.

The next year his son, John Noble, Jr., came and made a settlement, and, before 1712, twelve families had settled here on sites purchased by the Milford Company from the Indians, the purchases having been ratified by the Colonial Legislature; but, strange to say, only two of the twelve, Samuel Prindle and Isaiah Bartlett, came from Milford town.

Some thirty years previous, Henry Tomlinson and others of Stratford, Conn., had purchased from the Indians who assumed to be owners, this tract of land, and Mr. John Read, joint owner, representing them, came and laid claim to it.

It is said that Zachariah Ferriss, a brother-in-law of Mr. Read, came here in 1706, before any other white man, and plowed a piece of land where Roger Sherman Hall now stands, in order to claim title to the land under the deed of the Stratford Company.

He was sued for trespass by the Milford Company, but won his suit, Mr. John Read being his counsel.

Mr. Read built a house on or near the site of the Knapp residence, in which he lived, meanwhile prosecuting his claim to the title of the land. He obtained a verdict in his favor fifteen times, but the sixteenth time the General Court ruled against him; and he, being discouraged, soon after removed to Lonetown, now Redding, named for him.

The Colonial Government soon set off to him a large tract of land in what is now the town of Kent, of which the Scaghticoke Indians long after held possession, Mr. Read having exchanged it for territory in the town of Redding.

Mr. John Read was a notable man. He was well educated in theology and in the law, being a graduate of Harvard College, and is said to have preached the first sermon in this place. He was under thirty years of age when he came here. He married a daughter of Major John Talcott, was held in high esteem by the Governor of the Colony, and was appointed by him to many important positions. He held the office of Queen's Counsel under the reign of Queen Anne. His son, widely known as Colonel John Read, was for many years very prominent in the Colony.

Other settlers came through the wilderness and erected their rude houses. The next thing these pioneers and pilgrims did was to petition the Assembly for the power and privileges of a township, which were granted, conferring authority relating to ecclesiastical matters. They then formed themselves into a church, and called a minister to settle over them.

"What sought they thus afar?
Bright jewels of the mine?
The wealth of seas, the spoils of war?
They sought a Faith's pure shrine.

"Ay, call it holy ground,
The soil where first they trod.
They left unstained what there they found,
Freedom to worship God."

They called Mr. Daniel Boardman to be their minister, and built the meeting-house and the schoolhouse, for these two institutions went hand in hand throughout New England, and formed the characters of their descendants.

These early settlers of our town were busy men. They had

MINOT S. GIDDINGS
Chairman Historical Committee

DR. GEORGE H. WRIGHT
Chairman Loan Committee

THE KNAPP RESIDENCE

hard work to perform in those early days to subdue the wilderness, to plant and cultivate the corn and the rye for their sustenance, to raise the flax and the wool which the womenfolk made into garments. Mechanics, artificers, and wheelwrights were at a premium. The village blacksmith was a most important and necessary person, and concessions were made and land given to induce blacksmiths to settle in the community.

Small manufactories were soon established on every considerable stream. The grist mill, the saw mill, the flax mill—these were important institutions. The spinning wheel was in every house, and the loom was set up in every neighborhood. It remained for our day to develop the immense manufactories situated near the large marts. Those were days that developed brawn and brain—two hundred years ago.

What were the deeds our fathers performed in those strenuous times? They have told us but little; a few things were recorded in the town books of record. They were too busy making history to expend much time in writing it. They cleared and fenced the fields; they built the town and the village.

They did not pretend to great academic learning, but they had good common sense which served them well. They went out to drive off the French and Indians who harried their borders in their peculiar savage way. They rallied to defend their liberties in the great War of the Revolution, for which they poured out their blood and treasure, more than two hundred and twelve from the town serving in that war.

Referring to the founders of this country, a noted orator said, "How little did these rulers of the Old World—James the First seeking to strangle the liberties of England, or Richelieu laying his plans to build up a kingly despotism—realize that a little group of English yeomen were founding a colony in a Western wilderness, from whose vigorous loins would spring a mighty nation to dominate the world when the Stuart and the Bourbon were alike forgotten!"

Of these Puritans and their English brethren, King James had scornfully said, "I will make them conform, or I will harry them out of the land." He did indeed drive these Pilgrim Fathers from his land; but within five generations thereafter their descendants had harried the English Government from these shores, and, within another five generations, had compelled not only England, but the whole world as well, to conform to America's principles of free government, to America's ideas, to America's commercial predominance.

Those early days of New Milford produced some noted men, whose lives and example did much to mould the characters of the inhabitants. The names of Boardman, Taylor, Noble, Gaylord, Bostwick, Canfield, Baldwin, Griswold, Sherman, Sanford, Mygatt, Marsh, Hine, Turrill, and others of the same stamp will be recalled as those of leaders in the affairs of the town and the church.

The greatest and the most celebrated man that ever honored the town with his citizenship was Roger Sherman. He came from Newton, Mass., in 1743, at the age of twenty-two years, and was active and influential in affairs of the town and church; but the town could not retain him long. Of him Edward Everett Hale said: "They say dear Roger Sherman was a shoemaker. I do not know, but I do know that every central suggestion in the American Constitution, the wisest work of men's hands, that was struck off in so short a time, is the suggestion of this shoemaker, Roger Sherman."

It was said that Roger Sherman was placed on every important committee while in Congress, and that no law, or part of a law, that he favored failed to be enacted. John Adams said that Chief Justice Ellsworth told him that he made Roger Sherman his model in youth.

The Fathers of New Milford wrought wisely and well in establishing the religious and civic institutions. They built well the town and wide the streets, and their descendants have enlarged and improved so much that this little village has the name far and wide of being one of the most beautiful spots in New England.

Remembering these hardy pioneers, their devotion to righteousness, their perseverance amid discouragements, and their

many virtues, we all—the loyal sons and daughters of New Milford, those who went forth to make homes for themselves elsewhere and have now returned hither, and the strangers from foreign shores who have settled here—join together this beautiful month of June to celebrate the founding of the town, two hundred years ago.

MINOT S. GIDDINGS.

GLIMPSES OF OLD NEW MILFORD HISTORY

Contributed by Charlotte Baldwin Bennett

FEW contrasts could be more striking than our beautiful village of to-day against the background of the place John Noble, the first white settler, found two hundred years ago. An unbroken wilderness met his eye, save for the Indian settlement across the river on Fort Hill, where the smoke, curling from many wigwams, marked the homes of over two hundred warriors with their families.

Even four years later, when the white man's plantation included twelve settlers and about seventy souls, we find it a rather dismal picture. An irregular cart path, winding in and out among stumps of newly cut trees, formed the Main Street. A narrow road led from the north end of this street to the river, then followed the river bank a mile north to the rapids, the general crossing place. The first bridge over the Housatonic was built at New Milford, but not until 1737.

John Noble's house, the first in the town, stood on the site of Mr. Levi P. Giddings' present residence. At the time it was built, it was the last house this side of Albany, and fourteen miles from any white man's dwelling. The original "Town Plot" was on Aspetuck Hill, our forefathers evidently being impressed even then with the beauty and healthfulness of the hilltops. What is now Park Lane was also in the first century of the town a more populous neighborhood than the one in our village. But the valley offered more shelter and protection in the rigorous winters, and doubtless the toilsome life of the pioneer made the hill-climbing a heavy burden; so the valley triumphed at last, and claimed the larger population

In 1712 the "New Milford Plantation" became a town, the inhabitants having petitioned the General Court to that end In this year, also, "Mr. Daniel Bordman was called to preach ye gospel at New Milford." Previous to this, except for occasional preaching here, the people had been obliged to go to Woodbury or Derby for church services. John Noble became a member of the Woodbury Church in these first years. When we recall what was meant by that long journey of twenty-eight miles through the wilderness, in which the narrow Indian trail was the only path, we bow in reverence before the faith and sturdy manhood that laid a sure foundation for the blessings that have come down to us. John Noble was a tower of strength to the little community during his brief life here.

He was evidently a modest man, who did not exalt his own deeds; but we may read between the lines a story of noble service and heroic courage. He fortified his house as a refuge for the people in times of danger from hostile Indians. He was the first town clerk elected by the town, and a surveyor of lands. When he died, in 1714, there must have been sincere mourning in the little community. He was the first adult person to be buried in the little graveyard. All honor to John Noble, our first citizen!

The first sermon preached here was by John Read, who had studied for the ministry, and who resided here from 1708 to 1711. His house, where Ingleside School now stands, was used, for several years after he left, as a meeting-house.

In 1713 the town voted to pay the expense of a minister; also to lay out a pastor's lot, and to dig and stone up a well for Mr. Boardman, if he became a settled minister. This recalls one of the first necessities of the new community—pure water. Strangely enough, this well is the only vestige now remaining of that earliest settlement. It is on the lawn of Mrs. W. D. Black's residence.

The town, meantime, allowed five shillings and sixpence a week for the minister's board. His salary was to be paid one-third in grain and two-thirds in labor, linen, or pork. This gives a pitiful glimpse of the slender resources of the people, but we remember with pride that there is no record of the church here ever receiving aid from any outside source. In 1716 the church was organized, and, on November 21 of that year Mr. Boardman was ordained. The first meeting-house was commenced in 1718, but was not open for worship till 1720, and was then quite unfinished, the floor not being laid till 1723. It stood on the highway on Aspetuck Hill, a little north of the Knapp house.

Until 1745 the Congregational Church was the only one in the town, and every person was taxed for its support.

There was no Ecclesiastical Society till after 1750. The town was the Society, and provided for all expenses of public worship. It has been remarked of these early New England towns that " one might almost say that the church had selectmen and the town had deacons, so closely were the two united." From 1750 to 1790 those who aided in supporting other churches were relieved of the tax for the support of this one, and, from 1800, only members of this society were taxed for its benefit. The renting of pews began in 1854.

Before this, committees had " dignified the meeting-house." All persons of the age of fifty-six years and upwards were assigned to the first rank of seats, and all others were seated " according to the taxes they have paid toward building said Meeting-House." We are told that in the early days of the colony the " dignifying the meeting-house," that is, the seating people by certain grades of wealth, was unknown. It became common only after slavery was an established institution.

The people were for many years called to church by the beat of the drum. An appropriation was made for this when the church was organized, and, annually, the town appointed a person to beat the drum, and voted to pay him for the same.

This method may have been employed to remind the people that they belonged to the church militant. Certain it is, that the marching with measured tread to the martial sound was a fitting prelude to the grim and lengthy service awaiting them.

The meeting-houses were not heated till 1823, when two box stoves were put in the second meeting-house. No wonder our forbears developed strong and decided traits of character under such Spartan training!

The tithing man was an important factor in church work. As early as 1729 it was voted in town meeting " that James Hine have oversight of the female sex during exercises on the Sabbath." We are left in painful doubt as to whether the " female sex " needed more oversight than the men. But a later vote recorded relieves our minds, for " two men were appointed to oversee the youth (males), and one for the female sex," during service. So we may conclude our foremothers needed only *half* as much watching as the fathers and sons.

The law requiring the appointment of tithing men was passed in 1721. Earlier, it was customary in New England to appoint an officer to keep people from sleeping during the delivery of the sermon.

In 1745 the town voted that " any farmers, inhabitants, have leave to build a small house to repair to on the Sabbath Day, on the common land, provided the public is not damnified thereby." This building was " north of the meeting-house on the side of the hill." After the second church was built, in 1754, on " The Green," opposite the spot now occupied by Mrs. Henry Bostwick's residence, the Sabbath Day house was built on the site of Mr. James Orton's present home on Bridge Street. These " Sabba' Day houses," as they were called, were an important institution in the Sunday life of those old days.

Here those living at a distance stored loads of wood and barrels of cider, refilled their foot stoves and rested between services.

This little intermission, in which the settlers took breath after the two hours' sermon of the morning, and gained strength for the ninthlies and tenthlies of the afternoon, is a pleasant picture in the midst of the rigorous Sabbath. We like to think there was a little relaxation for the housewives in exchanging their doughnuts and Indian bread, and comparing receipts for the same, and, *perhaps*, indulging in a little week-day gossip, when James Hine was not at hand to " oversee."

The most notable figure in the town was always the minister.

He was *the* person, the "parson." Even the "divinity that doth hedge a king" commands hardly more reverence than that which was paid to the early New England minister. The very children were taught to make obeisance to him as he passed along the street. An early rule of the New England churches read as follows: "If any person or persons shall be guilty of speaking against the minister, in any shape, form or manner, or of speaking against his preaching, said person or persons shall be punished by fine, whipping or banishment, or cutting off of ears."

Mr. Orcutt, in his "History of New Milford," says that Episcopal Church services were held here as early as 1742, perhaps earlier, Rev. Mr. Beach of Newtown conducting occasional meetings. The first resident Episcopal clergyman was Rev. Solomon Palmer, who came in 1754. The second Episcopal church stood on the lower end of "The Green." It was consecrated in 1793, though begun many years before.

The Separatists, or Strict Congregationalists, as they were called, built a house of worship in 1761, near the entrance to the present cemetery. They disbanded in 1812. The Baptists had a small church in "The Neck," now Bridgewater, in 1788, but soon moved away. The Baptist Church in Northville was formed in 1814. In 1825 the Methodist Church was established at Gaylordsville. The Methodist Church in this village was erected in 1849.

The Quakers were early in the field, their first meeting-house in the south part of the town being built about 1742.

The present Congregational Church edifice was built in 1833. In 1883 the beautiful new St. John's Episcopal Church, which is one of the chief ornaments of our Main Street, was completed. All Saints' Memorial Episcopal Church was organized in 1880. The beautiful church building was erected later on Aspetuck Hill, in memory of the late Judge David C. Sanford, by his wife. It was consecrated in 1888. The Church of St. Francis Xavier, Roman Catholic, was built about 1860, and has a large and flourishing congregation. The most recent addition to our list of churches is the Advent Church, which has done an excellent work already in our community. It was built in 1901.

From very ancient times it seems to have been ordained that harmony and discord should go hand in hand in the churches, for no subject was more prolific of disturbance than the singing. In the first days of New Milford the deacons led the singing, standing in front of the pulpit. There seems to have been a difference of opinion as to any change, for, in 1739, a meeting was held " to consider about the singing of God's praises in the congregation," and it was voted " that we should ' half ' the time; that is, to sing one day all the old way, and the next Sabbath all the new way, for the space of one year, and then have a reconsideration of the matter." Samuel Bostwick was chosen chorister for the new way, and " Nathan Botsford second, in case of the other's absence."

The difference continued, for the following year a meeting was called to " agree about the singing in church." It was put to vote that all in favor of singing all together the old way should go to the east end of the meeting-house, and those for the new way to the west end. On being counted, thirty favored the new way, against sixteen for the old. They peaceably voted that the majority should rule.

Eight years later a new trouble arose as to using Dr. Watts' version of the Psalms. It was voted " that Dr. Watts' version be sung the last singing in the afternoon on the Sabbath and at lectures." The next year it was voted to sing from the old version in the morning, and from Dr. Watts' version in the afternoon, for one year, and then altogether from Dr. Watts. Who could imagine Dr. Watts as a dangerous innovation!

Up to this time no reference is found here to any musical instrument but the pitch pipe. The bass viol and the rest of the stringed instruments must have come into use in the church services soon after. How the old fugue tunes, with the parts chasing each other all the way through, must have shaken the rafters and waked all the sleepers, without the help of the tithing man!

This town very early began to uphold morality and order.

In that first century it fined certain persons " for bringing into the town unwholesome inhabitants."

The care with which the town guarded its temporal interests is shown by an early vote, " that a black bonnet, a red woman's cloak, and a worsted gown belonging to Hannah Beeman, deceased, be kept for her daughter till she is of age; if she die under age, the town to have them."

The cause of education went hand in hand with that of religion in those early days. When there were but twenty-five families in the town, a public school was ordered. In town meeting, September, 1721, it was voted that a school be maintained for four months, the town to bear half the charge. The next year a committee was appointed to raise money to hire a schoolmaster three months in winter, and a schoolmistress three months in summer. One of these early schoolmistresses was the little daughter of John Noble, who had come hither with him alone through the wilderness. Deacon Sherman Boardman, son of the Rev. Daniel, mentions going to school to her, and says she was an excellent teacher. The " little red schoolhouse " was preceded by the log schoolhouse, which was soon a frequent landmark through the town. The town was often divided into new districts. In 1782 there were twenty-one school districts. In 1787 a new building for townhouse and schoolhouse together was erected at the north end of the Main Street.

The singing schools were a pleasant feature of early days, and, in a time of few pleasures, afforded a harmless enjoyment. They were usually held in the schoolhouses, but sometimes at a dwelling in the neighborhood. In 1792 Mr. Cyrene Stilson is recorded as beginning a singing school at a private house. There are to-day treasured in many of our homes, brass candlesticks that were kept bright by our grandmothers to carry to the schoolhouse for the evening singing school. They suggest many bits of romance. When the boys were privileged to walk home with the girls, they carried the candlesticks, we hope, and they doubtless lingered on the broad doorstep sometimes, in spite of zero weather.

CONGREGATIONAL CHURCH

HOME OF NATHANIEL TAYLOR, JR.
Gen. LaFayette lodged here for a night during the Revolution

HOME OF REV. NATHANIEL TAYLOR
Count Rochambeau spent a night here during the Revolution

One of the brightest spots in New Milford history is the patriotism the town has shown through all its generations. This sentiment seems to have been a perennial spring in the hearts of the inhabitants, ready to burst out into action whenever a crisis arose.

The long list of soldiers in the wars is proof of this. The War of the Revolution called out a host of brave men from New Milford. Not less patriotic was the minister, Rev. Nathaniel Taylor. He had long before served as chaplain in the French and Indian War, and, in 1779, he remitted his entire salary to alleviate the suffering caused by the war. It is inspiring to read that in this same year the county treasurer at Litchfield received the sum of ninety-four pounds sixteen shillings, by the hand of Col. Samuel Canfield—money contributed by the first Ecclesiastical Society of New Milford, for the relief of the distressed inhabitants of the towns of New Haven, Fairfield, and Norwalk.

The actual conflict came no nearer than Danbury. A large number of our citizens participated in that battle. The sending out of troops, and the mourning in many households for those who did not return, must have kept the war very near to the hearts of all the inhabitants of the town. Furthermore, the presence of three brigades (nearly 5000 men) in camp on Second Hill, for nearly a month in the autumn of 1778, brought the war atmosphere almost to their very doors.

Once during the war Lafayette and Rochambeau were entertained over night here; Rochambeau, at the home of Rev. Nathaniel Taylor, north of the present Congregational Church, and Lafayette, at the house of the son of Rev. Nathaniel, Nathaniel, Jr., south of the church.

There was a pretty romance of the war here also. Major Jones of Virginia, in charge of the commissary stores kept here the summer after the burning of Danbury, fell in love with pretty Tamar Taylor, the minister's daughter. We have the story from Mrs. Helen Carr, the granddaughter of Tamar Taylor, as she heard it from the lips of her grandmother. The Major's affection seems to have been returned, but her parents frowned upon the affair for the sole reason that they could never let their daughter go to that far country—Virginia. The wooer was said to be "a very fine man, who won golden opinions from everyone," the question of distance being the only obstacle to parental consent.

Four years later Major Jones wrote to Daniel Everett of New Milford, his sweetheart's brother-in-law and his near friend, from Yorktown, during the siege, shortly before the surrender of Cornwallis. Even that exciting and arduous time seems not to have made him forget the young lady, for he says: "She is never out of my mind, though it seems Fortune has not been so favorable as to allot us to the possession of each other in this short transitory life, or if she has, parents seem to clash. . . . I wish I had time to write you fully on a subject that floats in my head, the last when I go to bed and the first when I awake, but must omit it till a future opportunity."

After the war was over and the country had become settled, Major Jones, with his body servant, journeyed on horseback from his Virginia home to New Milford; but the journey was in vain, and he went sorrowfully home alone. Pretty Temmie Taylor seems not to have been inconsolable, for she was happily married later to the Hon. Nicholas Masters of this place. Mrs. Carr still cherishes the ring and locket given her grandmother by the earlier lover; and when we touched the ancient tokens, the long years fell away, and we, too, seemed to live in the love story of olden time.

New Milford was on one of the regular post roads from Philadelphia to Boston, and, if the old highways could speak, they might tell many stories of distinguished men who have travelled over them. We read in the letters of John Adams of his going through this town on his way to the Congress in Philadelphia. During the war there was frequent passing through the place of both British and Continental troops.

When the war was over there was still further expression of the patriotic sentiments of the people in a vote "that none of those persons who have voluntarily gone over and joined the enemy, shall be suffered to abide and continue in the town during the present situation of our public affairs." A committee was appointed to carry out these resolutions, with the result that several never came back, and their lands were confiscated by the State.

We learn of much pleasant social life in the peaceful days following the war. There were the "assemblies." An invitation card for one of these functions is for "Friday Evening, July third next, at six o'clock." What would the young people of our day think of that? Another is for a "Quarter Ball, at Mr. G. Booth's Assembly Room, on June 3d at three o'clock, P. M."! In winter there were merry sleighing parties to neighboring towns. Often large companies in twenty or thirty sleighs enjoyed an early supper together, getting safely home before ten o'clock.

Afternoon teas were frequent; not like yours, dear up-to-date woman of to-day, but "tea-drinkings," where the women took their knitting work and spent long afternoons in visiting. Mrs. Nathaniel Taylor had on one occasion such a company. The parson, in his study overhead, was greatly interested in the fragments of conversation that floated up to him. Each woman had some exciting tale of her domestic experiences to relate. One quiet sister, unable to hold her own in the babel of tongues, tried again and again to tell her story, beginning, "My goose———." But each time the quiet voice was drowned, and the story never proceeded further.

When good Parson Taylor was summoned to the tea table he said: "Ladies, I have been so interested in your conversation, I thought it worth preserving. So I wrote it down and will read it to you." Great was the amusement when he read the persistent efforts of their friend to tell the story of "My Goose." After all, human nature is much the same in all generations.

The town enjoyed in the old days quite a reputation for good living, and many were the notable feasts cooked over the great fireplaces and in the huge brick ovens before the days of stoves and ranges. What an amount of seasoned hickory logs went up the chimney in smoke to cook them! Forty cords of wood, the record gives, as one item of the minister's salary for the year.

The means of transportation in early times furnished one of the most serious problems. The Housatonic Railroad was not completed till 1840. Before this, all transportation of produce and merchandise was by wagons to Bridgeport, and thence by sloop to New York. The mail also came in much the same way, being brought here from Bridgeport by a carrier on horseback. Our old friend, the late Colonel Wm. J. Starr, remembered the postman of his childhood days, who announced his arrival by shouting as he rode, "News! News! Some lies and some trues!"

We owe to Colonel Starr a vivid picture of the Main Street of the village nearly a century ago, as he recalled it. It is not an agreeable picture. Pigs were kept in the street, and before almost every house was a long trough, where twice a day they were fed. We can hardly wonder that fevers broke out mysteriously. Geese also roamed at will, and mischievous youths were known to play a practical joke on some unpopular man by penning all the geese in the village into his front porch during the night.

Many of the front yards were adorned with huge woodpiles. A part of the street was a swamp, through which ran a crooked water course that, after a shower, left pools of mud, in which pigs and cattle cooled themselves, for "The Green" was also a cattle pasture. The story is told of a dignified gentleman of the old school, who, dressed in immaculate white on a summer Sunday, was hastening across "The Green" to church, making his way among the puddles, when a large hog, frightened from a pool, ran violently against him. He had an unsought ride on its back across the street, and was deposited in a puddle, in full view of the waiting congregation gathered on the church steps.

In 1838 the open-paved watercourse through "The Green" was constructed and was regarded as a grand improvement.

The Village Improvement Society was organized in 1871,

JEHIEL WILLIAMS, M. D.
An early and beloved physician. B. 1782, d. 1862.

and, a little later, under its auspices, "The Green" was put in its present attractive condition, a covered brick sewer being laid to replace the open-paved watercourse which previously ran through the center of the street. This was accomplished on the initiative, and largely though the instrumentality, of Mr. and Mrs. William D. Black, whose efforts and energies were always directed for the benefit of the village. A large and successful fair to raise money for this purpose was held in a tent on "The Green" in July, 1872, and the residents of Main Street accepted a voluntary assessment of a large amount to perfect the work.

A familiar and welcome sight of long ago was the village doctor on horseback with his saddlebags. He was the friend of everyone, beloved and venerated next to the minister. His store of huge pills and herbs and simples carried healing and comfort to all the countryside. Dr. Jehiel Williams was the last of these old-time doctors in New Milford. He is still remembered by many with reverent tenderness. His kindness knew no bounds, and his hearty laugh carried cheer wherever he went. A cautious man he was. Even his most cherished opinions were always prefaced with "I 'most guess." He was cautious also in his remedies, and the overworked woman of this busy age would hardly accept his cure for nerves and sleeplessness: "Take a hop, put it in a teacup and fill the cup with hot water. Drink it at night and I 'most guess you will feel better." It was whispered that his huge pills were often made of bread, when he felt none were needed.

He rode up and down the hills for a lifetime, charging twenty-five cents for a visit, fifty cents when the journey was long—afterwards sixty-two and a half cents! On one occasion he rode five miles to find that his patient had been already relieved by some housewife's simple remedy. He declined any fee, merely saying, "What I have learned in this cure is worth far more to me than the trouble of coming."

He was friend and helper to three generations, and when, at last, full of years and honors, he went to his well-earned rest, every household of the town mourned his departure.

Slavery existed here, as elsewhere in New England, in the first century of the town. A written advertisement for a runaway slave, offering a reward for his capture, and signed, "Gideon Treat, New Milford, September, 1774," is still in existence. It sounds strange enough to twentieth century ears. Judging from the records, slaves were generally well treated in New Milford, and many owners freed their own negroes long before the days of slavery were over.

A woman is recorded as the first in our town to free a slave. Mary Robburds, in 1757, gave her negro servant Dan his freedom. Partridge Thatcher, a lawyer here, was especially noted for his kindness to his slaves. Judge David S. Boardman wrote concerning him: "He had no children, but a large number of negroes whom he treated with a kindness enough to put to shame the reproaches of all the Abolitionists of New England." And he freed them all during his lifetime.

But the sins of old days in this matter were somewhat atoned for in after years by the zeal of the Abolitionists of New Milford in aiding runaway slaves to reach Canada and freedom. In the later days of slavery in the South there were several stations of the Underground Railroad in this vicinity. Mr. Charles Sabin's house in Lanesville was one, and the house of Mr. Augustine Thayer on Grove Street in this village was another. Mr. Thayer and his good wife devoted their lives to the Abolition cause. They helped many poor slaves on their way, rising from their beds in the night to feed and minister to them, and secreting them till they could be taken under cover of darkness to Deacon Gerardus Roberts' house on Second Hill, from there to Mr. Daniel Platt's in Washington, and so on, by short stages, all the way until the Canadian border was reached.

The spirit and courage of the fathers have descended to the sons through many generations. This has been proved again and again in later years, notably in our Civil War. During all the dark four years from the terrible day when the flag fell at Fort Sumter to the memorable rejoicing over the fall of Richmond, there were not wanting brave sons of this old town

SALLY NORTHROP
Born 1776, died 1870
A resident of New Milford for One Hundred Years

DAVID CURTIS SANFORD
Born 1798, died 1864
A Justice of the Supreme Court of Connecticut

HENRY SEYMOUR SANFORD
Born 1832, died 1901
Son of David C. Sanford; Attorney at the Fairfield and Litchfield County Bars

WILLIAM DIMON BLACK
Born 1836, died 1889
Member of firm of Ball, Black & Co., New York City; for eighteen years a resident of New Milford and active in the devolpment of the town till his death, 1889

to offer their lives, and fathers to give of their substance. The daughters of the town vied with each other in loyal labors for their country, and gave their time with their hearts to loving ministry.

In recent days the courage of our citizens has been "tried as by fire." The great conflagration of May, 1902, swept away the entire business portion of the village; yet the Puritan fathers could not have met disaster more stoically than our brave men of to-day. The cheerful optimism that built "Shanty Town" on "The Green" while the ruins were still smouldering showed that the stout hearts of old New Milford were the same in the *new*, and that noble lives have been its inheritance through all its years.

We smile as we recall the old days and ways, but we bare our heads reverently before those godly men and women whose hardships meant a better way for us. Two hundred years hence others will read *our* record, and smile, perhaps. Will it be as worthy?

THE OWNERS OF NEW MILFORD

NAMES OF THE PROPRIETORS IN THE MILFORD COMPANY, WHO, UNDER A DEED OF DATE OF JUNE, 1703, WERE THE OWNERS OF THE TOWN OF NEW MILFORD

COMPILED AND ARRANGED BY GENERAL HENRY STUART TURRILL [*]

THE following were proprietors to the amount of £1 4s.: Col. Robert Treat, Mr. Thomas Clark, Ensign George Clark, Lieut. Joseph Treat, Ensign Joseph Peck, Jonathan Baldwin, committee; Capt. Samuel Eells, Sergt. Edward Camp, Rev. Mr. Andrews, Thomas Wlech, James Prime, Stephen Miles, Barnabas Baldwin, John Woodruff, Mr. Richard Bryan, Daniel Terrell, Samuel Brisco, Timothy Botsford, Sergt. Daniel Baldwin, Mr. Robert Treat, Deacon Platt, Thomas Clark, Mr. Samuel Clark, Jr., Samuel Buckingham, Thomas Buckingham, John Buckingham, William Wheeler, Nathaniel Farrand, Sr., George Allen, Samuel Camp (mason), John Smith ye 4th, Samuel Clark, Sr., Ephraim Burwell, Joseph Beard, Joseph Camp, Samuel Camp (Lanesend), Nathaniel Farrand, Jr., Thomas Tibbals, Thomas Canfield, John Merwin, Samuel Smith (West end), William Gold, Joseph Wheeler, John Prince, Samuel Camp, (son of Edward Camp), Eleazor Prindle, Lieut. Camp, William Scone, Samuel Baldwin (wheelwright), Lieut. Joseph Platt, Sergt. Miles Merwin, Samuel Sanford, Sr., John Beard, Mr. Samuel Andrews, Sr., George Clark, Sr., Joseph Clarke, Joseph Peck, Jr., John Camp, Sergt. John Smith, Jonathan Law, Jr., John Allen, Hugh Grey, Joseph Ashburn, John Summers, James Fenn, Zachariah Whitman, William Adams, Joseph Rogers, Samuel Stone, Jonathan Baldwin, Jr.; Jesse

[*] Henry Stuart Turrill, Brigadier General United States Army, a native and former resident of New Milford, enlisted in the army, 1863, retired. 1906, died suddenly May 24, 1907, while dictating his reminiscences for this volume.

Lambert, Frederick Prudden, Sergt. Zachariah Baldwin, Benjamin Smith, Sr., John Smith, Jr., John Platt, Josiah Platt, Richard Platt, Samuel Prindle, Sergt. Samuel Beard, Sergt. Samuel Northrope, George Clarke, Jr., Samuel Coley, Samuel Merwin, Lieut. Samuel Burwell, Samuel Miles, James Beard, Samuel Nettleton, Joseph Treat (son of Lieut. Treat), Jeremiah Canfield, Thomas Smith, Nathaniel Baldwin, Jr., Jeremiah Beard, Bethel Lankstaff, Andrew Sanford, Sr., Nath. Sanford, John Merwin, Joseph Tibbals, Billin Baldwin (in right of her father, Sergt. Timothy Baldwin, deceased), and Mr. Samuel Mather.

The following were proprietors to the amount of 12s.: Mr. Robert Plumb, Andrew Sanford, Widow Mary Baldwin, James Baldwin, Nathaniel Baldwin (cooper), Henry Summers, Samuel Smith (water), John Clark, and William Fowler.

TWO HUNDRED YEARS AGO

Contributed by Sarah Sanford Black

Upon this hilltop stood the doughty priest
And bade his minions, men of brawn and bone,
To dig for water ere the frost should come
To lock the land and shroud the hill in snow,
  Two hundred years ago.
And here they labored long and valiantly,
Till far beneath the sod a rill arose
And 'twixt the rocks a stream broke forth
And sparkled in the Autumn evening glow
  Two hundred years ago.

"Thank God for water pure and clear," he cried,
And in the twilight grey the good priest stood
And looking off beyond the valley fair,
To where the same hills which we love and know,
  Two hundred years ago
Seemed to touch Paradise, as now, he called
On God, the wanderers' God, to bless the well
Which was to them that day, the most desired
Of all the gifts which man or beast could know,
  Two hundred years ago.

The years have passed, two hundred years,—and now
We stand beside the well, which was the first
Our village knew,—"The Ancient Boardman Well";
To-day the bucket dips, the waters flow,
  Just as they did
  Two hundred years ago.
We look where purple hilltops touch the sky,
We kneel and thank our God for all the past—

THE FIRST WELL IN THE TOWN OF NEW MILFORD
Dug by Priest Daniel Boardman. The property is now owned by Mrs. William D. Black, and known as " Hickory Hearth "

Two Hundreds Years Ago

They clasped His hand as we do, tho' that day
All that their future held they could not know
   As we know now,—
   Two hundred years ago.

We thank our fathers' God for all His care,
For smiling fields and busy haunts of men,—
For all the gifts of Science and of Art,—
For lives whose deeds His loving guidance show
   Brave as those lives
   Two hundred years ago.
All are from Him, these works of hand and brain
His love has made men wise, has kept men true,
Since first upon this hilltop life began,
And water in the wilderness did flow
   Here at this well
   Two hundred years ago.

THE TWO ABIGAILS

REMINISCENCES OF A TYPICAL NEW MILFORD FAMILY

Contributed by General Henry Stuart Turrill

CALEB TERRILL, eldest son of Daniel and Zorvia (Canfield) Terrell, was born in Milford, Connecticut, December 3, 1717. Nearing his majority, he was given the right of land in New Milford of which his grandfather, Daniel, Sr., was the original proprietor. The first allotment to this right was made April 14, 1729, and consisted of about forty-two acres of land on Second Hill, fronting the old Bostwick place. Here, in the spring of 1738, Caleb built his house, cleared a little part of his land and planted a small garden. Late in the summer he returned to Milford. In September he married, in Stratford, Abigail, daughter of Josiah and Alice (Canfield) Bassett, his first cousin, and, in a few days, returned with his bride to the little home on Second Hill. On this spot he lived until his death, February 29, 1796.

This house was the home of his youngest son, Major Turrill, until his death in 1847. Among my very earliest recollections, is a visit to this old place. It was in 1846. I had just passed my fourth birthday, and spent my first day at school. So I, as the youngest of my name, was taken by my father to pay my respects to the oldest living member of my family. I think that this visit produced one of the most lasting impressions of my childhood. I can recall it now, sixty years after. At that time Major Turrill was seventy-eight years old. The large splint-bottomed chair in which he was seated had four enormous legs, seemingly six inches in diameter at least, the two in front continuing up to support the broad arms on which his hands reposed, the two behind extending far above his head. As he rested his head against the broad splint back, he produced the effect of a grand old gentleman in a rustic frame. Major Turrill was a broad-shouldered man of medium height, very upright even in his seventy-eighth year. He had a large, well-formed head and a strong face of a rather stern cast of countenance, while his hair, which was abundant, was steel gray rather than white. My father presented me to him as the youngest of the race, who had just commenced his life work by his first day at school. He called me to him and, placing a broad hand upon my head, said to my father, "A fine little lad," then turning to me he said, "You must grow up as fine a man as your grandfather, and stand for your country as he stood for it."

The marriage of Caleb and Abigail, descended as they were from some of the most important of the founder families (she, from the Baldwins, Bryans, Bruens, and Schells, he, from the Fitches, Pratts and Uffords, and both, from the Canfields, the Mallorys and the Cranes), was an event of great importance in Stratford and Milford; and, when it was known that Caleb was to take his bride to the new Plantation of the Weantinaug, the interest in the affair was much deepened. The conditions in those days were quite different from what they are at present. There were no parlor cars, nor honking autos to whisk the blushing bride, amid a shower of rice and old shoes, to the seclusion of the city hotel, there to hide her nuptial joys among the unknown multitude. So Caleb and Abigail were married in that pleasant Stratford home, she, surrounded by the friends of her girlhood, who, if the records are to be believed, were about the whole community, and he, supported by his three stalwart brothers and troops of cousins. A few days were passed in all the feasting and gayeties of the times, after which the young couple, surrounded by a band of the Stratford friends, started on their wedding journey. At the ferry across the "Great River," they were bidden farewell on the Stratford bank, only to be received on the Milford shore by an equally enthusiastic band of Milford friends, and to be escorted to Caleb's home in Milford. This was the founder home of Roger, and Caleb was the fourth generation to bring a bride to its shelter. His bride was a namesake of an earlier

Abigail, who, ninety-nine years before, had come with her life mate to the then wilderness of Milford. Now, this second Abigail, this tenderly reared girl of scarce eighteen summers, was starting with her life mate, for another wilderness—the New Milford.

After a short stay at the old Tyrrell home, the wedding journey was resumed, up the "Great River" to the Weantinaug country. The "house plenishing," demanded by the customs of those days, had been furnished by Josiah Bassett, and had been securely packed in a stout boat to be rowed and poled up the river, this being, at that time, the only means of conveying heavy articles to the settlements above. The various animals necessary to farming, although scarce in the New plantations, were plentiful in the older ones; and, since Daniel Terrell was a man of "much substance," as the records say, an abundant supply had been assembled at the usual starting place for the journey up the river to the "Cove," just above Goodyear's Island. On a bright September morning, surrounded by brothers and sisters from both families, and a large company of friends and relatives, the newly-married pair set forth.

The accompanying friends went as far as the first "nooning," somewhere below Derby. There, the last farewells were said, and Caleb, with his sweet girl wife on the pillion behind him, journeyed to their future home. They moved up the river, camping at night in some quiet nook, their boat, with their provisions and camp equipment, securely fastened to the river's bank. The bright camp fires flashed out from under the dense foliage of the grand old primeval forests that lined the banks of the Great River, while this pair of children strolled in the deepening gloom, whispering their love, their plans and their hopes of happiness in their home in the wilderness. For four days they thus leisurely journeyed towards the cot on Second Hill, reaching the Cove about noon of the fifth day.

By the mouth of the little brook that falls into the Cove, just at the foot of "Lovers' Leap," they made their last camp, while their boat was being unloaded and a more permanent camp

FALLS BRIDGE AND THE GORGE

established, for it would be several days before their belongings could be conveyed to their home. As the sun was sinking toward the cover of Green Pond and Candlewood Mountains, Caleb led his bride up the winding trail that mounts the southern face of the grand old cliffs of Falls Mountain to Waramaug's Grave; and, from that sightly place, she had her first view of the beautiful Weantinaug Valley. Waramaug's grave has ever been held an almost sacred spot by the descendants of Caleb and Abigail. In my early youth, on just such another September afternoon, I was taken by my father up this winding trail, and sitting on the grass by the side of those honored stones, was told the tale I have been relating, as each succeeding generation of the name had been told it before me.

The wedding journey ended in that rough little home on Second Hill. There, the pair lived for fifty-eight years in happy wedlock; there, they reared a family of fourteen children (eleven sons and three daughters) of whom all came to manhood and womanhood; and, thence, in 1796, at nearly four score years, Caleb went to his eternal rest. Abigail survived him more than twenty years, in the full possession of all her faculties, and, at the extreme age of ninety-seven years, seven months, and eleven days, was laid beside the husband of her youth and the loving companion of so many years.

A wonderful life was that of grandmother Abigail. She lived through four French and Indian wars, and two wars with England. She saw one son go to the last French war and return from the decisive battle on the Heights of Abraham. She saw six sons go to the Revolution, and, having faithfully performed their part in their country's struggle—at the siege of Boston, in the battle of Long Island and White Plains, in the crossing of the Delaware and at Valley Forge with Washington, in the battles of Trenton, Saratoga, Princeton, Monmouth, and Germantown—return victorious and unscathed. She also saw Stephen and Isaac return from the successful and conclusive struggle at Yorktown. Finally she saw four of her grandsons return from the second contest with England.

It would be hard to find in American history two more remarkable women than the two Abigails of the Tyrrell family. The first, Abigail Ufford, leaving a happy English home in Essex, braving the trials and privations of the American voyage of 1632, lived through the horrors of the Pequot War, and went with her young husband to found a primitive home in Milford. She stood among that company, which, under the umbrageous trees of Peter Prudden's home lot, listened to the stately Ansantawa, as, plucking a branch from a tree and gathering a grassy clod from the earth, sticking the branch in the clod and sprinkling it with water from the Milford River, he waved it in the air, declaring that he " gave to them forever, the earth with all thereon, the air, and the waters above and below." In this home, thus acquired, she lived for fifty-five years, rearing eleven children; saw her sons go to King Philip's War; and saw them when they had reached man's estate, start off with their loving helpmates, as their father had done before them, to found other homes—in Southold, in Newark, in Stratford, and in Woodbury. Ninety-nine years after, comes into that Milford home the second Abigail, to venture forth in her turn, like the first Abigail, into the wilderness.

NEW MILFORD IN THE WARS

By General Henry Stuart Turrill

For the first fifty years from its settlement by John Noble, the town of New Milford had very little concern in the military affairs of the colonies. The Colony of Connecticut furnished soldiers in the war of 1711 and in 1713; and, in 1721, occurred a great outpouring of Connecticut colonists for foreign service. In 1745 a call came to Connecticut from the sister colonies for large numbers of troops for service outside her borders, and, again, in 1755. In response to these calls, New Milford seems not to have sent any men. The defense of their own town and of its outlying districts was about all the colonists of New Milford undertook in a military way, this being sufficiently strenuous to engage their entire attention.

We are inclined, in these later days, to smile at the train-band of the ancient times, but the train-band service of our Colonial fathers was one of exceeding severity.

The first company in New Milford was organized in 1715, and was commanded for twenty years by Captain Stephen Noble. The service for the guarding of the frontier towns in the colony of Connecticut was an exceedingly arduous one. Every male citizen, except the aged, the infirm, and the ministers, was obliged to do military duty. These militia-men had to provide their arms and equipment at their own expense, and, if any business required their absence from the town, they were obliged to provide a substitute and to pay, themselves, for his services. The arms which each soldier furnished consisted of a musket or rifle, a bullet pouch containing twenty bullets, a powder horn containing twenty charges of powder, and such an amount of cloth or buckskin as would make sufficient wadding for this number of charges. These requirements were constant, and frequent examinations were made to see that all of the men of the company complied with them.

As New Milford was, during most of these first fifty years of its existence, a frontier town, a line of guards was established which reached across the country from Woodbury to the New York boundary, and the members of the company had to take turns in patrolling this line.

The second company in New Milford was organized in 1744, and both of these companies continued to exist until the Revolution.

The first recorded service of the New Milford men beyond their own borders occurred about 1758. The greatest accumulation of men found on the record is a company raised for the French and Indian War in 1759. It was commanded by Captain Whiting and was known as the "Tenth Company of Colonel David Wooster's Third Regiment of Connecticut Levy." The New Milford men were First Lieutenant Hezekiah Baldwin, Sergeant Israel Baldwin, Corporal John Bronson, Drummer Zadock Bostwick. The privates were Isaac Hitchcock, Barrall Buck (there are two mentions of Buck, he being recorded also as David Buck), Martin Warner, David Hall, Dominie Douglas (whether Dominie stood for minister or was just the baptismal name, I do not know), Thomas Oviatt, Daniel Daton, Joseph Lynes, Ashel Baldwin, Elnathan Blatchford, Ebenezer Terrill, William Gould, David Collings, Joseph Jones, Moses Fisher, Zachariah Ferris, Jesse Fairchild, Joseph Smith, Benjamin Wallis, Benjamin Hawley, Moses Johnson.

The Colonial Records do not show where this regiment was used. Colonel Wooster had a long Colonial service and marched with several expeditions toward Canada. How far these men marched is not on record. They were enlisted in the spring, and seem to have returned to their homes in the fall. Whether they went as far as the expedition of that year toward Canada does not appear. Possibly family traditions might throw some light on the matter.

In the Eleventh Company of the Second Regiment, Colonel Nathaniel Whiting commanding, Ruben Bostwick was ensign, and the records show that Private James Bennett went from the town in 1760.

In the calls from New Milford of 1759 and 1761 occur the names of Hezekiah Baldwin, Second Lieutenant, Second Company, Third Regiment (Lieutenant Colonel Hinman commanding), Israel Baldwin, and Josiah Baldwin. The records show that, in the same year, Ashel Turrell, son of Nathan, with his brother Nathan, went from the town to the army in New York or Canada. Caleb Turrill, Enoch Turrill, Isaac Turrill, sons of Caleb Terrell, also went in the same organization. John Terrell is mentioned as being in the war (1761), but I judge that to be a mistake, as there was no John Terrell in the town of New Milford of age sufficient to answer that call.

The Eleventh Company of the Fourth Regiment was commanded by Captain Josiah Canfield, the Regiment being commanded by Colonel Wooster. There appear the names of Ashel, son of Nathan Terrell, and of Enoch, son of Caleb Turrill.

In the Tenth Company of the Second Regiment (Colonel Nathaniel Whiting's) commanded by Captain Gideon Stoddard, the name of William Drinkwater appears. The following New Milford names are scattered through the Second, Third and Fourth Connecticut regiments: Bronson, Baldwin, Beach, Bardsley, Beebe, Bennett, Boardman, Booth, Buck, Buell (David, afterward a Revolutionary soldier) Bostwick, Camp, Comstock, Couch, Crane, Curtis, Drinkwater, and Ferris.

Captain Joseph Canfield raised a company in 1758, of which Jeremiah Canfield was the drummer. The last edition of the Colonial Records (issued only a year or so ago), the best existing authority upon the period, gives merely the names of the members of this company and the length of their service, with dates of enlistment and of discharge. Exactly what rôle they played it is impossible now to find out. There are many traditions in the families of their doings, but these family traditions are not as full as those of the Revolution, which, following so quickly, effaced memories which would otherwise have survived. There are some tales of Bill Drinkwater, of

Stephen Terrell, and Thomas Drinkwater, but they are so indefinite that all which can be gleaned from them is that these men went as far as Quebec, and were in the battle on the Heights of Abraham, and, possibly, in some of the others.

Most of the members of this company must have returned, as their names appear in the town affairs after this period. There is no record of any loss of life, so far as I have been able to find, among the New Milford men who participated in the French and Indian War. Very little disturbance from Indians occurred in the vicinity of New Milford during this war; there is but one instance of trouble, I think, recorded. A very good understanding with the Indians was attained by the warm friendship between Waramaug, chief of all the tribes of the region, and the New Milford minister, Rev. Mr. Boardman, who attended old Waramaug on his deathbed. Quite an interesting tale is told of his death, but that will probably be recorded in another place. After the close of the French and Indian War there seems to have been little military activity in New Milford, except the keeping up of the two companies under the rigorous acts of the Colonial Guard. These were officered and drilled as they had been from their formation. It is not till the period of the Revolution is reached that the town takes on very much of a military character.

Canfield, Bostwick and Noble seem to have been the most prominent names in military affairs during the Colonial period.

The first company of which mention is made in connection with the Revolution is that of Lieutenant Ebenezer Couch, who served in the regiment of Colonel Andrew Ward. This company does not appear at all in either the Connecticut War Book or the rolls of the Connecticut Historical Society. The first notice of Ebenezer Couch in the Connecticut War Book is of his commanding a company of Colonel Canfield's regiment at West Point and Peekskill in 1777. The only record of the company is in a roll which was in the possession of the late Colonel William J. Starr of New Milford, and which, I suppose, was among his papers when he died. It was raised in May, 1775. The names of its members are given in the roll of New Milford men in the Revolution, which is appended to this article and need not be repeated here.

Its history is rather indefinite. It seems to have been raised for the Lexington alarm, but, being too late for that purpose, it probably went to the Sound or to New York. The date of its discharge does not appear on any record, but most of the men are soon found on the rolls of other companies in the service.

In July, 1775, a company was formed in New Milford, commanded by Captain Isaac Bostwick, who was first commissioned on the sixteenth of that month and, later, was recommissioned at Boston. It joined the regiment of Colonel Charles Webb, under the name of the Seventh Connecticut Levy, served along the Sound, and then went to the siege of Boston. Its term of service was to expire in December, 1775. About the time it was to be discharged, it was reorganized as the Nineteenth Regiment of Connecticut Line, enlisted for one year. Most of the men of Captain Bostwick's company, as well as those of Lieutenant Couch's company, appear in the new organization. The company and regiment remained at the siege of Boston until after the evacuation of that place by the British, when they accompanied General Washington to New York, going by land as far as New London and thence by boat. They were put to work at first upon the fortifications of New York, then, on the completion of that work, they were taken over to Brooklyn, and were employed, on the left of the line, in completing the fortifications there. They were not engaged in the battle of Long Island, but they covered the retreat, after that disaster, and played an important part in the subsequent movements about New York. They rendered some aid to the Brigade of Connecticut Militia in the disastrous affair of Kipp's Bay, moved with the army across the Harlem to Westchester, and were hotly engaged, with considerable loss, in the battle of White Plains.

After this battle, and before the capture of Fort Washington, they were brought down to Spuyten Duyvil creek, just at its junction with the Hudson, and were kept there furnishing guards, orderlies and escorts for the movements about the fort. While the Jumel mansion (then the old Morris house) was being used as the American Headquarters, many of Captain Bostwick's men were frequently on duty about the place as guards and orderlies. The following is a tradition for which the only authority is the stories told by the old soldiers around John Turrill's fireside many years after: During the engagement of the British with Fort Washington, a sergeant's guard under the command of David Buell of New Milford, which had been placed at a picket station near the base of Inwood Hill, were separated, by the rapid advance of the Hessians up the Harlem River (a movement, which, but for the quickness of a soldier's wife at the Morris house, would have resulted in. the capture of General Washington), from their regiment across the creek and obliged to fall back to Fort Washington. Being hotly pursued by the advancing enemy, they were forced to take cover under the banks of the Hudson, to avoid the fire of almost an entire regiment. A small party of the Hessians endeavored to cut off their retreat to the fort and one of them succeeded in jumping down the bank in front of the New Milford men. Roger Blaisdell was in the advance, and, as the German stumbled down the bank in front of him, pushed him with a thrust of his bayonet into the river and the party reached temporary safety in Fort Washington.

The Fort was soon captured by the British, however, and our New Milford men found themselves in the unfortunate position of prisoners of war.

The prisoners, according to the stories told by them afterward, were moved down to a point about where Union Square is now, and were there confined in a barn, for three days, before any food was given them. Then, wagons from the British slaughter-houses arrived, loaded with the hock bones of the cattle killed for the British troops. These wagons having been backed up to the door of the barn, the hock bones were shoveled in on the floor, while the prisoners scrambled for what they could get. It is said that their hunger was so great that they seized the bones and gnawed them as a dog would.

They were kept for three days in this barn, and were then conveyed down to that much-dreaded place of confinement, the Old Sugar House Prison, a sugar store-house, which was between Ann and Fulton streets. It was a building with a large central portion, and had two wings which projected on either side of a little courtyard. There were no cellars and the floor was of puncheons (hewn logs eight or ten inches thick) laid loose on the floor timbers. It was very strongly constructed in order that it might sustain the weight of the heavy casks of sugar and molasses which came from the West Indies.

The place where our twelve New Milford men slept was just inside one of the doors. The two projecting rooms on either side were occupied by the guard of the prison and the officers, respectively. A sentry paced up and down the front from the guard room to the room of the officers. The provisions furnished to the prisoners were exceedingly scanty and of so poor a quality that they had been condemned as unfit for the use of the soldiers and sailors of the British army. Their rations consisted mainly of moldy and wormy pilot bread. This régime, following the "bone diet" of the barn, soon reduced them to the verge of starvation. These poor Continentals had little or no money with which to purchase favors and they were soon in a very bad way. The British profited by this situation to try to get the Americans to renounce the Patriot cause and enlist in the British army. A guinea a head was offered to each British soldier who would induce a rebel to join their cause. The English guard was well fed and it was very tantalizing to our New Milford men to see the burly Englishmen enjoying their abundant repasts. Necessity is the mother of invention, however, and our men soon formed a plan to obtain some of the much coveted food. The cooking for the guard was done in the room occupied by them and a limited amount of provisions was, from time to time, brought there. Late one afternoon, a half-barrel of mess pork was brought in and opened for use, and left standing under the charge of the sentry for the night. This was our boys' opportunity and, as soon as the other prisoners were sound asleep, they very quietly raised one of the logs in their floor space and scooped out a little hole in the sand underneath. A place having been thus prepared for their expected booty, they then proceeded to get the much desired pork. The night was so dark that a man could not be recognized at any distance and this was much in their favor. Roger Blaisdell quietly approached the sentry and, explaining that he was tired of starving, asked to be told where he could go to enlist in the British army, adding that he did not dare to come when the other prisoners were awake. The sentry, overjoyed at the prospect of the guinea, and fearing that, if he let the man go, some other would secure the much-coveted prize, told Blaisdell to walk up and down his beat with him until he should be relieved, when he would take him to the officer of the day. Accordingly, they paced up and down the sentry's beat until, when a good opportunity occurred at the point farthest from the quarters of the guard, Blaisdell hit his companion a blow behind the ear which would have felled an ox and which knocked the sentry senseless. The men, who were on the watch, rushed to the pork barrel, scooped out an armful of pork each, quickly deposited it in the hole that they had prepared, replaced the plank, and dropped down upon it, snoring to beat a bass drum. Of course an alarm was raised and the prisoners were turned out, but the sentry was too much shaken up by the blow to be able to tell much about the matter. The loss of the pork was not discovered that night, if at all, so there was nothing to direct attention to the men, and they escaped detection. Each night, while the other prisoners were sleeping, the enterprising twelve would quietly raise the plank and have a meal of raw salt pork. In after days, those of the group who survived the prison experiences (particularly Sergeant David Buell) used to refer to their prison pork as the sweetest food that they had ever eaten, and for years the standing toast at their reunions was, "To Roger Blaisdell's pork barrel."

Within the last few months I have compared my recollections with those of other descendants of these men and have found that the traditions of these events agree so nearly as to warrant the belief that there was much truth in the stories told by the old veterans.

After being confined for a number of weeks in the sugar house, the prisoners were taken to the prison ship *Dutton*. Two hundred of them were transported to Milford and put ashore there. Twenty were dead before the vessel arrived and twenty more died very soon after. All the forty are buried in the graveyard of that place. Of the twelve men of New Milford, tradition narrates the return of only four, Roger Blaisdell, David Buell, William Drinkwater and Lyman Noble. Through friends in Milford, they were able to secure a horse, and thus worked their way back to New Milford, reaching there about March, 1777. This group was eliminated from Captain Isaac Bostwick's company and did no further service until their companions came home from the successful fields of Trenton and Princeton. Shortly after the fall of Fort Washington, the regiment containing Captain Bostwick's company was ordered to Philadelphia. It was with Washington at Germantown before the army went into winter quarters at Valley Forge. Its term of service was to expire December 20, 1776. But Washington was then planning the move which ended in the crossing of the Delaware at Trenton, and many of its members remained in service, at his personal request, for a six weeks' campaign.

Most of the men of Captain Bostwick's company were with Washington and crossed the Delaware on the twenty-fifth of December, 1776, and, on the early morning of that day, they were in the battle of Trenton, where they assisted in the capture of the Hessian regiment. They were engaged in the succeeding battle at Princeton, January 3, 1777, and were finally discharged on the first of February, 1777, when they returned to New Milford.

Captain Bostwick appeared as a leader in the Danbury alarm. With him was John Terrell and David Buell, who had so far receovered from his prison experiences as to join his old companions on that occasion. Roger Blaisdell does not appear, but Bill Drinkwater does. With them was a New Milford man who had been in Captain Couch's first company.

one Ruben Phillips. Ruben Phillips was a colored man, living in New Milford, who had evidently been the cook in Captain Bostwick's company. The descendants of Ruben Phillips were living, in my time, in the little house where the road goes up Chicken Hill toward Bridgewater, and this family knew that their ancestor had been in the Revolution with my grandfather. A descendant of this Phillips, Chester Phillips by name, volunteered in the Twenty-ninth Connecticut Infantry in the War of the Rebellion and was killed in front of Petersburg, Virginia. Truly the Revolutionary blood of New Milford was as good in the black man as in the white.

The group from Captain Bostwick's company were engaged four days in the Danbury alarm. The following story regarding this little band is extant: The British had commenced their retreat from Danbury by way of Ridgefield and these men were following them up very earnestly, pressing close upon a grenadier regiment which was the rear guard of the British force. John Terrell, William Noble, Bill Drinkwater and David Buell rushed together up one side of the famous rock in Ridgefield, while the grenadiers were still on the other side. One of them (which one I do not know), showing himself imprudently, was shot by the British grenadiers. Of the truth of this story I have never been able to learn. It is firmly believed in and about Ridgefield and also in New Milford. There is a plate on the rock, I think, commemorating the death of one of the company.

A number of men from New Milford were in the company of Captain Daniel Pendleton of Watertown, which belonged to the regiment of Colonel Judthon Baldwin, a regiment of artificers that served under the direction of the Quarter-Master-General as a Construction Corps. This regiment was in all the engagements of the war except those about Boston and those of the northern army above Albany, in more engagements, in fact, than any other body of Connecticut troops. In 1780, when General Green took command of the Southern Department, he requested that Captain Pendleton's company be sent to him. The company joined him, as requested, and was the only body of Connecticut men that served south of Virginia. It was on duty there until the disbanding of the army in November, 1783.

This was the only considerable group of men that went as a body from New Milford after the first two companies; perhaps it might be called the third company. The enlistments were for short periods and the changes were quite frequent, until 1778 and 1779, when enlistments began to be made for three years or the war.

New Milford is credited on the Connecticut War Records and the Connecticut Historical Society's rolls with two hundred and eighty-five men in the war, many of whom served two and three, and some even four terms of enlistment.

While these soldiers of the Revolution were in the field doing military duty, their fathers and brothers were at home laboring for their support; not so easy a task when it is remembered that in the first three years of the war the Colony of Connecticut paid for the maintenance and equipment of her troops in the field, for the damage to her people in the British raids of Danbury and Norwalk, the immense sum of £516,606. During the last four years of the war the Continental Congress fixed Connecticut's share of the expenses of the war at $1,800,000 a year. At times the tax rates were three shillings on the pound. The eight years of the war were years of toil and suffering to those on the sterile hill-farms, where the striving and stress were about as great as in the midst of the dangers of the battle-field. Indeed, much of the war had come to these farmers' very doors, for the Tories of Squash Hollow and the Quakers of Quaker Hill and Straits Mountain had not proved themselves exactly the men of peace that they professed to be.

The leading family of New Milford in the Revolution was the Bostwicks. There were ten of the name in the service during the war—Amos, Benjamin, Elijah, Elisha, Ebenezer, Isaac, Israel, Joel, Oliver and Solomon. The next was the Turrills, of whom there are nine on the records—Ashel, Caleb, Ebenezer, Enoch, Isaac, Joel, John, Nathan and Stephen. The Canfields have seven names to their credit—Amos, Ezra,

John, Josiah, Moses, Nathaniel and Samuel—and the Baldwins, four—Jared, John, Jonas and Theodore.

It would be impossible to give all the actions in which New Milford men were concerned during the Revolution without giving a history of the entire war. Some of the marked battles in which they were engaged were those about Philadelphia, the Mud Forts, Germantown and Monmouth. They participated in the crossing of the Delaware from Princeton and, later, were at the surrender of Germantown. New Milford men were with Morgan at Saratoga and tradition says that they were at the capture of Ticonderoga and Crown Point, with Ethan Allen. Colonel Warner of Roxbury, the companion of Allen, who was well and favorably known in New Milford, had many friends, some of whom may have gone with him on that expedition. There may be some truth in this story, therefore, as it is extant.

According to one of the legends current in Western Connecticut, a troop of New Milford and Roxbury men on their way to the Hampshire Grants to join Ethan Allen, assembled at New Milford. Their first morning's march was up the Housatonic to a little spring which comes out near the present railroad a short distance below Merwinsville. There, they were met by Deacon Gaylord, who had crossed the river from his place in a canoe, with a lunch, which included a bottle of applejack, and a jug of hard cider. He distributed these liquid refreshments so freely, deacon though he was, that the party were quite jolly before they moved on to their night camp, which was to be at Bull's Bridge. Whatever may be the truth of this story, it is evident that the New Milford men's eyes were turned very much toward the Northern Department, and that many of them served in the operations of that department.

New Milford men were present at the famous charge of Mad Anthony Wayne at Stony Point. A company of pioneers was selected to go forward and cut away the pickets in order to facilitate the advance of the charging column up into the fort. There is a tradition that Lieutenant David Buell was one of these pioneers, and, as he was in the engagement, the tradition is probably correct. The pioneers, having cut away the pickets, scattered to the right and left, in accordance with their orders, leaving the way open for the charging column, which began the ascent. The cannoneer of the fort was swinging his linstock to fire a cannon which pointed right down the line. History gives it that, at this critical moment, one of the pioneers rushed forward with his axe and knocked the cannoneer over before he was able to apply the linstock, thus saving the expedition; and legend claims that this pioneer was Sergeant David Buell. Legend goes on to say that, in the fort at Stony Point, the Continental soldiers found a number of Tories (some from the vicinity of New Milford) who had retired thither for protection. These Tories were paraded about the fort with ropes around their necks and David Buell, as a mark of distinction, led the procession, holding a rope around the neck of the most valiant and troublesome Tory. David Buell received a pension for his services and was long a resident of New Milford, where, I believe, he is buried. His house was on Second Hill, and, in his advanced years, he did little but travel about among his friends, frequently stopping for some time with a sister who lived in " Pug Lane " (now Park Lane). His favorite resort, when he was with his sister, was Mr. Cushman's Tavern, which is still standing on the road going up to Second Hill and Northville. It was his morning custom to go over to the tavern and meet his friends there. It was observed that, whenever an Englishman and Tory happened into Cushman's place, David Buell immediately left. He would go home and say " Umph! an Englishman was there; I could not stay." Another favorite gathering place of many of these old soldiers was at the home of John Turrill, and it was there that they celebrated the anniversaries. Their habit was to gather in the morning, go and make a call on Captain Isaac Bostwick, drink a glass of wine, and then return to dinner at John Turrill's home, where they would afterward tell their stories. Many of these stories were quite lurid, possibly by reason of the quantity and quality of John Turrill's hard cider and applejack; for John, although extremely temperate himself, is said never to have stinted his former companions in arms either in food or drink.

Stephen Turrill was another noted man in the regiments. He belonged at first to the company of Ebenezer Couch, but, soon after drifted into a number of organizations from New Milford which served about West Point. He was in that part of the country for nearly two years. There are numberless stories of his encounters with the Tories. One of these is as follows: A band to which he was attached, while marching through the lower part of the Debatable Land, came to the house of a Dutch Tory. They wanted something to eat and asked the woman of the house if she could give them some milk or anything. She very gruffly told them that there was nothing in the house to eat, that she had nothing for the Rebels. Just then, something called her out of doors for a minute, and the soldiers saw that, over the fireplace, in a large pot, the dinner was boiling. Stephen Turrill's inquisitive mind determined to know what was in that pot. Accordingly, he pulled off the lid, saw a fine bag pudding, pulled it out, put it in his haversack, and marched away. The woman quickly discovered her loss and came crying that the Rebels had stolen her pudding. The sergeant in command marched by his men and then told the woman there was no evidence of her pudding there; but, after she had retreated a short distance, he said "Turrill, did you get that woman's pudding?" "Yes," said he, "here it is in my haversack." The company passed on and dined sumptuously.

Scattered over the Debatable Land were little guard houses, in each of which a guard was kept for a week at a time, to intercept the approach of British or Tories. These guard houses usually consisted of two rooms, a front and back one. On one occasion——

[General Turrill's narrative of "New Milford in the Wars," was tragically cut short at this point by his sudden death in the office of the Grafton Press, where he was dictating it. It has seemed more fitting to leave this narrative in its unfinished condition, as a sort of memorial to him, than to have it completed by another. Any inconsistencies that may exist in it may be attributed to the fact that it did not have the benefit of his correction and revision.—EDITOR.]

HENRY STUART TURRILL
Brig. Gen. U. S. Army

THE COLONIAL WARS

The names given in the rolls of the Connecticut Historical Society are as follows:

RANK.	NAME, COMPANY, AND REGIMENT.	LEVY.
Privt.	Ashmon, Justus, 11th Co., 4th Reg.	1758
Sergt.	Baldwin, Israel, 11th Co., 3rd Reg.	"
Lieut.	Baldwin, Hezekiah, 10th Co., 3rd Reg.	1759
Privt.	Baldwin, Ashael, 10th Co., 3rd Reg.	"
"	Baldwin, Benjamin, 3rd Co., 1st Reg.	1762
"	Baldwin, Joseph, 10th Co., 4th Reg.	1758
"	Ball, Joseph, 1st Co., 2nd Reg.	1759
"	Baker, Thomas, 11th Co., 4th Reg.	1758
"	Bartholomew, Lemuel, 2nd Co., 2nd Reg.	"
"	Bartholomew, Noah, 11th Co., 4th Reg.	"
"	Beach, John, 1st Co., 4th Reg.	"
"	Beardsley, Amos, 2nd Co., 2nd Reg.	"
"	Beecher, Nathaniel, 11th Co., 4th Reg.	"
"	Bell, Robert, 11th Co., 4th Reg.	"
"	Benedict, Ezra, 11th Co., 2nd Reg.	"
"	Beeman, Benjah, 11th Co., 4th Reg.	"
"	Bisbee, Joseph, 11th Co., 4th Reg.	"
"	Bliss, Gillum, 11th Co., 4th Reg.	"
"	Botchford, Elnathan, 11th Co., 4th Reg.	"
"	Bostwick, Elijah, 2nd Co., 3rd Reg.	"
"	Bostwick, Joseph, 11th Co., 4th Reg.	"
"	Bostwick, Robert, Jr.*	
Drummer	Bostwick, Zadoch, 10th Co., 3rd Reg.	1759
Corp.	Brownson, Benjamin, 10th Co., 3rd Reg.	"
Privt.	Brownson, John, 11th Co., 4th Reg.	1758
"	Brownson, Abram, 11th Co., 4th Reg.	"
"	Brownson, Israel, 11th Co., 4th Reg.	"
"	Brownson, John, 11th Co., 4th Reg.	"
"	Birch, Joseph, 11th Co., 4th Reg.	"
"	Bradley, Jahuel, 11th Co., 4th Reg.	"
"	Bryan, Augustus, 11th Co., 4th Reg.	"

* In Orcutt's "History of New Milford," but not in the Connecticut Historical Society Rolls.

RANK.	NAME, COMPANY, AND REGIMENT.	LEVY.
Privt.	Buck, Bethial, 11th Co., 4th Reg.	1758
"	Buck, David, 11th Co., 4th Reg.	"
"	Buck, Daniel, 11th Co., 4th Reg.	"
"	Botchford, Elnathan, 11th Co., 4th Reg.	"
"	Buell, David, 6th Co., 2nd Reg.	1759
"	Buell, Abel, 6th Co., 2nd Reg.	"
"	Bunce, John, 11th Co., 4th Reg.	1758
Capt.	Canfield, Joseph, 11th Co., 4th Reg.	"
Privt.	Canfield, Nathan, 11th Co., 4th Reg.	"
Drummer	Canfield, Jeremiah, 11th Co., 4th Reg.	"
Privt.	Canfield, Josiah, 2nd Co., 4th Reg.	"
Lieut.	Castle, Phineas, 11th Co., 4th Reg.	"
Privt.	Carter, Elezer, 11th Co., 4th Reg.	"
"	Chittenden, Isaac, 6th Co., 2nd Reg.	1759
"	Chittenden, Timothy, 6th Co., 2nd Reg.	"
"	Clark, Roger, 11th Co., 4th Reg.	1758
"	Colhoon, David, 11th Co., 4th Reg.	"
Drummer	Cogswell, Edward, 11th Co., 4th Reg.	"
Privt.	Cogswell, Asa, 11th Co., 4th Reg.	"
"	Collengs, Daniel, 10th Co., 3rd Reg.	1759
"	Curtis, Elezer, 11th Co., 4th Reg.	1758
"	Daton, Amos, 11th Co., 4th Reg.	"
"	Dayton, Daniel, 10th Co., 3rd Reg.	1759
"	Dean, John, 11th Co., 4th Reg.	1758
"	Deveraux, Jonathan, 11th Co., 4th Reg.	"
"	Divine, Timothy, 11th Co., 4th Reg.	"
"	Divene, Nathaniel, 11th Co., 4th Reg.	"
"	Dean, Uriah, 11th Co., 4th Reg.	"
"	Dinsmore, Samuel, 11th Co., 4th Reg.	"
"	Douglas, Dominey, 10th Co., 3rd Reg.	1759
"	Downs, David*	
"	Drinkwater, Thomas, 10th Co., 2nd Reg.	1758
"	Drinkwater, William, 10th Co., 2nd Reg.	"
"	Durkee, David, 11th Co., 4th Reg.	"

* In Orcutt's "History of New Milford," but not in the Connecticut Historical Society Rolls.

New Milford in the Wars

RANK.	NAME, COMPANY, AND REGIMENT.	LEVY.
Privt.	Downs, Jonathan, Col. Nath. Whiting's Reg.	1762
"	Fairchild, Jesse, 10th Co., 3rd Reg.	1759
"	Ferris, Zachariah, 10th Co., 3rd Reg.	"
"	Fisher, Henry, 11th Co., 4th Reg.	1758
"	Fisher, Moses, 10th Co., 3rd Reg.	1759
"	Foot, David, 11th Co., 4th Reg.	1758
"	Galusha, Jacob, 11th Co., 4th Reg.	"
"	Gould, William, 11th Co., 4th Reg.	"
"	Green, David, 11th Co., 4th Reg.	"
"	Gurney, John, 11th Co., 4th Reg.	"
"	Guthrie, Ephraim, 11th Co., 4th Reg.	"
"	Hamblin, Simon, 11th Co., 4th Reg.	"
"	Hamlin, Joel, 11th Co., 4th Reg.	"
"	Hawley, Jeptha, 11th Co., 4th Reg.	"
"	Hawley, Benjamin, 10th Co., 3rd Reg.	1759
Corp.	Hawkins, Zadoc, 11th Co., 4th Reg.	1758
Privt.	Harris, David, 11th Co., 4th Reg.	"
Clerk	Hine, Abel, 11th Co., 4th Reg.	"
Privt.	Hall, David, 10th Co., 3rd Reg.	1759
"	Hitchcock, David, 11th Co., 4th Reg.	1758
"	Hitchcock, Isaac, 11th Co., 4th Reg.	"
"	Hill, Silas, 11th Co., 4th Reg.	"
"	Hinman, Benjamin, 11th Co., 4th Reg.,	"
"	Hurd, Lovel, 11th Co., 4th Reg.	"
"	Hurd, Noah, 11th Co., 4th Reg.	"
"	Hurlbutt, Aaron, 11th Co., 4th Reg.	"
"	Hurlburt, Elijah, 11th Co., 4th Reg.	"
"	Hurlburt, Josiah, 11th Co., 4th Reg.	"
"	Johnson, Moses, 11th Co., 4th Reg.	"
"	Jones, Joseph, 10th Co., 3rd Reg.	1759
"	Lake, Gresslone, 11th Co., 4th Reg.	1758
"	Latimer, Thomas, 11th Co., 4th Reg.	"
"	Lynes, Joseph, 10th Co., 3rd Reg.	1759
"	Manville, Daniel, 11th Co., 4th Reg.	1758
"	Manville, John, 11th Co., 4th Reg.	"
"	Mun, Gideon, 11th Co., 4th Reg.	"

RANK.	NAME, COMPANY, AND REGIMENT.	LEVY.
Privt.	Murray, John, 11th Co., 4th Reg.	1758
"	North, Thomas, 11th Co., 4th Reg.	"
"	Oviatt, Thomas, 11th Co., 4th Reg.	"
"	Owen, David, 11th Co., 4th Reg.	"
"	Parish, Jacob, 11th Co., 4th Reg.	"
"	Peet, Jaihael, 11th Co., 4th Reg.	"
"	Pike, Daniel, 11th Co., 4th Reg.	"
"	Phelps, James, 11th Co., 4th Reg.	"
Sergt.	Prindle, Joseph, 11th Co., 4th Reg.	"
Privt.	Read, David, 11th Co., 4th Reg.	"
"	Robbards, Eli, 11th Co., 4th Reg.	"
Capt.	Ruggles, Benjamin, 12th Co., 2nd Reg.	1759
Privt.	Rayment, Samuel, 11th Co., 4th Reg.	1758
"	Sanford, Nathan, 11th Co., 4th Reg.	"
"	Sanford, ( )ade, 11th Co., 4th Reg.	"
"	Sawyer, Jess., 11th Co., 4th Reg.	"
"	Squire, Solomon, 11th Co., 4th Reg.	"
"	Smith, Joseph, 10th Co., 3rd Reg.	1759
"	Stone, Benjamin, 11th Co., 4th Reg.	1758
Chaplain	Taylor, Rev. Nathaniel, 2nd Reg.	1762
Privt.	Taylor, Abram.*	
"	Terrell, Nathan, 2nd Co., 4th Reg.	1758
"	Terrell, Ashael, 11th Co., 4th Reg.	"
"	Terrill, Ebenezer, 10th Co., 3rd Reg.	1759
"	Turrill, Enoch, 11th Co., 4th Reg.	1758
"	Turrill, Caleb, 11th Co., 4th Reg.	"
"	Turrill, Isaac, 7th Co., 2nd Reg.	1759
"	Turrill, Stephen.†	
"	Tuttle, Andrew, 11th Co., 4th Reg.	1758
"	Walker, Gideon, 11th Co., 4th Reg.	"
"	Walker, Zachariah, 11th Co., 4th Reg.	"
"	Warner, Benjamin, 10th Co., 3rd Reg.	1759
"	Warner, Martin, 10th Co., 3rd Reg.	"
"	Warner, Solomon.*	

* In Orcutt's "History of New Milford," but not in the Connecticut Historical Society Rolls.

† Tradition that he was in Canada, but there is no record.

RANK.	NAME, COMPANY, AND REGIMENT.	LEVY.
Privt.	Wallis, Benjamin, 10th Co., 3rd Reg.	1759
"	Welton, John, 11th Co., 4th Reg.	1758
"	Wright, Solomon, 11th Co., 4th Reg.	1758
"	Wood, Elisha, 11th Co., 4th Reg.	"

THE REVOLUTION

The following is the roll of men on the various records as having had service in the Revolution who are accredited to New Milford:

Muster roll of a company said to have been raised in New Milford and to have formed a part of Colonel Andrew Ward's regiment of Connecticut Militia, as given in Orcutt's New Milford:

Lieut. Ebenezer Couch, Lieut. Elizur Bostwick, Ensign Noble Hine, Clerk Benjamin Bostwick, Sergt. David Whittlesey, Sergt. Benjamin Weller, Sergt. Mathew Bronson, Sergt. Oliver Bostwick, Corp. Gideon Morgan, Corp. Uri Jackson, Corp. Nathaniel Cole, Corp. William Nichols, Corp. Lemuel Thayer, Drummer Eleazer Hendrix, Fifer David Ruggles, Fifer John Couch.

Privates—Nathan Averill, Benjamin Adams, Salmon Bostwick, John Baldwin, John Beach, Israel Bostwick, David Buell, Jared Baldwin, David Bosworth, Caleb Barnes, Mathias Beeman, Stiles Bradley, Joel Bostwick, John Canfield, Jesse Camp, Jonathan Crittenden, Elija Cary, Israel Camp, Samuel Copley, Ezra Dunning, Jedadiah Durkee, Caswell Dean, Thomas Drinkwater, Stephen Evitts, Asa Farrand, William Foot, Jonathan Gray, Epenetus Gunn, Elnathan Gregory, Liverus Hawley, Ashael Hotchkis, Lewis Hunt, Richard Johnson, John Keeler, Nathan Keeler, David Keeler, Jonathan Lumm, Joseph Mygatt, Lyman Noble, Ephram Minor, David Porter, Samuel Prince, Amos Prime, Ruben Phillips, William Peet, John Rood, Isaac M. Ruggles, Aziah Robbards, Nathan Rowley, Liffe Sanford, Asa Starkweather, Jonah Todd, Ebenezer Trowbridge, John Turrill, Stephen Turrill, William Whitley, Nathan Wildman, Cooley Weller, Abel Wilkins.

Roll of Captain Isaac Bostwick's company, Seventh Company, Sixth Regiment, of Connecticut Line: Colonel Charles Webb; Capt. Isaac Bostwick; Lieut. Hulbutt; Ensign Amos Bostwick; Sergts. Gideon Noble, Simeon Porter, Simon Mills, Elisha Bostwick, Sowl. Barnum; Corps. Samuel Bennett, Harmon White, Ebenezer Barnum, Seth Hall; Drummers Eleazor Hendrix, Calvin Pease; Fifers Nathan Avery, Theodore Baldwin, David Roch; Privates Nathan Avery, Theodore Baldwin, David Beach, Elizur Bostwick, Joseph Bates, Jonathan Brown, Reuben Bellamy, Ashel Case, John D. Comstalk, Timothy Cole, Aaron Curtis, Hedekiah Clerk, Thadeus Cole, Charles Chapen, Joseph Clerk, Ashael Dean, Jeremiah Douchey, David Everist, James Gates, John Green, Hedakiah Gray, Daniel Grinnel, Amaziah Griswold, Joseph Hawley, Levit How, William Hale, Abner Kelsey, John Lewis, Simeon Lyman, David Lyon, Joseph Murray, Samuel Millar, Ruben Mager, Josiah Munger, Ruben Philips, Rufus Partridge, Howard E. Prince, Jeruel Philips, Phineas Palmer, John Smith, Cordeal Smith, Isaac Smith, Caleb Swetland, Job Tousley, Ruben Taylor, Absolem Taylor, Gamaliel Terrey, Benjamin Thomas, John Walter, Thomas Woodward, Cornelius Whitney, Samuel Waters.

Men who crossed the Delaware with Capt. Isaac Bostwick of New Milford, December 25, 1776, and were in the battle of Trenton and the succeeding battle of Princeton, January 3, 1777: Lieuts. Hulbutt, Elisha Bostwick; Sergts. Brownson, Beach; Ensign Amos Bostwick; Corps. Thayer, Grover, Bell; Drummer Gunn; Fifer Humstead; Privates Jeptha Bartholomew, Luther Bartholomew, Isaac Brownson, Moses Camp, Moses Canfield, William Cressey, Jonathan Crittenden, Hezakiah Clark, Jonathan Davidson, Francis Fields, Aaron Foot, Moses Hurd, Robert Nichols, George Norton, Elisha Phiney, Ruben Pitcher, Asa Prince, Wills Sherwood, John Turrill.

Officers and men from New Milford who served in the Sixth Company of the Fourth Regiment, Continental Line: Capt. Josiah Starr; Sergt. John Stevens; Privates Oliver Bostwick, Josiah Buck, Dar. Barns, William Beal, Asa Beal, Michael Beach, Amos Beach, Jas. Brown, Josiah Brooks, Herman

Smith, Ephram Alderman, Domini Douglass, Jabes Frizbee, Oring Ferriss, Elihu Grant, Levi Hunt, Christo. Hington, Geo. Lummis, Eben Lewis, Jere McCarte, Nathan Nichols, Oliver Phelps, Jos. Phelps, Lemuel Peete, Timoth. Stanley, Benajah Smith, Geo. A. Smith, John Seeley, Nathl. Stewart, Enos Scott, Zimri Skinner, Joseph Thair, John Tuff, Ezekiel Towner, Lem Walter, Jos. Worden, Amos Mc'Kinnee, Robt. Brown, William Drinkwater, Jonathan Mayo.

New Milford men who served in Lieutenant-Colonel Josiah Starr's Regiment, Connecticut Line: Lieut. Col. Josiah Starr, Comd. Reg. and Co.; Lieuts. Augustine Thayer, James Bennett; Ensign Josiah Buck; Sergt. Oliver Bostwick; Privates Caleb Maxfield, Leef Sanford, Eleazor Hendricks, Ebenezer Bostwick, Solomon Bostwick, David Cole, Prince Crosley, Leverus Hawley, Samuel Hubble, Prime Hubble, Sep Hubble, Titus Heart, Stephen Headges, James Higgins, William Handy, Ira Hotchkis, Benjamin Heart, Aaron Hall, Ely Nichols, Robert Nichols, Samuel Nettleton, Holan Nettleton, Samuel Phillips, Jurel Phillips, Elijah Parker, Elab Parker, Nehimiah Piffany.

New Milford men who were in Lieutenant-Colonel Samuel Canfield's Regiment of Connecticut Militia, at West Point, in 1781: Lieut-Col. Samuel Canfield, comd.; Quartermaster Jonah Baldwin; Surgeon Dr. George Hurd; Capt. Ebenezer Couch, Comd. Co.; Privates Ruben Brownson, Elijah Hoyt, John Case, Andrew Merwin, Stephen Bennett, Benjamin Mead, Ebenezer Couch, Jr., Asa Read, Simeon Taylor, David Merwin, Henry Straight, Ruben Hurlbut.

New Milford men who served in Connecticut Regiment of Pioneers: Colonel Judthon Baldwin; Capt. Daniel Pendleton, Comd. of Co. in which the New Milford men were engaged; Sergt. David Porter; Privates Jessie Cole, John Eggleston, Isaac Turrill, Jonathan Wilkinson, Ashael Turrill, James Bradshaw, John Turner, Lyman Mott, Samuel Oviatt, Abel Wilkenson, Isaac Mott, Samuel Turner.

New Milford men who served in Col. Moses Hazen's Regiment, Connecticut Militia: Capt. Jeremiah Parmelie's Co.: Michael Welch, Jabes Tomlinson.

New Milford men who served in the Fifth Troop, Shelden's Dragoons: Sergt. Liffe Sanford, David Buell.

New Milford men who served in Second Regiment, Connecticut Line: Col. Herman Swift; in Capt. Samuel Comstalk's Co., Squire Davenport; in Capt. Richard's Co., Ezerah Canfield, David Cole; in Capt. Belden's Co., David Johnson, Moses Scott, Mathew Stewart.

A company of forty volunteers was raised in the towns of New Milford, Newtown, and Danbury, in December, 1776. The officers were: Capt. Benjamin Brownson, Lieut. Shadrack Hubble, Ensign Benjamin Seeley. The names of the privates are not given in the records.

In General David Waterbury's State Regiment, Captain Charles Smith's Company, were the following New Milford men: Sergt. Josiah Barnes; Drummer Eleazer Hendricks; Fifer Oliver Mead; Privates Nathan Murray, Benton Buck, John Ingersol, Achillies Comstalk, Amos Canfield, Daniel Davis, Jonathan Beecher, Isaac Utter, Mingo Treat, John Warner, Jonathan Jessup.

In Lieutenant John Phelps' Troop of Horse was Private Nathaniel Canfield of New Milford.

In Colonel Benjamin Hinman's Fourth Regiment, Continental Line, Sixth Company, Capt. Josiah Starr, were the following New Milford men: Sergt. John Stevens; Privates Oliver Bostwick, Herman Smith, Asa Brownson, Josiah Brooks, Ephraim Alderman, Josiah Buck.

In Colonel Herman Swift's Second Regiment, Continental Line, in Captain Kimberly's Company, served from January until June, 1783, the following New Milford men: Sergeants Charles McDonald, Ebinezer Bostwick; Drummer Job Hawkins; Privates Isaac Lockwood, Bostwick Ruggles, and John McCoy.

The following New Milford men served under Lieutenant Colonel Canfield in the Tryon invasion: Benjamin Stone, Nathaniel Barnes, William Cogswell, Ebenezer Couch, Noble Hine, Ruben Bostwick, Adam Hurlburt.

The members of the Society of Cincinnati from New Milford were Colonel Josiah Starr, Lieutenant James Bennett, and Lieutenant David Beach.

THE WAR OF 1812

The list of men from New Milford who served in the regular army during the War of 1812, taken from the rolls of the Adjutant General's office, is as follows:

Lieutenant Thomas Weller; Privates, Hedekiah Baldwin, Theopholus Baldwin, Joseph C. Barnes, Rufus Beeman, Samuel Bunnel, Charles H. Crampton, Kneeland Edwards, Philo Gregory, Joseph Hawley, Stephen Hawley, Abram Hunt, Warren Hyde, Ithamer Lane, Benjamin Lee, James Lee, Stephen Lyon, Seth Nelson, Ebinezer Reynolds, John Saxton, Stephen Seignor, Caleb Shelden, Peleg Slocum, Levi Smith, Eliakim Stow, Samuel Summers, Jonathan Tharrs, Benjamin Warner, Harry Wakelee, William S. Wakelee, Thomas W. Way, Squire Whitney, Shelden Wooden.

The War Records of Connecticut do not give the places from which the Militia and Volunteers came, so it is impossible to tell exactly how many New Milford men participated in the war. The names of Baldwin, Barnes, Bartholomew, Bassett, Beech, Buck, Buell, Bostwick, Booth, Canfield, Comstock, Noble, Starr, Taylor, Turrill, and many other New Milford names are upon the rolls, but just how many are to be credited to the town it is impossible to say.

THE MEXICAN WAR

The names of the men from New Milford who served in the Mexican War, taken from the rolls of the Adjutant General's office, were:

Henry Burrhants, Sherman Crosby, Albert Morey, Abner M. Philips, Ruben W. Phillips, Warren S. Tenbrok, James Schemmerhorn.

Two other men from the town were, I believe, in that war: Henry Soul, son of John Soul, who lived at the point of Buck's Rocks, and Charles Ford, who afterwards served in the war of 1861.

THE CIVIL WAR

Allen, Charles J., Mus. Co. I, 8th Inft., Dis. Disa., R. E. Co. D, 28th Inft., deserted.

Allen, William, Pvt. Co. A, 8th Inft., deserted.

Anderson, Charles F., Sergt. Co. H, 2d h. Art.

Atkins, James, Pvt. Co. D, 6th Inft.

Bailey, Andrew E., Mus. Co. H, 2d h. Art.

Bailey, Joseph A., Pvt. Co. D, 28th Inft.

Baldwin, David A., Pvt. and Lt. Co. I, 8th Inft.

Baldwin, Francis E., Mus. 4th Penn. Cav.

Banker, Miles N., wagoner, Co. E, 12th Inft.

Banker, Philo, Pvt. Co. I, 13th Inft, R. E. V. Co. B, died in service May 6, 1865.

Bartram, Andrew, Pvt. Co. I, 17th Inft., deserted.

Bartram, Ashbel E., Pvt. Co. I, 8th Inft., Dis. Disa.

Bartram, Charles E., Pvt. Co. D, 28th Inft.

Bartram, Charles M., Pvt. Co. I, 14th Inft., missing at Chancellorsville, May 3, 1863, supposed dead.

Bartram, Ferdinand, Mus. 4th Penn. Cav.

Bartram, Oscar F., Pvt. Co. I, 8th Inft., Dis. Disa.

Beardsley, Daniel S., Petty Off. U. S. Navy.

Beeman, Charles E., Pvt. Co. H, 2d h. Art.

Beeman, John A., Pvt. Co. H, 2d h. Art.

Beeman, Rufus, Pvt. Co. H, 2d h. Art.

Benedict, William E., Pvt. Co. C, 17th Inft., died at Folly Island, S. C., Nov. 17, 1863.

Bennett, George D., Pvt. Co. I, 2d h. Art.

Bemus, Charles F., Pvt. Co. D, 28th Inft., killed at Port Hudson, La., June 14, 1863.

Bennoit, Antone, Pvt. Corp. and Sergt. Co. H, 11th Inft.

Birch, George, Pvt. Co. I, 8th Inft., killed at Sharpsburg, Md., Sept. 17, 1863.

Bishop, Orange P., Pvt. Co. I, 11th Inft., deserted Apr. 4, 1863.

Booth, Charles M., Mus. Band 4th Penn. Cav., Lt. Co. D, 28th Inft.

Booth, Henry, Pvt. Co. D, 28th Inft.

CHARLES D. BLINN
Colonel of 13th Conn. Vols.

New Milford in the Wars

Breen, John, Pvt. Co. K, 15th Inft., Trans. to Co. K, 7th Inft., Sub.

Briggs, Daniel, Pvt. Co. D, 13th Inft., R. E., Pvt. Co. K, 2d h. Art., Dis. Disa., May 4, 1862, Wd. Cedar Creek, Oct. 19, 1864.

Bingham, Charles, Pvt. Co. D, 6th Inft., Sub., deserted Nov. 9, 1864.

Bright, John, Pvt. Co. A, 7th Inft., Sub., deserted March 23, 1865.

Breunel, Charles, Pvt. Co. H, 2d h. Art., Dis. Disa. May 29, 1865.

Bronson, Andrew A., Pvt. Co. H, 2d h. Art., deserted Aug. 11, 1865.

Bronson, Doctor, Pvt. Co. H, 2d h. Art.

Bronson, Charles R., Pvt. Co. C, 3d Inft.

Bronson, Francis H., Pvt. 14th Reg. Inft., U. S. A.

Bronson, William N., Pvt. Co. D, 28th Inft., died in service July 28, 1863.

Brown, Jackson J., Pvt. Co. I, 8th Inft.

Brush, Joseph, Pvt. Co. I, 8th Inft.

Buck, Andrew N., Pvt. Co. I, 8th Inft., Dis. Disa. May 11, 1862.

Buckingham, Andrew, Sergt. Co. I, 11th Inft., Dis. Disa. Oct. 24, 1862.

Buckingham, Clark, Band 4th Penn. Cav.

Buckingham, Earl, Band Leader, 2d Lieut. 4th Penn. Cav.

Buckingham, Irwin C., Corp. and Sergt. Co. H, 2d h. Art., Wd. Oct. 19, 1864, Cedar Creek, Va., Dis. Disa. May 23, 1865.

Buckingham, Orlo H., Mus. and Corp. Co. H, 2d h. Art.

Burk, Joseph, Pvt. Co. A, 10th Inft., Sub., deserted June 15, 1865.

Burke, Nicholas, Pvt. Co. M, 2d h. Art., deserted March 25, 1865.

Burns, Edward C., Pvt. Co. C, 8th Inft., Sub., deserted to enemy March 21, 1865.

Burr, Thomas, Pvt, Co. B, 29th Inft., Col'd., Dis. Disa. May 28, 1864.

Cady, Cyrell, Pvt. Co. I, 11th Inft., Dishon. Disc. Dec. 28, 1863.

Caldwell, Smith P., Pvt. Co. K, 13th Inft., Dis. Disa. Jan. 19, 1863.

Calnen, Thomas, Pvt. Co. F, 2d h. Art.

Camp, Edwin, Pvt. Co. D, 28th Inft.

Camp, Edwin T., Pvt. Co. C, 13th Inft., Dis. Disa. Feb. 17, 1863.

Campbell, James, Pvt. Co. A, 5th Inft.

Canfield, William E., Pvt. and Corp. Co. H, 2d h. Art.

Carman, George, Pvt. Co. C, 5th Inft., Sub., deserted Nov. 1, 1863.

Carpenter, George E., Sergt. Co. F, 29th Inft., Col'd., Dis. Disa. May 21, 1864.

Carroll, Edward, Pvt. Co. H, 5th Inft., deserted from 14th Inft. March 29, 1863; Sub., deserted Oct. 5, 1864.

Clark, Titus, Corp. Co. D, 28th Inft.

Cleggett, Louis A., Corp. Co. K, 29th Inft., Col'd., died Dec. 25, 1864, Point of Rocks, Va.

Cole, Ferdinand, Pvt. Co. H, 2d h. Art., deserted July 27, 1865.

Cole, Henry S., Pvt. Co. D, 7th Inft., deserted Nov. 11, 1864.

Cole, Hobert, Pvt. Co. D, 28th Inft.

Conlon, John, Pvt. Co. K, 14th Inft., Dis. Disa. Dec. 12, 1863.

Conley, Daniel, Pvt. Co. K, 2d h. Art., Dis. Disa. May 11, 1864.

Copley, George D., Band 4th Penn. Cav.

Corcoran, William, Pvt. Co. D, 20th Inft., Sub., deserted Oct. 5, 1864.

Conkwright, Alexander, Pvt. Co. D, 28th Inft., died July 13, 1863, at Barancas, Fla.

Cummings, James P., Pvt. Co. G, 28th Inft.

Disbrow, David B., Pvt. Co. I, 8th Inft., R. E., Pvt. Co. H, 2d, h. Art., Dis. Disa. Jan. 15, 1863.

Disbrow, Henry S., Corp. Co. I, 8th Inft.

NEW MILFORD IN THE WARS

Disbrow, William E., Corp. Co. H, 2d h. Art.
Dix, William, Pvt. Co. E, 8th Inft., Sub., shot for desertion Jan. 8, 1865.
Doane, Edward, Corp. Co. D, 13th Inft., Dis. Disa.
Dodge, Robert, Pvt. Co. D, 28th Inft., injured at Port Hudson, La., July, 1863.
Driscoll, Cornelius, Pvt. Co. G, 1st Reg. Cav., Sub., deserted July 1, 1865.
Dubois, Hiram, Corp. Co. K, 2d h. Art.
Dunham, Benjamin F., Pvt. and Corp. Co. H, 2d h. Art.
Durand, William, Pvt. Co. I, 11th Inft., Sub., deserted Aug. 25, 1865.
Dutcher, William P., Pvt. Co. I, 8th Inft., Wd. May 7, 1864, Walthall Junc., Va., Dis. Disa. July 15, 1865.
Erwin, George S., Corp. Co. H, 2d h. Art.
Erwin, Robert, Reg. Qm. Sergt. and Co. Qm. Sergt. Co. H, 2d h. Art., Wd. Oct. 19, 1864, at Cedar Creek, Va.
Evans, James H., wagoner Co. C, 13th Inft.
Evits, Oliver B., Pvt. Co. H, 2d h. Art.
Farrel, John, Pvt. Co. I, 8th Inft., Sub., deserted Feb. 18, 1865.
Farrell, William, Pvt. Co. A, 6th Inft., Sub.
Ferris, Hilliard, Pvt. Co. I, 8th Inft., died in New Milford July 27, 1862.
Ferris, Jay, Pvt. Co. D, 28th Inft., died at New Orleans, La., June 1, 1863.
Ferris, John, Pvt. Co. C, 13th Inft.
Ferris, Robert, Corp. Co. I, 8th Inft., killed at Sharpsburg, Md., Sept. 17, 1862.
Ferris, Stephen, 1st Sergt. Co. D, 28th Inft.
Finn, John, Pvt. Co. I, 10th Inft., Sub.
Fisher, James, Pvt. Co. I, 14th Inft., Sub., deserted Aug. 14, 1864.
Ford, Aaron N., Mus. Co. D, 28th Inft., died at Brashier City, La., May 22, 1863.
Ford, Charles, Mus. Co. I, 8th Inft., Dis. Disa.
Franklin, Henry J., Pvt. Co. K, 29th Inft., Col'd.

French, Francis L., Pvt. Co. H, 2d h. Art.
Fuller, Alfred E., Mus. Co. D, 28th Inft.
Garlick, Charles, Pvt. Co. I, 8th Inft., Wd. at Antietam, Md., Sept. 17, 1862.
Gaylord, Charles H., Sergt. and 1st Sergt. Co. C, 13th Inft.
Goodsell, Jerome, Pvt. Co. D, 28th Inft., deserted Nov. 16, 1862.
Graves, Franklin S., Corp. Co. B, 2d h. Art.
Green, George A., Pvt. Co. K, 28th Inft.
Gregg, John, Pvt. Co. H, 5th Inft.
Gregory, Charles B., Corp. Co. D, 28th Inft., died at Baton Rouge, La., July 30, 1863.
Gridley, Henry S., Corp. Co. H, 2d h. Art., Wd. Oct. 19, 1864, Cedar Creek, Va.
Griffin, Edward, Pvt. Co. K, 2d h. Art., killed June 1, 1864, at Cold Harbor, Va.
Harrington, George W., Pvt. Co. K, 2d h. Art., died Feb. 25, 1864, at Alexandria, Va.
Hartwell, Willis, Pvt. Co. H, 2d h. Art., died Oct. 28, 1864, at Martinsburgh, Va.
Hatch, Calvin B., Sergt. and Lieut. Co. A, 2d h. Art., killed at Cold Harbor, Va., June 1, 1864.
Heacock, Richard, Pvt. Co. K, 29th Inft., Col'd.
Healy, James, Pvt. Co. A, 10th Inft., Sub.
Hess, Christian, Pvt. Co. G, 10th Inft.
Higgins, John, Pvt. Co. I, 5th Inft., Sub., deserted Oct. 1, 1863.
Hill, Samuel R., Pvt. and Corp. Co. H, 2d h. Art.
Hine, Frederick R., Pvt. Co., 11th Inft., died Feb. 1, 1864, at Alexandria, Va.
Hoag, David D., Capt. Co. D, 28th Inft., killed at Port Hudson, June 14, 1863.
Hoag, George W., Pvt. Co. I, 6th Inft., Wd. at Drewry's Bluff, Va., May 16, 1864.
Hodge, Homer W., Pvt. Co. K, 2d h. Art., Wd. at Cold Harbor, Va., June 1, 1864.
Hoffman, Herman, Pvt. Co. H, 2d h. Art.

New Milford in the Wars

Hoyt, Charles A., Pvt. Co. K, 2d h. Art., Wd. at Cold Harbor, Va., June 1, 1864.

Hoyt, Denman, Pvt. Co. D, 28th Inft.

Hoyt, Henry R., Corp. and 1st Sergt. Co. H, 2d h. Art.

Hoyt, Horatio S., Pvt. Sergt. and 1st Sergt. Co. H, 2d h. Art.

Hunt, Gideon L., Pvt. Co. G, 23d Inft.

Hunt, Merritt, Mus. Co. G, 28th Inft.

Hurd, Charles A., Pvt. Co. H, 2d h. Art., Wd. at Cedar Creek, Va., Oct. 19, 1864.

Hurd, Robert B., Pvt. and Corp. Co. E, 1st h. Art., deserted July 28, 1865.

Hutchinson, John, Pvt. Co. I, 2d h. Art., Wd. at Cold Harbor, Va., June 1, 1864, at Cedar Creek, Va., Oct. 19, 1864.

Irwin, Charles N., Sergt. and Lieut. Cos. I and E, 8th Inft., Wd. at Antietam, Md., Sept. 17, 1862, killed at Chapin's Farm, Va., Sept. 29, 1864, he having Vol. to remain for that battle after Exp. of his term of service.

Jacklin, Philip H., Pvt. Co. I, 8th Inft., died at Newbern, N. C., Sept. 23, 1862.

Jackson, Charles W., Pvt. Co. H, 2d h. Art., killed at Cold Harbor, Va., June 1, 1864.

Jackson, Henry F., Pvt. and Corp. Co. C, 29th Inft., Col'd.

Janks, August, Pvt. Co. B, 11th Inft., Sub., deserted Sept. 6, 1865.

Jennings, Alvin H., Pvt. Co. I, 8th Inft.

Jennings, David J., Pvt. Co. A, 2d h. Art.

Jennings, Jay, Pvt. Co. I, 8th Inft., Dis. Disa. Dec. 11, 1862.

Jones, Horace E., Pvt. and Corp. Co. H, 2d h. Art.

Judson, Charles, Pvt. Co. D, 28th Inft., died, Aug. 10, 1863.

Karge, Earnest, Pvt. Co. C, 11th Inft., Sub.

Kinney, Andrew S., Pvt. Co. H, 2d h. Art., Dis. Disa. Feb. 6, 1863.

Knowles, David W., saddler Co. C, 1st Cav.

Lake, David, Corp. and Sergt. Co. I, 8th Inft., killed at Antietam, Md., Sept. 17, 1862.

Lampson, Charles E., Pvt. Co. H, 2d h. Art.

Lampson, Frederick G., Pvt. Co. I, 8th Inft., R. E. Pvt. Co. C, 2d h. Art., Dis. Disa. Feb. 3, 1863.

Lampson, William, Pvt. Co. G, 28th Inft., died July 21, 1863, at Port Hudson, La.

Lapoint, Joseph, Pvt. Co. E, 6th Inft.

Lathrop, Herman S., Pvt. Co. A, 2d h. Art.

Lathrop, Orrin F., Pvt. Co. F, 6th Inft.

Lathrop, William G., Pvt. Co. D, 28th Inft.

Law, Sidney A., Pvt. and Corp. Co. K, 2d h. Art., died Jan. 29, 1865.

Lawrence, Thomas, Pvt. Co. E, 8th Inft., Trans. to Co. A, 10th Inft., Sub.

Lefever, Adolph, Pvt. Co. D, 10th Inft., Wd. at Ft. Gregg, Va., Apr. 2, 1865.

Logan, Frederick J., Pvt. Co. H, 2d h. Art., Dis. Disa. Apr. 12, 1863.

Logan, George E., Pvt. Co. I, 8th Inft., died at Weaverstown, Md., Nov. 15, 1862.

Loverage, Joseph R., Pvt. Co. H, 2d h. Art., died at Washington, Sept. 12, 1864.

Loverage, Remus, Mus. Band 4th Penn. Cav.

Loverage, Romulus C., Sergt. and Lieut. Cos. H and B, 2d h. Art.

Loveridge, Royal T., Pvt. Co. E, 1st h. Art.

Lyon, Edward F., Corp., Sergt., and 1st Sergt. Co. H., 2d h. Art.

Lyon, James, Pvt. Co. D, 1st h. Art., Sub., deserted May 21, 1865.

Mallett, Henry W., Pvt. Co. H, 2d h. Art., Wd. at Winchester, Va., Sept. 19, 1864.

Malloy, William, Pvt. Co. L, 2d h. Art., died Aug. 22, 1864.

Marsh, Albert N., Pvt. Co. H, 2d h. Art.

Marsh, Charles N., Corp. Co. D, 1st Cav., Wd. and Cap.

at Gordonsville, Va., Aug. 7, 1862, Cap. at Thoroughfare Gap, Oct. 7, 1862, awarded Medal of Honor.

Marsh, Daniel E., 1st Sergt. and Lieut. Co. H, 2d h. Art.

Marsh, Decater D., Corp. Co. D, 28th Inft., died at Barancas, Fla., Apr. 12, 1863.

Marsh, Edward W., 2d Lieut. Co. H, and Capt. Co. M, 2d h. Art.

Marsh, George W., on Orcutt's Rolls as being from New Milford, but on the Conn. Offl. Rolls, as a deserter from Co. A, 7th Inft., and a Sub. from Southbury, and as an unassigned recruit to 18th Ill., who failed to report.

Marsh, Irwin G., Band 4th Penn. Cav.

Marsh, Philip G., Pvt. Co. I, 5th U. S. Art., on Orcutt's Rolls, not on Conn. Rolls.

McBath, David, Pvt. Co. A, 2d h. Art., Wd. at Cold Harbor, Va., June 1, 1864.

McHenry, Hugh, Pvt. Co. A, 1st h. Art., Sub., deserted July 29, 1865.

McKeagany, William, Pvt. Co. C, 1st h. Art., Sub., deserted July 10, 1865.

McLoy, John, Pvt. Co. C, 8th Inft., Sub., deserted Jan. 15, 1865.

McMahon, Joseph, Pvt. Co. G, 28th New York Inft., Sergt. Co. A., 2d M. R. of N. Y., died in Serv. in N. M., July 17, 1864.

McMahon, Michael, Pvt. Co. F, 2d h. Art., Wd. at Petersburg, Va., Aug. 31, 1864.

McMahon, Michael, 3d, Pvt. Co. F, 2d h. Art., Wd. at Winchester, Va., Sept. 19, 1864.

Mehan, John, Pvt. Co. H, 11th Inft., Sub., deserted, confined, escaped.

Meney, Francis, Pvt. Co. A, 13th Inft., Sub., Wd. at Winchester, Va., Sept. 19, 1864, deserted Oct. 31, 1864.

Merwin, Garwood R., Sergt. Co. H, 2d h. Art., died Jan. 25, 1863, at Alexandria, Va.

Mintsch, John L., Pvt., Co. D, 28th Inft. and Pvt. Co. A, 2d h. Art.

Monroe, Edward, Pvt. Co. K, 2d h. Art., Dis. Disa. Jan. 25, 1864.

Monroe, John, Pvt. Co. A, 11th Inft., Sub., Dis. Disa. Nov. 11, 1865.

Moore, Frank, Pvt. Co. I, 10th Inft., Sub., deserted March 8, 1865.

Morehouse, Frank, Pvt. Co. D, 28th Inft.

Morehouse, Lyman F., Pvt. Co. A, 2d h. Art., Wd. at Cold Harbor, Va., June 1, 1864, Dis. Disa. June 21, 1865.

Morehouse, Henry S., Pvt. Co. H, 2d h. Art.

Morgan, William, Pvt. Co. C, 5th Inft., Sub., deserted Nov. 1, 1863.

Morrison, William E. L., Sergt. and Pvt. Co. I, 29th Inft. Col'd., Wd. at Kell House, Va., Oct. 27, 1864, died Nov. 12, 1864.

Mosher, James D., Corp. Co. C, 13th Inft., died at Brasier City, La., Aug. 6, 1863.

Mosher, Lewis W., Corp. and Sergt. Co. H, 2d h. Art., Wd. at Cold Harbor, Va., June 1, 1864, Dis. Disa. May 24, 1865.

Munson, John, Pvt. Co. K, 2d h. Art., Wd. at Cold Harbor, June 1, 1864, died from wounds, Aug. 30, 1864.

Murphy, Michael, Pvt. Co. C, 5th Inft., Sub., deserted Nov. 1, 1863.

Nichols, Ezra L., Pvt. Co. K, 29th Inft., Col'd.

Nichols, Orlando, Pvt. Co. G, 10th Inft., Sub.

Noble, Andrew B., Pvt. Co. D, 28th Inft.

Noble, Henry C., Corp. and Sergt. Co. H, 2d h. Art., Dis. Disa. Feb. 4, 1865.

Northrope, Lawrence, Mus. Band 4th Penn. Cav.

O'Callaghan, Timothy O., Pvt. Co. F, 2d h. Art., killed at Winchester, Va., Sept. 19, 1864.

Odell, John, Pvt. Co. C, 13th Inft.

O'Niel, William, Pvt. Co. E, 10th Inft., killed at Fort Gregg, Va., Apr. 2, 1865.

Parkes, Joseph P., Sergt. and 1st Sergt. Co. A, 2d h. Art., killed at Cold Harbor, Va., June 1, 1864.

Phillips, Chester, Pvt. Co. K, 29th Inft., Col'd., killed at Petersburg, Sept. 23, 1864.
Phillips, Henry, Pvt. Co. I, 11th Inft., deserted Dec. 16, 1861.
Pike, Luther M., Corp. Co. D, 28th Inft.
Plumb, Alonzo, Pvt. Co. D, 28th Inft., died Aug. 21, 1863.
Plumb, Harvey G., Pvt. Co. D, 28th Inft.
Plumb, Henry, Surgeon 2d h. Art.
Plumb, Harvey G., Pvt. Co. I, 123d New York Vol.
Potter, George D., Pvt. Co. H, 2d h. Art.
Potter, George H., Corp. Co. H, 2d h. Art.
Purdy, Charles, Pvt. Co. I, 8th Inft., Wd. at Fort Huger, Va., Apr. 19, 1863, Dis. Disa., Apr. 4, 1864.
Randolph, Harvey J., Pvt. Co. K, 29th Inft., Col'd.
Read, Herbert H., Pvt. Co. H, 2d h. Art., Pris. at Ford's Mills, Va., June 14, 1864, died in Andersonville, Ga., July 3, 1864.
Rice, Levi, Pvt. Co. H, 2d h. Art., appears on Orcutt's Rolls, but not on Government Rolls.
Roach, Thomas, Pvt. Co. D, 8th Inft., Sub., deserted Dec. 2, 1864.
Roberts, Andrew, Pvt. Co. I, 8th Inft., died at Newbern, N. C., Apr. 1, 1862.
Roberts, Henry M., Pvt. Co. I, 8th Inft., died at Newbern, N. C., Apr. 6, 1862.
Roberts, William J., 1st Lieut. and Capt. Co. I, 8th Inft., Wd. at Fort Harrison, Va., Sept. 29, 1864, Dis. Jan. 31, 1865.
Rogers, Austin V., Pvt. Co. K, 2d h. Art.
Root, Nathan H., Corp. Co. H, 2d h. Art.
Ruby, Eli, Pvt. Co. D, 13th Inft., Dis. Disa. Sept. 29, 1862.
Ruby, George M., Pvt. Co. D, 13th Inft., deserted Aug. 27, 1864.
Sanford, Isaac L., Pvt. Co. A, 2d h. Art.
Savage, Edward P., Pvt. Co. G, 8th Inft., deserted Aug. 19, 1865.

Shultz, Myron, Pvt. Co. I, 8th Inft., Dis. Disa. Feb. 24, 1863.
Sherman, Lucius S., Pvt. Co. H, 2d h. Art., Wd. at Cedar Creek, Va., Oct. 19, 1864.
Sherwood, Asahel, Pvt. Co. D, 28th Inft.
Sherwood, Reuben H., Pvt. Co. H, 2d h. Art.
Schook, Louis, Pvt. Co. E, 8th Inft., Sub., deserted July 24, 1864.
Shove, Henry, Sergt. Co. D, 28th Inft.
Smith, Charles H., Corp. Co. K, 11th Inft., Sub.
Smith, William, 1st, Pvt. Co. F, 10th Inft.
Soule, David E., Corp. Co. H, Lieut. Co. F, 2d h. Art.
Soule, Henry, Band 4th Penn. Cav.
Sparks, Edwin, Pvt. Co. I, 8th Inft.
Spengler, Edward, Pvt. Co. E, 8th Inft., Sub., killed at Fort Harrison, Va., Sept. 29, 1864.
Stephens, Edgar, Pvt. Co. K, 2d h. Art.
Stephens, Henry L., Pvt. Co. D, 28th Inft.
Stephenson, William, Pvt. Co. A, 5th Inft., Sub., deserted July 11, 1865.
Sterling, Homer, Pvt. Co. H, 2d h. Art., Dis. Disa., Apr. 18, 1864.
Stevens, Franklin B., Pvt. Co. B, 2d h. Art., killed at Cold Harbor, Va., June 1, 1864.
Stevens, George, Pvt. Co. E, 6th Inft., Sub.
Stevens, William H., Pvt. Co. K, 2d h. Art., Wd. Cold Harbor, Va., June 1, 1864, Dis. Disa., June 6, 1865.
Stokes, Henry, Pvt. Co. A, 5th Inft., Dis. Disa. Jan. 30, 1862.
Tallman, Martin N., Corp. Co. K, 29th Inft., Col'd.
Tarr, James, Pvt. Co. E, 11th Inft., Sub., deserted July 7, 1865.
Taylor, Joseph, Pvt., Corp., and Sergt. Co. C, 13th Inft.
Thayer, Edward A., Pvt. Co. B, 20th Inft., deserted Sept. 29, 1862.
Thayer, John Q., Pvt. Co. I, 8th Inft.
Thompson, Edward E., Pvt. Co. H, 2d h. Art.

Tibbetts, Charles E., 2d and 1st Lieut. Co. C, 13th Inft.
Treat, Frederick M., Pvt. Co. D, 28th Inft., Wd. at Port Hudson, La., June 14, 1863.
Turrill, Henry S., 1st Lieut. and Asst. Surg. 17th Inft., Cap. and held Pris. in Macon, Savannah, and Charleston.
Van Anden, William, Pvt. Co. D, 28th Inft.
Vanderwater, William G., Pvt. Co. H, 13th Inft., Wd. at Irish Bend, La., Apr. 14, 1863.
Van Lone, Peter, Pvt. Co. D, 8th Inft., Sub.
Vorey, Charles, Pvt. Co. D, 11th Inft.
Walden, Edward, Pvt. Co. F, 2d h. Art., Wd. at Winchester, Va., Sept. 19, 1864.
Walker, Albert, Pvt. Co. D, 7th Inft., died on Morris Island, S. C., Sept. 18, 1863.
Warner, William C., Pvt. Co. H, 2d h. Art., died at Washington, D. C., Dec. 23, 1862.
Waters, Alexander, Pvt. Co. C, 3d Inft.
Waters, Frank, Pvt. Co. G, 17th Inft., Sub.
Way, Charles A., Pvt. Co. H, 2d h. Art., Wd. at Winchester, Va., Sept. 19, 1864, at Salors Creek, Va., Apr. 6, 1865.
Welch, Patrick, 1st, Pvt. Co. F, 8th Inft., Trans. to U. S. Navy.
Weller, Chester A., Band 4th Penn. Cav., Pvt. Co. H, 2d h. Art.
Wentworth, Jacob, Pvt. Co. K, 2d h. Art., Wd. at Cold Harbor, Va., June 1, 1864, died June 20, 1864.
Wenzenger, Daniel, Pvt. Co. B, 8th Inft., Sub., killed at Ft. Harrison, Va., Sept. 29, 1864.
Wiedmore, Paul, Pvt. Co. D, 8th Inft., Sub., deserted Sept. 10, 1863.
Wiley, James, Pvt. Co. D, 8th Inft., Sub. deserted Dec. 1, 1863.
Williams, Burr, Pvt. Co. H, 2d h. Art., Dis. Disa. March 27, 1865.
Williams, George S., Capt. Co. H, 2d h. Art.
Williams, James, Pvt. Co. A, 5th Inft., deserted Oct. 3, 1863.

Williams, John F., Pvt. Co. H, 2d h. Art.

Wilson, John, Pvt. Co. C, 20th Inft., Sub., deserted Oct. 5, 1864.

Wentworth, Hiram, Pvt. 1st Conn. Lt. Batt., deserted Jan. 24, 1862.

Wooden, Charles E., Pvt. Co. D, 28th Inft., Wd. at Port Hudson, La., June 14, 1863, died of wounds, July 17, 1863.

Woodruff, Theron M., Pvt. Co. I, 2d h. Art., Wd. at Cedar Creek, Va., Oct. 19, 1864.

Worden, Richard T., Pvt. Co. I, 8th Inft., killed at Walthall Junc., Va., May 7, 1864.

Recapitulation: Number of men credited to New Milford, 282; killed in battle, 17; wounded in action, 34; died in service, 35; discharged for disability, 33; deserted, 44; dishonorably discharged, 1; shot for desertion, 1. Casualties, honorable, 119; dishonorable 46; total 165.

There were thirty-seven drafted men and substitutes credited to the town; of these, twenty-seven deserted, leaving seventeen as the number of the town's volunteers to desert their colors, and most of these were of foriegn birth.

THE SPANISH-AMERICAN WAR

Walter Campbell.
Wesley Collins.
Gabriel Erwin.
George Isaac Hine.
Charles A. Hull.
Charles Kellogg.
Andrew Nichols.
Cyrus Northrop.
Albert Piper.
Albert Timms.
Walter Thompson.
Arthur Wheeler.
Walter Wheeler.

RECOLLECTIONS OF OLD NEW MILFORD HOMES

CONTRIBUTED BY ALICE MERWIN BOSTWICK

INDELIBLY stamped on my memory are pictures of the old homes of my ancestors, and the simple life within them, in which it was my privilege to share in early childhood. These houses, built before the Revolutionary War, were of the " salt box " style, two stories high except at the back, where the roof sloped from the steep gables down so low that my grandfather, a tall man, had to bow his head to go under the eaves into the stoop. This made windows necessary on but three sides of a house, and was designed to evade the heavy tax on every pane of glass used. The shrewd colonist preferred to have less light, rather than add to the King's revenue. Every stick of timber was oak from the forest primeval, felled and hewed by the strong arms of the men who, with stout hearts, braved the perils and hardships of the wilderness for their altars and homes. Every shingle was " rived out " by hand. The laths, window sashes, doors, handles and latches, hinges and nails, were all hand-wrought.

How well our forefathers built, these old houses, still standing in good habitable condition, after braving the summer suns, winter winds, and storms of more than a century and a half, bear witness. The great stone chimney was a tower of strength from its foundation in the cellar, fifteen feet square, up to the garret, strong as granite rocks could make it. It anchored the heavy beams and roof timbers, giving ample space for the many fireplaces needed in the large rooms growing around it. The kitchen fireplace was like those we read of, but seldom see. At one side of the crane was a bench where I, as a child, often sat watching the building of the fire—a work of skill. The big green back-log was first rolled in; then, the back-stick, fore-stick, chips and kindlings were added—a veritable woodpile, which, when kindled by the aid of the bellows, sent sparks and flame crackling and roaring up the cavernous chimney.

There may have been much poetry in "the hanging of the crane." There surely was much prose in cooking for a family, in pots and kettles hung on its hooks and trammels, over the burning coals and smoke. Long-handled frying pans, spiders, skillets, turnspits, bake kettles, and Dutch ovens would be unknown quantities to graduates from modern cooking schools; but they, with all their science and new appliances, cannot surpass the savory dishes evolved by our grandmothers from the limited means at their command, with the aid of these same out-of-date utensils.

From out the arch-roofed old brick ovens came famous loaves of rye and Indian bread, biscuits, pans of pork and beans, cards of gingerbread, seed cookies, election and pound cakes, baked as none of our ranges can ever bake. They had a flavor all their own, a color golden-brown as the fallen autumn leaves of the maple trees, whose "fair white hearts" went up in smoke out of the doorway, while the long-handled iron peel spread the glowing coals over the worn floor of the old oven.

Those were not days of ease and idleness. From sun-up till sun-down, there was work for each and all, indoors and out. "Hired help" was scarce. Some neighbor, not so "well-to-do," who had more children than income, spared a daughter "to come as one of the family" to work for board, clothes and winter's schooling till of age. Then, she was paid five dollars a month, and, at her marriage, was given a black silk dress and a feather bed.

Country stores were few and far between. Every family made and kept on hand their own supplies, loaning and borrowing in time of need; exchanging spare-ribs, roasts of beef and lamb; arranging their "butchering" in rotation, to accommodate each other. Fresh meat was a luxury, salted meat, the main reliance. In the smokehouse hung hams, shoulders, beef, tongue and sausage. Under these it was my task to pile green hickory chips, pine sawdust and corncobs, which made a smoke of a peculiar, pungent, spicy quality and odor.

Tallow candles, the only light in the long evenings, were to be dipped; dozens and dozens, the whole year's supply. To run out of candles was " shiftless." A few, partly wax, for the tall silver and brass candlesticks on the mantels in parlor and keeping-room, were run in moulds and hung to bleach.

Soap was to be made, hard and soft. An empty soap barrel was thriftless. A cake of scented soap, brought from a distant city, was highly prized. Of spinning and weaving there was no end. The mother and daughters, instead of going to clubs and lectures, after the housework was done had their stents, so many knots of yarn to spin. No need to walk for exercise; back and forth they briskly stepped, as the wheel swiftly whirled, the rolls stretching into miles of yarn, " single twisted " for cloth, " double and twisted " for stockings and carpet warp. Then, the yarn must be scoured and dyed, not with " Diamond Dyes " from the drug store, but with vegetable dyes from fields and woods—white oak roots, butternut bark, chestnut burrs, sumach " bobs," onion skins, and the wonderful indigo " dye pot blue." Every good housewife was past master in the art of dyeing, and looked with pride on the line and fence draped with skeins of yarn of bright, unfading hues and shades. Flax wheels, not then strictly ornamental, hummed evenings by the fireside, while deft fingers drew from the flax-covered distaff fine linen thread for sewing, and for sheets, pillow-cases, towels, and all the underclothing of the family. The loom in the garret was never without its web of cloth in process of weaving—wool, linen, or wool and linen mixed (called linsey-woolsey). The linen was spread on the grass, bleached snowy white, then laid away in oaken chests, ready for the wedding " setting out " of the daughters, who made it up by hand, stitching " two threads over, two under," the rule of the good seamstress.

From " homespun fulled cloth " the " every day " suits of men and boys were made, with the help of the tailoress who came spring and fall with press-board, goose, tailor-shears, and rolls of patterns supposed to fit all figures. What wonder if these home-made garments looked their name! Bedquilts were pieced in intricate patterns—baskets of flowers, butterflies, peonies, chariot wheels, log-cabin, goose chase, double and single Irish chain—and quilted in shells, circles, squares, diamonds, sawteeth and herringbone. The quilt frames in the "spare bed room" usually had one of these marvelous constructions on, ready for a "Quilting Bee," after which the company gossipped over *their* cup of tea as we over *ours* after a card party.

The shoemaker came with work-bench, kit of tools, lap-stone and boot-trees to make the common boots and shoes for the family (strictly common sense, no French heels). A smell of leather and "black wax" pervaded the room where he hammered merrily away at the heavy shoe soles on the lap-stone, singing of "Captain Kidd as he sailed, as he sailed," and telling stories of haunted houses. One blood-curdling tale of a ghost in a cellar, seizing the feet of everyone who went upstairs after dark, still lingers in my mind—uncomfortably, if the truth be told.

The schoolmaster came, a welcome guest, "boarding around," a week for each scholar, and perhaps an extra week for the child of some poor widow needing kindly help.

There came homeless wanderers silently claiming lodging and food. Under the low sloping roof was the "Old Shack's Room," where a bed was always kept in readiness.

One whom we knew only as "Old Shiver-to-bits" had been "crossed in love" and his mind unbalanced. He never spoke, except to himself as he looked up to the sky, muttering, "The air is full of women, all shiver-de-bits." Another would sleep only on the floor by the kitchen fire, wrapped in a blanket, cooking his own food for fear of being poisoned. He was an astrologer and philosopher. A woman came, who wore a quilted hood, never taken off and kept drawn over her face, which was always averted when she was spoken to. None of these unfortunates was ever turned away from the open doors of those hospitable homes.

The Schaghticoke Indians, who came from the Reservation with squaws and hounds on their fishing expeditions to the "Eel Rocks" at the Great Falls, always expected the privilege of sleeping in the barn. Their desire for cider was greater than their desire for food. They willingly paid for both with splint baskets. Sometimes they became quarrelsome and noisy, and then the "riot act" was read to them, whip in hand.

The visits of the parson were prized events. An atmosphere of dignity and solemnity seemed to emanate from his black clothes, high stock and white cravat. A reverence now unknown was felt for him, and he was looked up to as the fountain head of theology and religion. The doctrines of election, predestination and eternal punishment were talked of, filling my childish mind with dire forebodings of literal fire and brimstone. After a "season of prayer," and dinner (always an extra good one), he drove away, to my great relief.

Visits in those days did not mean calls. Company came from miles away to spend the day, often uninvited, but not unwelcome. To "drop in and take pot luck" was not, as to-day, a figure of speech, but literally true, for a "boiled dish" was the regulation dinner. Corned beef, salt pork, and vegetables were served together on a big pewter platter, with a boiled bag-pudding of Indian meal. This may not sound as well as Beef *à la mode, entrées* and desserts; but, when well cooked, it was by no means to be despised; and on it our ancestors lived, thrived, and were content, thankful and happy. Possibly it *did* give them bilious and depressed views of the hereafter!

Sunday began Saturday night, when the sun went down behind the hills. With the lengthening shadows came a seeming stillness, in advance of the long day of rest to follow. The Sunday breakfast was early, giving plenty of time for the long drive to "meeting." Come sun, come rain, snow or wind, nothing but sickness excused absence from the two long sermons, morning and afternoon, with prayer meeting between. The day was kept to the very letter of the old Sabbatical law. Dinner was prepared Saturday, and eaten cold. For Sunday reading, the leather-bound Family Bible and Psalm Book were brought out; also Baxter's Saints' Rest, Pilgrim's Progress, and the Book of Martyrs. A walk beyond the garden and dooryard was not allowed, till after sundown; a drive, except in case of necessity, was never thought of. Only "York State folks" did that. A maiden aunt reproved me for cracking nuts on Sunday, giving me to read the Fourth Commandment, and Isaiah 58:13-14, "If thou turn away thy foot from the Sabbath, from doing thy pleasure on my holy day," etc. The remembrance of those well-kept, solemn Sundays still remains; and, to this day, my inherited New England conscience never fails to accuse any transgression of the Fourth Commandment. Howells says, "The devout spirit of the old Puritans remained to their descendants long after the stern creed that had embodied that spirit had passed away."

Fast Day, too, was strictly kept in Puritan households, without reference to Good Friday. We might ramble in the woods for wild flowers, however, gather wintergreen, birch and sassafras for root beer, and have fritters and maple syrup for supper.

Thanksgiving was *the* great feast day of the whole year. Then, the children to the third and fourth generation came trooping back, filling the low-ceiled rooms under the old rooftree; and for them high festival was held.

For days before, great preparations were made. The "buttery" was full of good things. On the shelves were rows of mince, pumpkin and tart pies, the last named made from cider apple sauce,—a lost art,—and pans of doughnuts and crullers, flanked by the sage cheese, ready to be cut. Baking in the brick oven was an immense chicken pie, made with cream crust,—another lost art,—and an Indian pudding rich with suet—still another lost art.

The turkey, the choicest young gobbler of the flock, stuffed with savory dressing, also a pig with an ear of corn in its mouth, were roasting in a Dutch oven on the hearth, all these together filling the house with an odor of good cheer.

Oscar, of the Waldorf-Astoria, can do mighty deeds in his line, but, with all his skill, cannot equal one of those real old-fashioned Thanksgiving dinners.

After all the kin had come and gone, there was abundant " skippin " for the worthy poor; yes, and for the unworthy, who might come to partake of the free bounty of the ever charitable.

The winters were long, shutting families indoors by themselves. Books and papers were few, but these early settlers kept abreast of the events of the day, and they had clear-cut, strong opinions, which they expressed with no uncertain sound. In the long evenings they gathered around the great fireplace, listening with never-failing interest to the oft-told tales of Indians, of Tory raids, and of hardships and suffering in camp and field.

> " Shut in from all the world without,
> They sat, the clean-winged hearth about,
> Content to let the north wind roar
> In baffled rage at pane and door;
>
> . . . . .
>
> And for the winter fireside meet,
> Between the andirons' straddling feet,
> The mug of cider simmered slow,
> The apples sputtered in a row,
> And, close at hand, the basket stood
> With nuts from brown October's wood."

If neighbors joined the circle, promptly as the tall clock in the corner struck nine they donned surtouts, mufflers and striped knit mittens, lighted the candle in the pierced tin lantern, and trudged away over the hills to their distant homes.

The back-log had by this time burned down to glowing coals, and from these the shining brass warming-pan was filled, to warm the bed of the great-grandmother, and the trundle-bed of the small great-granddaughter; the remaining coals being carefully covered to kindle the morning fire. " Early to bed and early to rise," was a lived-up-to motto. Each one of the household climbed the steep, draughty stairway, with flaring, flickering candles, which dimly lighted the cold bedrooms, with their frost-covered windowpanes. Hastily undressing, they hurried under the blankets, and, burrowing into the deep feather beds, were soon lost in sound sleep, such sleep as open air life, good digestion, and a clear conscience alone can give.

This life of the early days may seem dull and humdrum to us in the rush and whirl of ours. If it was sober by reason of struggles with the hard conditions and stern emergencies contended with, it was cheerful, kindly, dignified, full of high ideals, aims and works. Who shall say our life is better?

None of us would willingly go back to the " good old times," to their seeming narrowness, inconveniences and discomforts; yet let us not forget to give all honor to these, our forbears, through whose piety, loyalty, courage and toil *we* have received so goodly a heritage.

LEVI SYDNEY KNAPP
From a photograph taken about 1870, now in the possession of his son, Mr. Frederick Knapp

UNCHARTERED INSTITUTIONS

Contributed by Frederick Knapp *

AMONG the unchartered institutions of the New England town, none has had a greater influence than its general " sitting-down " place, where, by common consent, the leaders of all classes gathered. It was to the town what political and social clubs are to the city; it was an exchange place, a go-as-you-please Lyceum, a modern market-place, where the newspapers of the day were criticised, where affairs of Church and State had to be discussed, where politics and politicians were weighed, ticketed, and shelved for future reference, and where neighborhood events were gone over and approved or disapproved. War, domestic or foreign, and its generals, were subject to this trial by jury. The jury consisted of lawyers, doctors, bankers, merchants, farmers. Party-leaders of every shade of opinion—Whigs (later Republicans), Democrats, Abolitionists (brass-mounted, or not mounted at all), Prohibitionists, Independents—all met here on common ground. It was an intelligent, earnest crowd, always good-natured, whose " give and take " was without circumlocution or apology.

In no town in Litchfield County, I fancy, was there quite such a sitting-down place as the store of Mr. Levi S. Knapp on Bank Street in our own town of New Milford, which was conducted by him until his death at the age of ninety-three, and, afterward, by his son, Gerardus Knapp. The place was known to everybody in the towns around. During the Kansas-Nebraska troubles in the late " Fifties," a witty neighbor christened it " Topeka Hall "; and the name was accepted as quite the proper thing. For a half century, " Topeka Hall " was an informal congress, where earnest men threshed out the

---

* A native and former resident of New Milford, who now resides in Hartford, Connecticut.

problems of the hour. As our late Governor Andrews said of it, "It was the place where the world was wound up." Had it been honored by a historian, like the late George William Curtis, and a *Harper's Magazine* for record, its quips and repartees might have furnished the "Easy Chair" with abundant and amusing copy; and its "wise saws and modern instances" would fairly have covered the history of the town. While its good stories made fun for the day, the place became, none the less, an educator of public opinion, and wielded an influence second to no institution in the town.

The remarkable longevity of the men who assembled there is worthy of special record, covering, as it does, the greater part of the nineteenth century. Below is a list of several of the prominent men, and their ages at death. It is a matter of regret that a more complete list cannot now be made:

Col. William J. Starr, 97.
William Roberts, 92.
Royal I. Canfield, 76.
William N. Canfield, 86.
Ralph E. Canfield, 85.
Judge David C. Sanford, 66.
Sheldon Blackman, 69.
Eli Mygatt, 86.
A. B. Mygatt, 80.
Augustine Thayer, 70.
Rev. John Greenwood, 85.
Rev. David Murdoch, 76.
John S. Turrill, 64.
Benjamin J. Stone, 78.
John Peck, 81.
Cornelius W. Peck, 78.
Elijah Hall, 70.
William Hartwell, 87.
Theodore Buck, 78.
Charles H. Booth, 81.
Frederick G. Bennett, 74.

Col. Gerardus Roberts, 70.
Levi S. Knapp, 93.
Gerardus Knapp, 74.
Charles C. Noble, 72.
John Glover Noble, 77.
Hiram B. Noble, 70.
Van Rensselaer Giddings, 79.
Merritt Beach, 79.
William Bostwick, 80.
Ethiel S. Green, 84.
Rev. J. B. Bonar, 79.
John P. Treadwell, 64.
Isaac B. Bristol, 84.
Anan Hine, 71.
Dr. James Hine, 80.
William H. Hine, 77.
Clark Hine, 84.
Eli Clark, 87.
Charles Sabin, 74.
Royal Buckingham, 81.
Samuel Randolph Hill, 62.

ALANSON N. CANFIELD
Born Oct. 6, 1807. The oldest resident of New Milford

Albert N. Baldwin, 80.   Eleazer T. Brewer, 81.
James H. McMahon, 68.   Cyrus Northrop, 95.
Henry Merwin, 77.   Robert Irwin, 88.
Robert Ferriss, 87.   Ezra Ferriss, 90.
Joel W. Northrop, 74.

And, living with us to-day, the only survivor of the older men, Mr. Alanson Canfield,* who will be one hundred years old on the eighth day of October, 1907.

* Mr. Canfield viewed the various ceremonies of the Bi-Centennial Celebration from the veranda of his residence on the east side of " The Green." He received scores of visitors there with little apparent fatigue.—Editor.

TRAINING DAYS IN THE FORTIES AS TOLD BY AN "OLD BOY"

Contributed by Frederic Knapp

"I like boys, the masters of the playground and of the street —boys, who have the same liberal ticket of admission to all shops, factories, armories, town-meetings, caucuses, mobs, target-shootings, as flies have; quite unsuspected, coming in as naturally as the janitor—known to have no money in their pockets, and themselves not suspecting the value of this poverty; putting nobody on his guard, but seeing the inside of the show—hearing all the asides. There are no secrets from them, they know everything that befalls in the fire company, the merits of every engine and every man at the brakes, and how to work it, and are swift to try their hand at every part; so, too, the merits of every locomotive on the rails, and will coax the engineer to let them ride with him and pull the handles when it goes to the engine-house. They are there only for fun, and not knowing that they are at school in the courthouse, or the cattle show, quite as much and more than they were, an hour ago, in the arithmetic class."

Our Emerson was right: he knew boys. And at no place or time was the boy let loose to see and do, quite equal to the training days in the "Forties." This was his day, when school didn't count, when the schoolma'am or master wasn't in it, the day long anticipated. When the morning broke he was no laggard, but the wise mother would not allow him to skip or hurry his breakfast, for she knew that when the day was done her laddie would be too fagged to eat. So, breakfast over, she ties the ribbon in his broad turn-down collar, and the father gives him two fippenny bits for all his own to spend as he pleases, and then they launch him forth with a " good time " for a blessing.

At the hill's foot he meets his comrades, and, further down, more Johns and Jims and Sams and Bills, and then the fun begins. On the village Green things begin to take on a warlike aspect and the boys catch on to every movement and miss nothing; while the girls—pshaw! they ain't in it to-day—keep in yards or on church steps. The darkey boys, as happy as any, begin to bring on the warlike steeds, which are praised or jeered as appearances demand. Presently there is a drum-beat on the big bass drum, and every boy scampers for the band, which consists of a fifer, a snare-drummer, and Charles Ford to beat the big bass drum. And he just could beat it like Sam Hill! I tell you, if the Britishers could have heard those fellows play, they would have got right off from Bunker Hill, you bet! Sure! they all admit. Now, at the upper part of "The Green," a soldier in uniform appears, and soon another. It's nine o'clock, and the first parade begins at ten. Soon they come in, in squads, until "The Green" seems to be covered with the mounts, after which the soldiers dismount and take things easy. Our boys are in and out amongst the horses, scooting, howling, criticising, or jeering, when an officer rides up and gives an order. This means business, and the small boy "gits," nor does he "stand upon the order of his going, but goes at once," and the soldiers hold the field. This is only preliminary work, however, a shaking down of the files preparatory to the reception of the Colonel and his staff in the afternoon. This over, the troops are off duty.

The soldiers take their ease as they please, some on "The Green," but more over at the tavern, where the boys flock in amongst them, until the "barkeep" shouts to them, "Get out; there's too many of you!" It's lunch time, too, for the boys, who begin to mass around Aunty Thatcher's gingerbread stand feeling about their jackets for the small coin. Whether they have any or not—it's all the same. The boys are democratic and divide, paying just like grown-ups for what they buy with the coin of the realm. No line drawn to-day between the boy with money and the boy without, nor is the color line apparent. This cuts no ice with our boys. Here's Dandy Lazarus, Fred Wilson (afterward sold into slavery), Joe Bassett, and Phil Jacklin. Black or white, the boys never think, or care; so long as the fippenny bits last, no boy goes hungry.

Then they stroll over and wash the gingerbread down with some of Jennings' ginger pop, happy as lords. Simple pleasures these; but, as Josh Billings says, the boys then got more fun out of a quarter of a dollar than do boys now out of a five-dollar bill. The bugle sounds, and every boy is off, for now the Colonel takes command. This is the "crowner" of the day which no boy will miss. The troop is again in line, with sabres drawn to receive its Colonel. A shout from the boys, and down the line comes Colonel Starr with his staff. Hurrah! ain't it great! It's Napoleon, or Old Put, or Ethan Allen, or Lafayette over again! The Colonel is received and takes command. The small boy holds his breath, for now you'll see how it's done in battle. The Colonel gives his orders; by fours, by eights, they wheel, they turn, they go *en masse*—it's wonderful how they do it! Golly gracious! At last they return to place, salute their Colonel, clang their sabres back into the scabbards, and are dismissed, and Training Day is over. Our lads return to their homes to relate to the fathers and mothers the excitements and perils of the day.

Well, my lads of the Forties, you had your fun; but, without knowing it, you learned much more than the pleasures of the day. You learned patriotism, you learned what it was to subject yourselves to obedience for the common good; what team work was, to work together, shoulder to shoulder, for the achievement of a common purpose. You learned self-control and discipline, which stood you in good stead later, on the real battlefield, and for which we, the living, honor you as you sleep in God's acre, on each Memorial Day. And you also learned, without knowing it, what we older boys are slow to learn, that no man liveth to himself or dieth to himself, but that self-sacrifice, the greatest good to the greatest number, is the cornerstone of republics, the goal toward which the whole world is moving.

Lads of the "Forties," I sing the "Sabre Song" to your honor, and may "*Qui transtulit sustinet*" be your sheet anchor and your motto!

REMARKABLE LONGEVITY OF NEW MILFORD CITIZENS

A Partial List Compiled from the Records by Minot S. Giddings

Samuel Wheeler Smith, 83.
Eli Mygatt, Jr., 80.
Zephaniah Briggs, 101.
Nathan Gaylord, 81.
David Sterling, 81.
John Gaylord, 90.
Gideon Camp, 79.
Stephen Ferriss, 1st, 102.
Stephen Ferriss, 2d, 88.
Dea. Russell R. Pratt, 78.
Lewis Allen, 80.
Dr. George Taylor, 78.
Samuel Buel, 83.
Joseph Ferriss, 98.
Benjamin E. Bostwick, 83.
Henry Hoyt, 88.
Lyman Hine, 89.
Orrin B. Marsh, 94.
John B. Peck, 77.
Henry Camp, 78.
Wm. Albert Knapp, 86.
Jair Morehouse, 87.
Eli Gaylord, 76.
Jabez Morehouse, 79.
Amelia Gunn, 82.
Gracia Minerva Merwin, 78.
Sarah B. Allen, 80.
Henrietta Hine, 88.
Marcia L. Baldwin, 79.
David D. Northrop, 79.
James A. Giddings, 87.
Daniel Gaylord, 83.
Peter Gaylord, 95.
Peter Waller, 84.
David Marsh, 82.
William A. Lewis, 77.
Adolphus Hallock, 80.
Benjamin Buckingham, 84.
Seymour Buck, 81.
George A. Ferriss, 78.
George W. Mallory, 80.
Isaac Hine, 82.
Harvey Jennings, 78.
Daniel Marsh, 82.
William H. Fairchild, 81.
Northrop Dunning, 94.
Irwin B. Gaylord, 93.
Charles Lake, 83.
Benjamin Treat, 78.
Darius Williams, 88.
William Couch, 78.
Albert S. Hill, 85.
William Cummings, 78.
Eliza Leavitt, 86.
Hetty Mygatt, 82.
Janett Force, 82.
Polly Canfield, 88.
Thalia M. Nickerson, 80.

Chloe Nichols Turrill, 83.
Betsey Evitts, 88.
Betsey Sterling, 90.
Ann Brownson, 85.
Martha Bennett, 81.
Mary Ann Boardman, 80.
Eliza S. Knapp, 87.
Mabel Baldwin, 87.
Lucia Tomlinson, 93.
Eliza Roberts, 84.
Betsey Sterling, 90.
Martha Gaylord, 88.
Lucy F. Lathrop, 79.
Marinda Ruby, 81.
Jerusha Sanford, 97.
Catharine Lewis, 82.
Lamira D. Clark, 88.
Mercy Canfield, 94.
Emily Weaver, 81.
Loretta Geer, 85.
Helen C. Marsh, 80.
Charlotte Evans, 87.
Harriet Smith, 80.
Armida Giddings, 96.
Cornelia A. Morehouse, 82.
Salome Williams, 88.
Anna Walker, 91.
Martha E. Dewey, 81.
Susan Buckingham, 78.
Harriet Hoyt Addis, 86.
Elizabeth M. Northrop, 76.
Adeline Buckingham, 76.
Elizabeth S. Hine, 85.
A. Maria Garlic, 84.
Julia A. Garlic, 80.
Lucy L. Crofut, 78.
Helen M. Giddings, 75.

Polly Bull, 94.
Anna Sheldon, 86.
Urania Marsh, 82.
Elizabeth Morehouse, 92.
Martha Mygatt, 87.
Laura M. Hallock, 87.
Jerusha Roberts, 91.
Martha D. Mygatt, 90.
Marietta Bryan, 89.
Elizabeth Monihan, 92.
Elizabeth C. Miner, 78.
Phœbe R. Stillson, 89.
Electa Thayer, 92.
Sara A. Sabin, 88.
Rebecca Buck, 97.
Emily Bostwick, 97.
Eliza Bristol, 99.
Polly M. Bishop, 90.
Lois C. Fairchild, 80.
Abigail D. Sturges, 90.
Jane Jennings, 82.
Mary A. Haviland, 85.
Emeline C. Morrison, 85.
Phœbe Briggs, 101.
Sarah Ann Canfield, 80.
Elizabeth Briggs, 85.
Betsey Baldwin, 75.
Fannie C. Warner, 78.
Mary M. Hine, 83.
Lucy Morgan, 79.
Mary A. Treat, 82.
Mary C. Wooster, 76.
Julia Brewer, 84.
Henrietta Noble, 85.
Hannah Lake, 79.
Esther H. Wheeler, 83.
Laura M. Baldwin, 79.

Remarkable Longevity of New Milford Citizens

Maria Green, 84.
Nancy Newton, 83.
Eveline G. Marsh, 83.
Maria Marsh, 78.
Irene Hoyt, 82.
Betsey Platt, 77.
Minerva Franklin, 81.
Elsie Hoyt, 81.
Lucia H. Noble, 78.
Rebecca A. Phelps, 84.
Elsie O. Nickerson, 79.

Abigail Camp, 81.
Susan Merwin, 79.
Sophia McMahon, 89.
Mary Stephens Brewer, 81.
Mary Olcott, 82.
Sarah Kellogg, 77.
Laura L. Camp, 76.
Maria Gaylord, 83.
Caroline Erwin, 88.
Electa Morehouse, 84.
Eliza Roberts Knapp, 77.

Sally Northrop, 101.

ACTIVITIES OF NEW MILFORD IN LATER YEARS

CONTRIBUTED BY MINOT S. GIDDINGS *

THE town of New Milford originally was of much larger extent than it is at present. It contributed New Preston Society, on the northeast, to the town of Washington; Newbury Society, on the south, to the town of Brookfield; and "The Neck" (Bridgewater Society), in 1856, to form the town of Bridgewater. Notwithstanding this depletion, it is still one of the largest towns, territorially, in the State.

It is well watered and fertilized by the Housatonic River through the whole length of the town; by the Aspetuck River, East and West branches, from the north; by Still River and Rocky River from the south and west; and by other streams.

The hills and vales of its rolling landscape present to the eye a spectacle which equals, in some respects, the much-lauded scenery of the Old World.

The growth of the town has been slow but steady. Agriculture is the chief industry. The fertility of the soil and its adaptability to grazing purposes make the production of milk and butter profitable. There is a large creamery near the railroad in the south part of the village, where farmers of the surrounding country bring their milk, which is sent to the large cities. There is also a creamery at Gaylordsville, and there are two private establishments in the village to supply the local wants of the people.

Raising tobacco and preparing it for market are among the principal occupations of the inhabitants, the Housatonic Valley being celebrated for the fine quality and abundant growth of this plant.

* The writer of this article has endeavored to be accurate in his statements. He has sought information from various sources; from the town records, from files of newspapers of the town, from personal recollections, and from the "History of New Milford," by Rev. Samuel Orcutt, 1882.

NEW MILFORD HAT COMPANY

Vincent B. Sterling, who has been engaged with one of the large tobacco firms for many years, and is familiar with the tobacco business, has contributed the following regarding it:

"Like most great enterprises, the raising of tobacco in New Milford started from small beginnings. About the year 1848, the first tobacco in New Milford was raised by George McMahon, who was soon followed by Seeley Richmond and Elijah Hall. These three men were without doubt the pioneers of the tobacco-raising in the Housatonic Valley.

"From that time it has been cultivated with more or less success, until, to-day, it is the leading crop of the farmers of this and surrounding towns. The amount grown at present is about one thousand three hundred acres annually. The variety was Broad Leaf, up to 1883; since then, it has been almost exclusively Havana Seed.

"Probably the amount invested in tobacco in the early fifties did not exceed five thousand dollars per annum, while, at the present time, at least five hundred thousand dollars is used annually buying and packing it. No crop grown by the farmer requires such constant attention. From the sowing in April, through the transplantation in June, until the matured plant is harvested and placed in the curing sheds in August and September the greatest care must be exercised. 'Eternal vigilance' is the price of success, and a sharp hailstorm of a few minutes' duration may destroy the results of the summer's labor. During the early fall the plants are taken from the poles, the leaves are stripped from the stalks and packed in bundles, and the tobacco is then ready for the buyer.

"It is probable that tobacco was first assorted and packed in New Milford in 1848 by George McMahon, who was followed, a few years later, by Perry Hall. These men were the first packers in the Housatonic Valley. Space will not permit mention of the parties who have been engaged in the business since that time. At present, it is one of the leading industries of the town. There are twelve tobacco warehouses, employing through the packing season in the neighborhood of four hundred men.

"Most of the capital needed to pack the tobacco is furnished by the large tobacco jobbing firms of New York and Chicago, who employ local men as buyers and packers.

"The crop as a whole is an important source of wealth to the farmers, as is evidenced by the many thrifty and beautiful homes of the successful tobacco growers scattered over the hills and valleys of New Milford."

There are some notable manufacturing industries in this town.

The manufacture of wool hats here dates back nearly a century. Glover Sanford began making them in 1823, on a small scale, in Bridgewater Society. The business steadily increased and was carried on by himself and brothers till 1870, when the firm removed to Bridgeport, Conn.

Smith & Erwin opened a hat factory in Bridgewater in 1834, and removed to this village in 1855, occupying the long building now used as a store by the firm of Ackley, Hatch & Marsh.

Isaac Reynolds began hat manufacturing in Bridgewater in 1847, afterwards removing to Lanesville. Joseph Sanford, Lyman B. Stone, and Francis Callahan engaged in the business at different times. A company was organized there in 1853 under the name of the Union Manufacturing Company.

The modern hatting industry was established in this village in 1885. Some of the leading citizens donated to the firm of Bates & Green a piece of land on West Street Extension, where a building was erected, and the making of hats of fur was carried on in a moderate way until 1898, when a fire destroyed the plant. It was not rebuilt, but the business was reorganized as the New Milford Hat Company, which purchased a tract of land a short distance north of the village, near the mouth of the Aspetuck River, and erected there a large plant with modern improvements. The officers of the company are: Andrew G. Barnes, president; Seymour S. Green, secretary and treasurer, and William G. Green, superintendent. Under their able management the enterprise has been very successful. In 1906 the amount of business done was five hundred thousand dollars: the pay-roll amounted to one hundred and eighty-five thousand dollars, and there were two hundred and fifty employees.

HONORABLE ISAAC BALDWIN BRISTOL
President of First National Bank, 1902-1905, and of New Milford
Savings Bank at time of his death

Merritt W. Hill and E. W. Hanke formed a partnership and began making hats, about 1890, in the Randolph Hill mill building on Mill Street. At the end of two or three years they removed to the upper part of Maltby Leach's flour and feed store on Railroad Street, where they were incorporated as a stock company in 1894. This company was dissolved in a few years. Mr. Hill now has a jewelry store on Bank Street. Mr. Hanke went to Bridgeport, Conn., and is doing a flourishing hat business there.

The manufacturing of buttons from vegetable ivory was begun here in 1866 by Henry S. and Walter B. Bostwick, under the firm name of Bostwick Brothers. The ivory nuts were at that time brought to this country as ballast to ships and sold at a small price, so that the making of buttons from them was quite profitable. Bostwick Brothers erected a building on Railroad Street and carried on the business with great success till 1884, when the plant was damaged by fire. Soon after the firm dissolved. Walter B. Bostwick went to Bridgeport, Conn., where he engaged in business, became prominent and was elected mayor.

Buttons were made at the old hat shop, corner of Bridge and Railroad streets, for several years by Isaac B. Bristol, Robert H. Isbell, William Schoverling, Rufus Leavitt, and perhaps others. About 1878 the Noble Brothers purchased the business and carried it on for a few years. After that, various mechanical inventions were developed there. A few years ago, the building passed to the firm of Ackley, Hatch & Marsh, and is now used for a general store.

A button shop was erected in 1884 on West Street Extension, in which buttons were manufactured by William Schoverling, George W. Anthony, and David E. Soule till 1889, when it was burned to the ground. This put an end substantially to button making in the town, the cost of raw material having increased so much that it became unprofitable.

Making lounges was begun in a small way many years ago by De Watt Pepper. From this slight beginning, the business increased until it became necessary to establish a large plant to meet the growing demands of the trade. The Eastern Lounge

Company was first housed in William Schoverling's brick building on Railroad Street, occupying, in addition to that, the old hat building on the corner of Bridge Street. In 1895 the business was removed to the commodious plant built by William Schoverling, on the site of the West Street Extension button factory, where it has been large and flourishing. The company is composed of De Watt Pepper, president, Mrs. William Schoverling, vice-president, and William P. Landon, secretary and treasurer.

Roswell and Sheldon Northrop began in 1832 the manufacture of machinery in a building, in Maryland District, near where the trout pond of Turney Soule now is, using the water-power to carry on their business. In a few years they removed to the brook south, and erected a foundry and machine shop, enlarging the business and admitting a younger brother, David, to the firm. They made castings to order, cast-iron fences, and various kinds of machinery. Changes in the firm occurred from time to time, but it always continued in the Northrop family. In 1887 Jasper A. Northrop removed the business to this village on West Street Extension, erecting a foundry and machine shop. He invented and began making a heater for warming houses, which he named the "Unique." This heater is made for both water and steam, and is sold extensively in this region.

Paper making from straw and rags has been carried on in this town for many years. Albert S. Hill and Edward Barton erected a paper mill in 1852, about a mile above Northville, on East Aspetuck River, where they made straw-board paper for hat and dry goods boxes. This business was continued until within a short time. The site had been used for a saw-mill more than seventy years before the paper mill was erected.

Just below this mill, on the river, was a grist mill, which was purchased in 1862 by William W. Wells and his brother Edwin S. They ground flour and feed there many years, and also constructed a saw-mill. This property has been used as a mill site for more than one hundred and twenty-five years.

Justus Miles came from Milford in 1742 and purchased the farm in Park Lane where the old house known as "Miles'

UNITED BANK BUILDING

ACTIVITIES OF NEW MILFORD IN LATER YEARS 89

Tavern" still stands, and where, from an ancient sycamore, still hangs the old iron crane which bore the tavern sign a hundred years or more ago. He built the works known as the "Miles' Grist Mill" in 1748 "by the north end of Henry Garlick's home lot" on East Aspetuck River. Manufacturing of some kind has been carried on there ever since, paper having been made there for the last fifty years. A company organized as the "New Milford Paper Company" recently purchased the property, and is preparing to do a large business in making cardboard and paper.

The Merryall Plough Foundry was established soon after 1800 by Elijah Hall. He made castings for ploughs and invented the "Hall Plough," which was very popular among farmers for many years. Mr. Hall was the first man in the State to use bituminous coal for forge work.

In 1768 Angus Nicholson purchased land on West Aspetuck River, and, some time after, built what was known for a long time as Nicholson's Iron Works. He erected a square marble stone, which is now standing, on the corner of the road a short distance above Wellsville, with the following inscription: "To Wm. Nicholson's Ironworks, 2 miles from New Milford, 85 miles from N. York, 1788." On the east side of the stone, the words, "To Kent," are inscribed, with an index hand pointing northward.

The manufacture of wool and linen into cloth was begun in the town at an early date. Mills for that purpose were erected on various water courses. Such a business was carried on near the mouth of Rocky River.

About 1820 William Roberts erected cloth works at Gaylordsville. A dam across the river was constructed in the early part of last century, and a saw-mill put into operation on the west side by Homer Gaylord, and on the east side a grist-mill, by Peter Gaylord.

George Wells and brother established cloth works at Wellsville, where they manufactured cloths quite extensively from wool and from wool mixed with cotton. The plant burned down eventually, and was not rebuilt. The property subsequently passed into the hands of Chauncey B. Marsh, who erected a saw-mill and machine shop, which he carries on at the present time. Mr. Marsh is also engaged in large operations in wood and lumber.

As many of the hills about New Milford are of lime rock formation, the stone has been mined and burned for lime since an early date; but this business has been somewhat neglected in recent years. In 1893 Charles E. Griffin leased or purchased of Marshall Marsh a tract of land near Boardman's Bridge, much of which was composed of lime rock. There he erected buildings and lime kilns, quarrying and burning lime successfully until 1897, when a fire destroyed the property. It was soon rebuilt and carried on until 1902, at which time the plant became incorporated in the New England Lime Company. Under that name, the business has greatly increased, and a large quantity of excellent lime is produced.

The mill site at Little Falls, about one mile below the village, has from early times been used as a grist mill. It was first known as Ruggles' Mill, then, for fifty years, as Stillson's Mill, and, after that, as Giddings' Mill. The structure is substantially built of stone. In 1884, William D. Black joined with Levi P. Giddings in establishing an electric light plant there. Lewis F. Curtis joined the firm a few years later. The New Milford Electric Light Company was incorporated in 1893 by Lewis F. Curtis, Mrs. William D. Black, and Levi P. Giddings. A new dam of stone and concrete has been recently constructed across the river, which furnishes abundant water power. This company furnishes electricity for lighting the streets and public and private houses in the village. A few years ago, an acetylene gas plant was established, which is used to a limited extent.

For many years a company bought land and "rights" to use land on the Housatonic River from Falls Village southward as far as Newtown. The late Hon. Nicholas Staub was very active in this project. In 1898 a company was incorporated as the New Milford Power Company. This company built a high dam at Bull's Bridge and constructed a canal for about a mile down the river. At the lower end of the canal, on the border of this town, they built a power-house and established on the river electric machinery about one hundred and

MANUFACTURING PLANT OF THE BRIDGEPORT WOOD FINISHING COMPANY

ten feet below the level of the canal. Water is conveyed down this steep declivity to the wheels through a huge cylinder thirteen feet in diameter. The electricity generated here is carried on wires to Waterbury, Bristol, and other cities, and moves the trolley systems of those places.

A company was formed in 1888 for the purpose of making pottery. Buildings were erected a short distance east of Giddings' Mill, which received their power from the mill by means of a long wire cable connected with a water-wheel. Quite a large business was carried on for a few years; then the plant passed into other hands for other purposes.

George B. Calhoun contributes the following concerning one of the large industries of the town, the Bridgeport Wood Finishing Company:

"This company was incorporated in Bridgeport, Conn., on October 7, 1876, with a silex manufacturing plant at Fort Ann, N. Y. In 1881 the company removed to its present location at Still River, and erected there a large silex, filler and paint, and japan and varnish plant. The principal portion of this plant was destroyed by fire in February, 1902, and was rebuilt with better facilities for meeting its business requirements. The products of the company are ground silex and feldspar, Wheeler's Patent Wood Filler, Breinig's Lithogen Silicate Paint, Breinig's Water and Oil Stains, Japans, Varnishes, etc. The business of the company has steadily increased in volume from year to year, and its products now have a world-wide reputation, so that, at the present time, agencies have been established in all the principal cities of the United States and Canada, as well as in Porto Rico, South America, and the principal European cities. With an auxiliary silex manufacturing plant at Branchville, Conn., and branch offices and warehouses in New York City, Boston, Philadelphia, and Chicago, the company is well equipped to care for its largely increasing interests at home and abroad. The officers of the company are: David E. Breinig, president and general manager; Edward E. Porter, vice-president; George B. Calhoun, secretary; Henry S. Mygatt, treasurer."

The cause of education has always received the earnest attention of the citizens of New Milford, and the little brown schoolhouses, planted a few miles apart, in which the boys and girls received all their book learning, were landmarks in the New England colonies, as are to-day the more pretentious structures which have supplanted them. In the early days, the Bible was read every morning at the opening of school and religious instruction was given; it was also thought proper to invoke the blessing of the Great Ruler of the Universe.

New Milford was divided into twenty school districts, the schools of which taught the elementary branches. In later years, as the population increased and a greater desire for knowledge was manifested, private and select schools and academies were founded in different parts of the town; at Gaylordsville, at Northville, and in this village.

The most noted school, established in the early part of the last half century, was the Housatonic Institute, which was carried on many years by Benjamin J. Stone and Mary A., his wife. It was situated on the site now occupied by Memorial Hall. This school was known far and wide and received pupils from the surrounding towns. Many of the older people of the town received their education there.

A famous school for boys was the Adelphi Institute, which removed from Cornwall, Conn., to this town in 1860. Ambrose S. Rogers put up fine buildings on the sightly hillside southeast of the village, and conducted for many years an educational institution which took the form of a military school during the Civil War.

The Center School is graded. Its several departments range from the kindergarten to the high school, which last prepares students for college. It is estimated that there are about one thousand one hundred children in the town between the ages of four and sixteen years.

The first kindergarten school in the town was opened in 1873 by Mrs. Andrew Bristol, assisted by Miss Mary C. Wells. Miss Wells succeeded Mrs. Bristol in 1878, and removed the school to her own home on Elm Street. It is called "Sunny Nook." She prepared herself for teaching at the New York Normal

POST-GRADUATE DEPARTMENT

Ingleside School was established in 1892 by Mrs. William D. Black, a daughter of Hon. David C. Sanford and a native of New Milford.

It is a school for girls and has been patronized by prominent families in most of the states.

The literary standard is high. The best specialists are employed as teachers and the regular course exceeds the college entrance requirements. It is especially a finishing school and its Post-Graduate Department gives unusual opportunities for specializing in music, art, literature, languages, etc. Physical training is a popular feature. The number of pupils is limited to one hundred.

INGLESIDE BUNGALOW

FOUNDATION HOUSE
VIEWS OF INGLESIDE SCHOOL

Kindergarten, at which she graduated in 1878. Miss Wells conducts her school with great success.

The Ingleside School for girls, which was established by Mrs. William D. Black, in 1892, and is the pride of the town, is described in another place.

There are six churches in the village—the First* Congregational, the parent church; St. John's (Episcopal); the Methodist Episcopal; St. Francis Xavier (Roman Catholic); All Saints' Memorial (Episcopal); and the Advent Christian. There is a Baptist church at Northville, a Methodist Episcopal church at Gaylordsville, and the old Quaker Meeting-house at Lanesville. Boardman and Merryall have each a chapel, in which Sunday schools and religious meetings are held weekly. A Sabbath school is conducted in Chestnut Land District.

The Memorial Hall and Library was erected in 1897 as a memorial to the soldiers and sailors of New Milford. Egbert Marsh contributed ten thousand dollars toward the building and gave part of the lot. He also gave the fund for supplying books to the library. Individuals contributed the balance of the cost of this memorial. The upper story is the headquarters of Upton Post, Grand Army of the Republic, which was organized December 20, 1882, with twenty-six charter members.

The first newspaper in this village was the *New Milford Republican*, established in 1845, by J. K. Averill, who carried it on for a year, then removed to Litchfield, Conn.

Messrs. Bailey and Donavan of Danbury, publishers of the *Danbury News*, began, in 1872, to publish the *New Milford Journal*, which was soon after sold to J. R. Johnson, and, later, to Marcus L. Delevan, who changed its name to the *Housatonic Ray*. The *Gazette* was started by Gee and Hale in 1877, and passed shortly after into the hands of Robert Erwin. Joshua A. Bolles and Franklyn Henry Giddings of Great Barrington, Mass., purchased the *Ray* in 1882 and, a little later, the *Gazette*, and merged the two papers into the *New Milford Gazette*. Mr. Giddings soon withdrew from the paper, not finding sufficient scope probably as an editor of a country news-

* The Second Congregational Church was established in Bridgewater Society which became the town of Bridgewater in 1856.

paper for his great ability. He has since attained world-wide fame as Professor of Sociology at Columbia University, having written several works on sociology and kindred subjects, some of which have been translated into many languages. Mr. Bolles continued to conduct the *Gazette* with much ability till he was stricken with a disease which suddenly caused his death, to the sorrow of the whole community. The paper then passed into the hands of Philip Wells, the present proprietor.

New Milford has had a brass band most of the time during the last half century. The original band was organized in 1855 by Earl Buckingham, who was its first leader. At the breaking out of the Civil War, the band engaged with the Fourth Pennsylvania Cavalry. It was discharged by Act of Congress after having served about eleven months. In 1872, a reorganization was effected, with Winfred Soule as leader. Under different leaders, the band has continued, with occasional lapses, to the present time.

Roger Sherman Hall was built in 1875, at a cost of nearly fifty thousand dollars. It is of brick, and has a large hall on the second floor; a courtroom, probate, town offices, and a law library on the first floor; and a town courtroom and "lockup" in the basement. It stands on the site of William Sherman's store, where Roger Sherman had his shoe shop. On the twenty-sixth of October, 1897, a bronze tablet to the memory of Roger Sherman, which had been placed on the north side of the front entrance of the building, was unveiled in the presence of a large company. The tablet was the gift of the Roger Sherman Chapter, Daughters of the American Revolution, organized May 15, 1893. Mrs. Sara T. Kinney, State Regent, D. A. R.; Senator George F. Hoar, a nephew of Roger Sherman; Senator Joseph R. Hawley; and Henry S. Sanford made addresses.

The first bank was started here in 1852 with one hundred thousand dollars capital, under the name of the Litchfield County Bank. It occupied a small brick building near the Boardman residence on Main Street. Frederick G. Chittenden was president. The first cashier was A. McAllister of Bridgeport, Conn. George W. Whittlesey succeeded Mr. McAllister

ANDREW B. MYGATT
Born 1820, died 1901

ACTIVITIES OF NEW MILFORD IN LATER YEARS 95

as cashier, and Eli Mygatt and Henry W. Booth were successively presidents. In 1865 it was changed to a national bank and called the First National Bank of New Milford. The presidents were successively Daniel Marsh, Henry W. Booth, Andrew B. Mygatt, Isaac B. Bristol, and Henry S. Mygatt; the cashiers, John J. Conklin, Henry Ives, Henry S. Mygatt, and Everett J. Sturges. The present officers are: Henry S. Mygatt, president; Seymour S. Green, vice-president; and Everett J. Sturges, cashier. The clerks are Robert E. Murphy, Roland F. Mygatt, and Ray W. Leach.

The New Milford Savings Bank was organized in 1858. Eli Mygatt was president, Silas Erwin vice-president, and John S. Turrill secretary and treasurer. Mr. Turrill was succeeded by Charles Randall, who was succeeded, in turn, by his son, H. LeRoy Randall, the present incumbent. The present officers are: Turney Soule, president; Seymour S. Green, vice-president; H. LeRoy Randall, treasurer; Edwin J. Emmons, assistant treasurer. When Dr. James Hine was president, a fine building for the bank was built on Bank Street, which was destroyed in the great fire. On completion of the new United Bank Building, the bank was installed there.

The Agricultural Society of New Milford was formed in 1858, and, since that time, has held fairs and cattle shows each year—with a few exceptions. It now occupies a fine site at Conetia Park.

The New Milford Water Company was chartered in 1873, and organized with a board of directors. Charles H. Booth was chosen president, Charles H. Noble, secretary and treasurer, and Henry O. Warner, superintendent. A reservoir was located on the hill about one mile and a quarter northeast of the village, near the source of Cross Brook, which is fed by springs of pure water. Three other reservoirs have since been built of such capacity that the supply of water is ample for the public and private uses of the village. The present officers of the company are: Albert H. McMahon, president; Verton P. Staub, superintendent; and Harry S. Sanford, secretary and treasurer.

The first fire company, organized in 1830, was disbanded in

1863, and succeeded by the Water Witch Engine Company No. 2. This company was succeeded, in its turn, in 1876, by the Water Witch Hose Company, No. 2, which now occupies a commodious building on Church Street.

New Milford has had several ruinous fires in its history. A fire swept through Bank Street in 1860, and another, a few years later; but the most destructive conflagration occurred on May 5, 1902, when the village was startled by the ringing of bells, the tooting of steam whistles, and the cry of "Fire!" Smoke and flames were seen issuing from the stables back of the New Milford House. The hose company hastening to the scene put forth great efforts, and for a time seemed to have obtained control; but the flames spread in all directions, to the alarm of the inhabitants, who were removing their goods to supposed places of security. The solid block on Bank Street was soon in flames. Then, in spite of the strenuous exertions of the firemen, the fire leaped across the street to the north side and ignited the roofs of brick buildings where merchandise had been placed for safety. The neighboring city of Danbury sent a gallant band of firemen with one of their best engines, with which they labored with great zeal to subdue the flames. With the aid of our own brave boys, this was finally accomplished, but not until the whole block and both sides of Bank Street were smoking ruins. Three hotels, two bank buildings, the Post Office building, and the largest mercantile establishments in the town, with their contents, were destroyed. The only building in the whole square that was saved intact was the fine mansion on the southeast corner of Main and Bridge streets, the residence of State Bank Commissioner Charles H. Noble and his brother, Town Clerk Russell B. Noble—worthy descendants of the pioneer settler of the town.

Did the brave merchants and men of affairs, who could do nothing while they saw their property go up in smoke, sit down in despair? Not they! They cleared away the rubbish before it was cold. They worked with a will to bring order out of chaos. They erected on "The Green" cheap wooden buildings, in which they gathered the remnants of their goods; and

Photograph by C. D. Hine, May 7, 1902

NEW MILFORD AFTER THE FIRE

ACTIVITIES OF NEW MILFORD IN LATER YEARS

soon the beautiful square looked like a mushroom city in some mining district of the West. They named it "Shanty Town," and for several months business was transacted there.

After the fire, streets were improved, and the system of drainage was extended. Stores were enlarged—some to double their former size—their business increased, and in less than two years no trace of the terrible catastrophe was visible.

The town was rebuilt of brick, iron, and stone, more beautiful and substantial than before. The three hotels, which had been of wood, were replaced by much larger buildings of brick. On the site of that famous hostelry, the New England Hotel, now stands the magnificent United Bank Building, one of the best equipped banking establishments in Western Connecticut. The National Bank occupies one side, and the Savings Bank the other side of this structure, while in the second story are handsome, commodious offices.

The railroad station was partly burned, but was soon renovated, and at that point in the town great changes are now in progress. A new freight depot is being erected and more tracks are being laid. In the near future, a new passenger station is to be built, and other improvements will be made.

The population of the town is increasing, being estimated at the present time as fifty-five hundred inhabitants. A Board of Trade was organized many years ago. A commercial club now occupies the fine rooms over the new Post Office. The Town Court was established in 1901, and Postmaster George H. Jackson was appointed the first judge. J. Edwin Hungerford succeeded him, and J. Butler Merwin is the present incumbent. The wooden bridges that spanned the Housatonic, and were at times swept away by floods, have given place to graceful iron structures, which are above the reach of high water. The town possesses an excellent telephone system. The facilities for supplying all the needs of the inhabitants are adequate. In a word, to quote Newell Calhoun, "Wealth, learning, and religion have their abiding places here, and have helped to make this village the resting place of the weary, and the working place of the industrious."

THE STORY OF NEW MILFORD
TOLD IN CHRONOLOGICAL EPITOME

CONTRIBUTED BY RUSSELL B. NOBLE AND MINOT S. GIDDINGS

1702. Indian Deed to the Proprietors of New Milford was given, signed by fourteen Indians. Consideration, Sixty pounds current money of the Colony of Connecticut, and twenty pounds in goods.

There were 109 proprietors who owned Rights.

The Committee were Robert Treat, Sen., Thomas Clarke, Sen., George Clarke, Joseph Treat, Joseph Peck, Jonathan Baldwin.

New Milford was called a Plantation till 1712.

1703. The Legislative title called the "Patent" was granted by the Grand Court to New Milford.

1706. Zachariah Ferriss came to New Milford and plowed a piece of land near Roger Sherman Hall—the first work done by a white man here.

1707. The names of the three earliest settlers of New Milford are: John Noble from Westfield, Mass., John Bostwick, from Stratford, Ct., John Noble, Jr., from Westfield, Mass.

1708. Daniel Bostwick was born; the first male child born in New Milford.

Dea. Samuel Brownson, Farmington, Ct., Major John Bostwick, Jr., Stratford, Ct., and Zachariah Ferriss, Stratford, Ct., settled in New Milford.

1709 or 1710. Roger Brownson, Farmington, Ct.; John Weller, Springfield, Mass, and Thomas Weller, Westfield, Mass.,'settled in New Milford.

1710. Sarah Ferriss was born; the first female child born in New Milford.

1711. Benjamin Bostwick, Stratford, Ct; Isaiah Bartlet, and Samuel Prindle, Milford, Ct., settled in New Milford.

1712. The General Assembly of Conn. granted the powers and privileges of a Township.

1712 and 1713. Samuel Beebe and John Weller were chosen grand jury and sworn.

Benoni Stebbins and Stephen Noble were chosen haywards, or field-drivers.

William Gaylord was chosen inspector and brander, and sworn.

John Bostwick, Sen., was chosen Collector.

Voted: that the inhabitants should pay Six pounds, fifteen shillings towards the minister's board, Zachariah Ferriss, Jr., holder, Samuel Brownson, town treasurer.

1713. Ensign Wm. Gaylord came to New Milford, residing on the lot subsequently owned by Rev. Nathaniel Taylor.

The town voted to lay out a pastor's lot and dig and stone up a well for Mr. Boardman, if he became the settled minister.

Voted: to grant a twenty-four shilling lot to Mr. Daniel Boardman, a preacher of the Gospel at the said place, to his heirs and assigns forever, upon a condition that he shall become their settled minister of the place, and continue so for the space of twenty years, or during his natural life and ability so to be.

Voted: that a dwelling house, forty feet in length and twenty-one in breadth and two stories high, and fourteen feet between joints, be forthwith built upon the land at New Milford, proposed to be granted to Mr. Boardman.

John Noble was chosen the first Town Clerk. Zachariah Ferriss, Samuel Brownson, and Samuel Hitchcock were chosen Selectmen. John Bostwick was chosen constable and sworn. Zachariah Ferriss, surveyor. John Noble, Sen., and John Bostwick, Jr., were chosen collectors to join with Mr. Jonathan Law to collect 12 shilling tax for the year.

1714. Main Street, Bridge Street, Elm Street and Bennitt Street laid out.

Voted: that there shall be five shillings and sixpence allowed by the week for the minister's board for the time to come.

Voted: that there shall be six shillings cash allowed by the town to David Noble, in case he beat the drum the year coming upon all public meetings.

John Noble died Aug. 17. He was the first adult to be buried in the graveyard.

1715. In view of the need of a grist mill in the town, the proprietors, in a meeting held at Milford, Feb. 24, 1715, made this arrangement. Voted: that Ens. Samuel Clark, Sergt. Samuel Beard, and Samuel Brownson, are chosen a committee to agree with some person to build a mill on some part of Still river or elsewhere at his own charge.

1716. John Griswold came from Wethersfield and built a mill at what is now Lanesville.

The "First Church of Christ" was organized by Council on the day of the ordination of Mr. Boardman, and his call and acceptance of the ministry. Religious meetings were held in the house built by Mr. John Reed until a new meeting house was built.

The burying place laid out—Center Cemetery.

1718. Highway laid out from Danbury road to Mill at Lanesville.

Highway laid out across Indian Field from river on west side.

Highway laid out from Park Lane eastward.

1719. Highway from Main Street to Great Falls on east side river laid out 30 rods wide.

1722. June 12th, the New Milford North Purchase was made. It was taken from Waramaug's reserve.

The first highway on west side of river to New Fairfield line through Gaylordsville laid out.

Highway laid out on west side of Great River from Rocky River by marked trees to Winnisink Brook.

Highway laid out northward.

1723. Ensign Wm. Gaylord went to Gaylordsville and built a log cabin.

1724-5. Capt. John Warner was the first settler at the "South Farm" (lower part of New Milford).

1728. Ensign Wm. Gaylord erected a frame house which is still standing.

The first Grand List made in New Milford.

1730. John Noble, 2d, one of the first three settlers in New Milford, sold his house and lot in the village Nov. 6, to William Gillett of Milford, and soon after settled at Gallows Hill, New Milford plains, and resided there during his life. He was the first permanent settler below Gallows Hill.

1733. Capt. Joseph Ruggles was the third or fourth settler at the Iron Works (Brookfield).

1734. A burying place laid out in South Farms, New Milford, called Gallows Hill, lying on the country road to Danbury.

1736. "Capt. Stephen Noble, Dea. John Bostwick, Samuel Canfield, Sergt. Nathaniel Bostwick, and Joseph Ferriss were chosen a committee to order all the prudentials in building a bridge over the Great River in said New Milford at the place the town hath agreed upon, &c."

This was a free bridge and was partly carried away by the floods in about three years, when a toll bridge was erected in its place.

Rev. Daniel Boardman was granted the privileges of the bridge free of cost.

1737. The Great Bridge across the Housatonic river was built in 1737—the first to be built from its source to its mouth.

1741. The first Quaker Meeting House built in or about this year, on Danbury road west side of river, nearly opposite Little Falls.

1743. Roger Sherman came to New Milford from Newton, Mass.

Feb. 6. "Voted: that Mr. Roger Sherman shall pass and repass over the bridge and his family; he paying ten shillings."

December. "Voted: that the Indian natives shall pass and repass over the bridge toll-free."

December. "Voted: that all persons that shall pass or repass on the Sabbath or Lord's Day between sunrise and sunset, in order to attend the public Worship of God in a lawful congregation in New Milford, shall pass free from payment over the great bridge in said town for the coming year."

1744. Until 1744 there was but one military company in the Town. The officers were as follows: Capt. Stephen Noble (served 20 years), Lieut. John Bostwick, Ensign Wm. Gaylord, Capt. Theophilus Baldwin, Lieut. Joseph Bostwick, Ensign Samuel Canfield.

1746. The first Episcopal Church was established in New Milford about this time.

1746. Roger Sherman settled with his brother William on the west side of Winnisink brook, the place called New Dilloway.

1754. Rev. Solomon Palmer, the first resident Episcopal clergyman, came to New Milford.

Voted: " that the meeting-house —— shall be erected in the town street, east from Joseph Northrop's dwelling house and west from Samuel Comstock's well, where there is a heap of stones erected."

Voted: " that the inhabitants of this Society will raise the meeting-house by free will offering."

Voted: " that the committee shall provide what liquors they shall think necessary to be used at the raising of the meeting-house at the cost of the Society."

The second Congregational meeting-house was built.

The Newbury Society was incorporated.

1755. The bridge was carried away by flood, and a new bridge built by the taxpayers of the town, and the Assembly granted the privilege of taking toll of all persons except taxpayers.

Ezekiel Payne settled on the east side of the Housatonic, at Gaylords Ville.

Lazarus Ruggles settled at Lanesville and erected the Iron Works.

1756. " Voted: that the old meeting-house which belongs to this Society shall be disposed of as follows, viz.: three-quarters of the body seats and two pews shall be given to the Church of England, and the remainder of the body seats to the Quakers in this Society, and the pulpit to those of New-

CAPTAIN GARRY BROOKS
Grandson of Rev. Thomas Brooks, first pastor at Brookfield, Connecticut, and the oldest living person born in New Milford

bury (Brookfield), and the gallery seats to those of New Preston Society which belong to New Milford, and the remainder to be disposed of and the avails of it improved toward the new meeting-house in this Society."

1757. Mary Roberts gave her negro slave, Dan, his freedom upon his paying her £3, 2s. 5d. annually during his life.

The church was organized in Newbury Society Sept. 28th. Mr. Thomas Brooks was ordained the first minister.

1758. Capt. Joseph Canfield raised a company and served with them under Col. David Wooster. They marched to Albany in May.

1760. Gaylordsville School District laid out.

Upper Merryall burying ground laid out.

1761. The Separatists or Strict Congregationalists built a house of worship near the Center Cemetery.

An effort made to clear the Housatonic River for navigation. A committee appointed and liberty granted to raise 300 pounds money by lottery.

1766. The bridge was carried away and rebuilt, and in three years a part of it went off again. It was again repaired but did not remain a year.

1769. School District organized. Jared Lane introduced the Lombardy poplar tree into New Milford the latter part of the century.

1770. Voted: " that the town relinquish all their right to any part of the bridge to the proprietors, who shall rebuild the same in any place between Little Falls and Wannipee Island."

1771. School District on east side of the river laid out.

1774. Partridge Thatcher liberated his slave Sibyl on her marrying Amos Lewis, a negro man.

1775. Capt. Isaac Bostwick was sent with a company of sixty-five officers and men from New Milford to Boston in the autumn and winter of 1775, and remained there during January and February, 1776. They were in Colonel Webb's Regiment.

1776. Josiah Starr served in the Revolution. In May, 1776, he was appointed Captain. In June he was appointed Lieutenant Colonel, Commission dated January 9th, 1777, signed by John Hancock. He was commissioned as Colonel, 1780. Died Oct. 15, 1813.

1776. Capt. Couch's Company, in Col. Andrew Ward's Regiment, containing seventy-six officers and men, were sent to New York. The company was in the service two months and twenty-three days.

At an annual meeting of the inhabitants of the town of New Milford holden on the 9th day of December, 1776, the committee of Inspection and Correspondence appointed were: Mr. Samuel Comstock, Mr. Israel Baldwin, Capt. Abram Camp, Daniel Everitt, Esq., Capt. James Terrill, Mr. John Comstock, Mr. George Smith, Doct. Jonah Todd, Joseph Ruggles, Esq., Col. Bushnell Bostwick, Samuel Bostwick, Esq., Col. Samuel Canfield, William Cogswell, Esq., Abel Hine, Esq., Mr. Amos Northrop, Capt. Sherman Boardman, Mr. Reuben Booth, Mr. Asahel Noble, Dea. Benjamin Gaylord, Mr. Oliver Warner, Mr. Caleb Bennett, Mr. Samuel Warner, Dea. Ebenezer Hotchkiss.

1777. Public town meeting held Mar. 10. Voted: "That the regulations contained in the late Acts of Assembly respecting the laying of embargoes and the stating of prices now in force are good and wholesome, and such ought to be strictly adhered to and that it is the indefeasible duty of all informing and executive officers to prosecute in the most effectual manner all violations of said regulations; and that it is the duty of the inhabitants of this town to give all the assistance in their power to such officers in the discharge of their aforesaid duty."

Mar. 31. "Voted, that a committee be appointed according to the advice of His Honr., the Governor, &c., for the purpose of furnishing the quota of soldiers in the Continental service for said New Milford.

"Lt. Zadock Noble, Capt. Joseph Ruggles, Jr., Jeremiah Canfield, Mr. Ithiel Stone, Dea. Israel Baldwin, Mr. Thomas Brownson, and Mr. Zachariah Sanford, were chosen the committee.

"Voted, that the town of New Milford will give twelve pounds lawful money, bounty, for the first year's service in addition to all encouragement already given to such inhabitants of this town as shall enlist into the Continental service for three years, or during the present war, within ten days from this time, including those who belong to this town who have already enlisted, subducting only their wages from the time they enlisted to this day, and such private donations as they have received.

"That for the second and third years, said soldiers who shall so enlist shall have six pounds lawful money pr. year to be paid out of the town treasury."

Sept. 30. "Capt. Sherman Boardman, Mr. Samuel Warner, Mr. Simeon Baldwin, Capt. Benjamin Brownson, Capt. Ebenezer Couch, Mr. Ithiel Stone, Dea. Ebenezer Hotchkiss shall be a committee to procure clothing for the soldiers in the Continental service."

1778. A meeting held in January was recorded as follows:

"1st. The articles of *Confederacy* as proposed by *Congress* stiled, *The United States* of *North America*, was read in said meeting and taken into serious consideration by Articles separately, and in succession, and no objection made to said Articles, except some part of ye 5th Article, which respects the mode of choosing our *Delegates* in *Congress*.

"Voted: that the Freemen will always hold the Prerogative and sole power choosing our Delegates in Congress by vote.

"2d. Said Articles of Confederacy was approved as good, and adopted in full by the members of sd. meeting without one dissenting voice."

The Revolutionary Army under General McDougall encamped at Dea. Benjamin Gaylord's. Some time during the War Generals Washington and Layfayette were said to be guests of Dea. Benjamin Gaylord.

Army under General McDougall was encamped on Second Hill.

The committee of inspection and correspondence, which was a kind of home police of patriotism, were:

Capt. Elizur Warner, Lt. Isaac De Forest, Lt. Benjamin Seelye, Capt. Reuben Bostwick, Capt. Paul Yates, Mr. Daniel Everett, Capt. James Terrill, Mr. Amos Northrop, Mr. John Porter, Mr. Nathan Gaylord, Mr. Samuel Merwin, Jr.

The committee to procure supplies for the soldiers in the Continental army were: Capt. James Terrill, Mr. Reuben Booth, Lt. David Smith, Mr. Simeon Baldwin, Capt. Benjamin Brownson.

To provide clothing for the soldiers in the Continental army were: Ens. Jeremiah Canfield, Mr. Ebenezer Hotchkiss, Mr. Simeon Baldwin, Mr. Asahel Noble.

1779. Received, Litchfield, 28th Sept. 1779, of the First Society of New Milford by the hands of Col. Samuel Canfield, ninety-four pounds, sixteen shillings money, which was contributed by said Society for the relief of the suffering and distressed inhabitants of the towns of New Haven, Fairfield and Norwalk, £94-16.

Per Reuben Smith, County Treasurer.

Nathan Dayton purchased of Enos Camp a piece of land lying "southeast of the lime kiln," and on it his father and brother Abraham Dayton built a Saw Mill. Col. Josiah Starr and Abel Hine owned a grist-mill there at that time.

1780. The town voted that every soldier who shall voluntarily enlist to serve in the Continental Battalions for the space of six months, or until sooner discharged shall be paid four bushels of wheat or an equivalent in money in addition to the bounty already given by the State. They also voted to give three bushels of wheat or its equivalent in money to all militia men who might be called to serve one month, in addition to all other pay, and when they should serve more than a month, then three bushels of wheat for every month.

Two months later the town offered ten bushels of wheat per month for every soldier who should enlist for four months.

It was voted that none of the persons who had voluntarily gone over and joined the enemy, shall be suffered to abide and continue in the town during the present situation of affairs.

March 13. A committee of inspection on provisions, agreeable to a late act of Assembly, was chosen as follows: Mr. Simeon Baldwin, Capt. Noble Hine, Mr. Daniel Everitt, Capt. Paul Yates, Mr. Ebenezer Hotchkiss, Mr. George Smith, Capt. Sherman Boardman, Mr. Ithiel Stone, Mr. Thomas Lewis, Capt. Benjamin Brownson, Capt. Reuben Bostwick, Mr. Israel Baldwin, Joseph Hartwell, Doct. Reuben Warner, Benjamin Gaylord, Ebenezer Gaylord, Asahel Noble, Capt. Elizur Warner, Israel Camp, Lemuel Warner, Capt. Joseph Ruggles, Dea. Abram Camp, Ephraim Buck, Samuel Merwin, Martin Warner, Uri Jackson, Robert Bostwick, Nehemiah Hawley.

In June, upon the call from Congress for more soldiers, the town voted that "every soldier who shall voluntarily enlist to serve in the Continental Battalions for the space of six months, or until the first day of January next (unless sooner discharged) shall be paid out of the town treasury of said New Milford by the first day of January for every month they are in said service, four bushels of wheat, or an equivalent thereto in money in addition to the bounty and encouragement already given by the State."

The first burial in the Northville burying ground was that of Abraham Dayton.

Partridge Thatcher liberated his slaves Jacob and Dianah *gratis*.

Capt. Sherman Boardman liberated his negro slave Nehemiah.

John Treat liberated his negro man named Mingo.

1782. Jemima Wilkinson came to New Milford, held meetings, taught peculiar doctrines and gained some adherents. She was considered an impostor.

1788. The Society of Newbury was organized into a town and named Brookfield in honor of Rev. Thomas Brooks. The town was formed of portions of the towns of New Milford, Newtown, and Danbury. New Milford, Newbury Society contributed nearly one-half of the territory.

The Baptists built a small church in the "Neck," now Bridgewater.

Nicholas Wanzer deeded land to a Society of People called Quakers, it being the same on which the building known as the Quaker Meeting-house now stands.

1789. Town and School house built north of the cross highway at north end of Main street.

1790. Prof. Nehemiah Strong had a private school for boys about this date.

Rev. Stanley Griswold was ordained by the Consociation of Litchfield Co. Colleague pastor with Rev. Nathaniel Taylor of the First Church of New Milford.

A troop of horse formed, belonging to New Milford, Woodbury, and Litchfield; Captains belonging to the town, were William Taylor, Stephen Chittenden, Jr. & Hermen Canfield.

1792. Bridge built at Little Falls.

A company of Light Infantry was formed, of which the Captains have been Daniel Boardman, Nicholas S. Masters, Briggs Ingersoll, Abraham Hayes.

1793. New Milford divided into two military divisions, line running just north of the Levi S. Knapp residence. The new South Company was organized in that year and Nathan Bostwick was made Captain and James Hine, Lieutenant.

A company of militia was formed belonging to the "Neck" (now Bridgewater).

The second Episcopal Church begun in 1765 was finished and consecrated this year.

1794. June 19. A destructive tornado crossed New Milford; blew over houses, barns, apple trees, destroyed timber, killed a child of Mr. Cole; some others wounded, much grain destroyed.

New bridge across Great River in the neck.

1796. Watering place for horses and cattle established on Danbury road between Israel Camp's and Ephraim Buck's.

The Union Circulating Library established.

1797. Col. Samuel Canfield's name stands at the head of the tax list of the town. He was the son of Samuel Canfield,

Story of New Milford in Chronological Epitome 109

Esq., who was the first Canfield in New Milford and one of the Judges of the General Court.

At the annual town meeting, Dec. 11, question put, whether this meeting will remit and give in the fines which are laid upon a certain number of persons for laboring upon the Sabbath at harvest work the year past, and the town treasurer be directed to give up the obligations for sd. fines which are lodged in his hands. Voted in the negative.

1800. Up to this date there had been eight military field officers in the town, viz.: Major John Bostwick, Col. Bushnell Bostwick, Col. Samuel Canfield, Col. Josiah Starr (in ye Army), Col. Elisha Bostwick, Maj. Daniel Boardman, Maj. Reuben Warner, Maj. William Taylor.

The Merryall Plough Foundry established by Elijah Hall, the first foundry established in Conn., and the first that used Blacksmith coal (bituminous). Mr. Hall went about the country disposing of his own wares and, one trip, he collected a bushel basket of coppers in payment.

Perry Smith and William Terrill established a store near Upper Merryall.

1802. After stages began to run for carrying the mail, the bridge was carried away, and the Stage Coach Company sued the town for damages in failing to make a crossing. The town employed Homer Boardman to build a boat to be run across by a large rope to meet the emergency, and the next Spring they applied to the Assembly for the privilege of a toll-bridge.

1803 or 1804. Bridge built at Gaylordsville.

1807. A dam was built across the river. Saw mill erected and Grist mill at Gaylordsville.

Peter Gaylord built a store on the east side of the river about this time.

1809. Church organized in Bridgewater. Meeting-house begun to be built by lottery instituted 1807.

1810. St. Mark's Episcopal Church organized in Bridgewater.

1812. A fever epidemic occurred that carried off by death fifty-eight persons in two and a half months.

1814. St. Peter's Lodge No. 21, F. A. M. leased land of Eli Starr to build Lodge on.

1814. Baptists at Northville organized a Church known as the New Milford Baptist Church. Eleazer Beecher was licensed to preach the Gospel to them.

1816. Upon the petition of sundry inhabitants in the vicinity of what is called Gaylord's Bridge praying a grant of money from the town to rebuild the bridge upon Ousatonic River at Gaylords Falls, it was put to vote that a sum of $400 be granted which was negative; another vote was then put for a sum of $300 which was also voted in the negative.

1818. The New Milford and Sherman Turnpike Company incorporated.

1819. Wm. Roberts settled in Gaylordsville, erected clothing works.

1822. A convention of delegates met to consider the advisability of building "The Housatonic Valley Canal." Funds were raised and an estimate of the expense of construction made. The enterprise failed.

1823. A Baptist meeting-house erected near Lower Merryall burying place.

Glover Sanford began making hats in Bridgewater.

1824. The first Methodist Church organized by Rev. C. Silliman.

1826. Peter Gaylord appointed first Postmaster, Gaylordsville.

Union Church building erected, Gaylordsville.

The trustees of the Methodist Episcopal Church at Northville bought of Henry Benson a piece of land for erecting a house of worship.

1827. Sylvanus Merwin erected a store and hotel on west side.

1828-9. A Methodist meeting-house was built at the Corners at the old John Warner place in Lanesville.

1830. Anan Hine, James S. Clark, and George Taylor, and such other persons as they shall associate with them, not exceeding twenty in the whole, be and they and their successors

REV. NOAH PORTER, D. D., LL.D.
Pastor Congregational Church, New Milford, 1836-1843; President of Yale College, 1871-1886

are made a corporation by the name of "The New Milford Fire Company."

A Baptist Church was organized.

1832. Roswell and Sheldon Northrop started Machinery business and Foundry in Maryland District, now carried on by Jasper A. Northrop in this village.

1833. Congregational Church erected.

1835. New Milford Toll Bridge Company incorporated with liberty to erect and maintain two toll bridges, one at the present in the village, the other at the great falls.

1836. A special town meeting held February 29, to take into consideration the propriety of making an appropriation not exceeding $500 to defray the expense of surveying a route or routes for a railroad to pass through the town. It was voted that the Treasurer be authorized to borrow on the credit of the town a sum not exceeding five hundred dollars to be devoted to the accomplishment of this object.

1837. A special town meeting, May 12, voted to grant the request of New Milford and Sherman Turnpike Company upon the consideration that said company or some other company for that purpose to be formed shall build and keep in repair a toll bridge at the place commonly called Boardman's Bridge.

1840. The Housatonic Railroad was opened from New Milford to Bridgeport. Daniel Marsh was the first station agent.

Highway from near railroad station to village of Northville, laid out by commissioners, commencing at land of David S. Boardman.

1841. The New Milford Washingtonian Temperance Benevolent Society organized. Within three years 900 names were recorded as members.

1842. Town appropriated one hundred dollars to assist in paving water courses in village provided two hundred and fifty dollars be expended by the inhabitants of said village.

1843. Erected the Housatonic R. R. station which was called Merwinsville.

The first elm trees in the park were set by Solomon E. Bostwick in front of his residence.

Doct. George Taylor and Albert N. Baldwin appointed a committee to purchase a farm for the town.

1845. The *New Milford Republican*, the first newspaper in the village, was established by J. K. Averill.

1846-50. " The Housatonic Institute " erected.

1847. Highway laid out now called Bank street.

1849. Bridgewater and Brookfield Toll Bridge Company, incorporated.

1850. The present Methodist Episcopal Church erected.

1852. Bank of Litchfield County organized.

Albert S. Hill erected a paper mill across the road from the Wells Grist Mill.

Mr. and Mrs. B. J. Stone took charge of " The Housatonic Institute."

1854. The first week in May occurred a great freshet that carried away the dam at Gaylordsville; also the Boardman's bridge and the town bridge.

1855. New Milford Brass Band organized, Earl Buckingham leader.

1856. Bridgewater set off from New Milford as a separate town.

1858. The New Milford Savings Bank organized.

The Housatonic Agricultural Society formed.

1860. The Adelphic Institute established by Ambrose S. Rogers, A. M.

In Nov., fire destroyed business portion on south side of Bank St. and east side of R. R. St., to the property now owned by Ackley, Hatch & Marsh.

1861. The town voted to pay for the support of the wife, children, father or mother of those persons who enlisted, such sums as the Selectmen deemed necessary.

St. Francis Xavier's Church erected.

1862. The town voted a bounty of $200 for each resident who should enlist, for a certain time.

William Wells and Edwin S. Wells, sons of Philip Wells,

JOHN PRIME TREADWELL.
A Native of New Milford. Born 1812, died 1876

purchased the grist-mill on the Aspetuck River a mile above Northville.
1863. The town offered $300 to each person who might be drafted.
Water Witch Engine Company organized.
1864. The town offered a bounty of $500 for each soldier accredited to the town.
The town authorized the issue of bonds to the amount of $21,000 to meet war expenses.
1865. Bank of Litchfield County changed to First National Bank of New Milford.
1870. The Glover Sanford firm removed to Bridgeport, Conn.
Ousatonic Chapter, No. 33, R. A. M. organized.
1872. The *Housatonic Ray* (newspaper) established.
1873. Kindergarten school established by Mrs. Andrew Bristol, Miss Mary C. Wells, assistant.
The New Milford Water Company chartered, authorized capital $25,000.
1875. Roger Sherman Hall erected.
1877. The Good Shepherd's Lodge, No. 65, I. O. O. F., instituted.
The first New Milford Savings Bank building erected on north side of Bank St.
The *New Milford Gazette* established.
1878. Miss Wells established kindergarten school in her home in Jan.
1882. Upton Post, G. A. R., organized Dec. 20th, with 26 charter members.
St. John's Church erected.
All Saints Memorial Church erected.
1884. Sunday School established in Merryall.
1886. Board of Trade established.
1887. New Milford made a Shire town.
Iron bridge built at Boardman.
1888. The great blizzard, March 13.
1889. The New Milford Button factory burned.
1890. The new hose house built.

Union Chapel built, Lower Merryall.
1893. Roger Sherman Chapter, D. A. R., organized.
1893. Congregational Church remodeled at a cost of $18,300.
The New Milford Electric Light Company incorporated.
1897. Public Library and Memorial Hall erected on the site of Housatonic Institute, it being the same site that Eli Starr leased to St. Peter's Lodge No. 21, F. & A. M., to build lodge on in 1814.

Lime Works at Boardman destroyed by fire.

A bronze tablet to the memory of Roger Sherman was placed on Roger Sherman Hall by Daughters of the American Revolution.

1900. Great Fireman's parade, 1,300 men in line.
1901. A Town Court established. George H. Jackson, appointed first Judge.
1902. Great fire destroyed the business portion of the village, May 5.

President Roosevelt stopped at the station and made a speech.

The Boardman Sunday School Society organized.

Bridgeport Wood Finishing Company plant burned.

1903. The New Milford Power Company plant established at Gaylordsville.

RECORD OF THE PUBLIC SERVICES OF ROGER SHERMAN

AS REFERRED TO IN THE COLONIAL DOCUMENTS OF CONNECTICUT

CONTRIBUTED BY HON. EBENEZER J. HILL OF NORWALK, CONN.

OCTOBER, 1745, Roger Sherman appointed to be surveyor for the County of New Haven.

Roger Sherman, surveyor for the County of New Haven, appointed in October, 1750, to lay out lands for certain parties from ungranted lands of the Colony.

May, 1751, appointed to lay out certain lands for Williams and Crary.

May, 1751, appointed as one party to view and appraise certain lands in the town of Kent.

May, 1752, made Surveyor for Litchfield County, instead of New Haven.

May, 1752, paid £82, 9s. 10d., in full for his bill for laying out land and highways on the west side of Ousatonick River. As one of a Committee appointed previous October.

October, 1753, Roger Sherman, Surveyor for Litchfield County, ordered to run the Northwest line of town of Litchfield.

October, 1754, mentioned as the fifth Selectman of New Milford.

May, 1756, costs of £2, 17s. 4d., assessed against him and other proprietors of common land in New Milford in certain case.

May, 1755, Representative in Assembly for New Milford, 2d.

August, 1755, Representative in Assembly for New Milford, 2d.

October, 1755, Representative in Assembly for New Milford, 1st.

January, 1756, Representative in Assembly for New Milford, 1st.

February, 1756, Representative in Assembly for New Milford, 1st.

March, 1756, Representative in Assembly for New Milford, 1st.

February, 1756, ordered to eject one Macantire from certain public land.

October, 1756, ordered to inspect certain complaints in regard to land and report. Report made May, 1757.

May, 1755, Appointed Justice of Peace for Litchfield Co.

May, 1756, Appointed Justice of Peace for Litchfield Co.

October, 1757, Appointed to make deeds for certain public lands.

March, 1758, With others incorporated as Toll Bridge Company to own and maintain toll bridge over Ousatonick River in New Milford.

May, 1758, Representative for New Milford, 1st.

October, 1758, Representative for New Milford, 1st.

February, 1759, Representative for New Milford, 1st.

March, 1759, Representative for New Milford, 1st.

May, 1759, Representative for New Milford, 1st.

October, 1759, Representative for New Milford, 1st.

March, 1760, Representative for New Milford, 1st.

May, 1760, Representative for New Milford, 1st.

October, 1760, Representative for New Milford, 1st.

March, 1761, Representative for New Milford, 1st.

May, 1761, Representative for New Milford, 1st.

May, 1757, 1758, 1759, 1760, and 1761, Justice of Peace, Litchfield County.

October, 1760, 1761, 1762, 1763, 1764, 1765, 1766, and 1767, in Nomination for Governor.

October, 1762, Guardian of two Carpenter children authorized to sell land.

October, 1765, Appointed as Committee to investigate certain legal questions. Report made October, 1766.

October, 1764, Representative for New Haven, 1st.

May, 1765, Representative for New Haven, 1st.
October, 1765, Representative for New Haven, 1st.
May, 1766, Representative for New Haven, 1st.
May, 1766 and 1767, Chosen Assistant.
May, 1765, Justice of Peace for New Haven County.
October, 1765, Justice of Peace for New Haven County.
May, 1766, Justice of Peace for New Haven County.
May, 1766 and 1767, Judge of the Superior Court; also, May, 1773, 1774, 1775, 1776, 1777, 1778, & 1779.
May, 1768, 1769, 1770, 1771, 1772, 1773, 1774, 1775, 1776, 1777, 1778, 1779, Chosen Assistant.
Nominated for Governor, 1768, 1769, 1770, 1771, 1772, 1773, 1774, 1775, 1776, 1777, 1778, 1779, 1780.
October, 1768, Appointed to make index of laws.
May, 1769, Appointed to lay out highway from New Haven to Windham. Report accepted May, 1770.
May, 1771, Appointed to lay out highway, New Haven to East Hadam.
October, 1771, Appointed to purchase some elegant plate to present to Richard Jackson, Colonial Agent. Afterwards bought in England on account of duty if bought here.
October, 1771, Assessed in the construction of addition of Meeting-house.
October, 1772, One of joint Committee on Collegiate School.
January, 1774, One of Committee to adjust certain land questions near the Delaware and Susquehannah Rivers.
October, 1773, One of Committee to consider Earl of Dartmouth's letter.
April, 1775, Wrote and offered resolution appointing Committee to present letter of Gov. Trumbull to Gen. Gage, demanding explanation of attack of 19th of April and his future plans.
August 3, 1774, Chosen Representative in Congress.
February 27, 1775, Purchased 90 kegs of powder, 3,500 lbs. lead, 30,500 flints for the Colony.
October, 1775, Representative in Congress.

October, 1776, Committee to visit Army and grade the officers appointed by the Assembly.

May, 1777, Named as member of the Committee of Safety.

October, 1776 and 1777, Representative in Congress, 1st man.

July, 1777, One of a Committee to confer with Mass., New Hampshire, R. I., and New York on the state of the currency.

January, 1778, Committee to inquire into conduct of foreign traders in this State.

January, 1778, Commissioner to New Haven Convention. Chairman of Committee to draw report of Convention.

May, 1778 and 1779, Council of Safety.

October, 1778, Representative in Congress.

January, 1780, Representative in Congress.

February, 1780, Delegate to Philadelphia Convention to regulate prices.

Representative in Congress 1789 and 1791. Senator 1791 to 1793. Mayor of New Haven.

PART II
THE BI-CENTENNIAL EXERCISES

HENRY S. MYGATT
President of the Bi-Centennial Celebration

INCEPTION AND ORGANIZATION

Contributed by Charles N. Hall

In April, 1906, a call was issued in the columns of the *New Milford Gazette*, asking all citizens to meet at Mygatt's Hall, Bank Street, on Monday evening, April 30, to consider the project of celebrating the town's two hundredth anniversary.

About forty citizens responded to the appeal and met at the appointed time and place.

The meeting was called to order by Mr. William G. Green, and Mr. Henry S. Mygatt was appointed chairman of the meeting.

After full discussion as to the possibility and advisability of such a celebration as that implied in the call, the following preamble and resolution were adopted:

" Whereas, New Milford was first settled in the year of our Lord, 1707, and has from a humble beginning gone steadily forward in growth and prosperity, through the industry and patriotism of its sons and daughters, and the blessings of a Divine Providence:

" And Whereas, It seems fitting that the two hundredth anniversary of this town, now near at hand, should be recognized and celebrated by all its citizens in such manner as to confer proper dignity upon the occasion; to call together for a day all its children; to honor the memories of those who contributed to its past and present welfare; to show the industrial, agricultural, commercial, educational, and religious progress of the community throughout the past years; and to give due thanks to the Providence that has watched over it.

" Therefore it is Resolved: That during the year 1907, upon a date to be named at a future meeting, there shall be held a celebration to be known as the New Milford Bi-Centennial."

After further discussion as to forms of organization, it was voted:

"That in accordance with the spirit of the foregoing resolution, this meeting shall appoint a General Committee of Arrangements, said committee to have entire charge of all arrangements pertaining to the New Milford Bi-Centennial Celebration; to have power to make changes in and additions to its own numbers; to have authority to appoint and organize all necessary sub-committees, and the power to direct the work of such sub-committees, and to make removals and substitutions in such sub-committees; and to take any and all measures necessary to carry the foregoing resolution into effect."

The meeting then appointed a Nominating Committee consisting of C. M. Beach, W. G. Green, H. L. Randall, S. S. Green, G. M. Breinig, and Rev. Marmaduke Hare, to present to the meeting the names of those who should constitute the General Committee of Arrangements.

After consultation, the Nominating Committee presented a list of those persons who should constitute the General Committee, and those so named were by vote declared appointed as the General Committee of Arrangements, with the powers and duties above set forth.

It was then voted:

"That when this meeting adjourns, the chairman of this meeting shall have authority to call, at his pleasure, a meeting of the General Committee of Arrangements."

The meeting then adjourned.

The General Committee of Arrangements met on July 6, 1906, about one hundred members being present. At this meeting a permanent organization was effected, officers elected, sub-committees appointed, and a date set for the celebration.

The officers elected were:

Permanent Chairman and President, Henry S. Mygatt; Vice-Presidents, Andrew G. Barnes, Francis E. Baldwin, Stephen C. Beach; General Secretary, Charles N. Hall.

It was voted:

"That the Celebration be held on Saturday, Sunday, Monday, and Tuesday, June 15, 16, 17, 18, 1907."

It was voted:

Inception and Organization

" That Sub-Committees be created as follows:
An Executive Committee,
A Finance Committee,
A Committee on Exercises,
A Committee on Refreshments,
A Committee on Decoration,
A Committee on Publicity,
A Committee of Invitation, Reception, and Entertainment;
A Committee on Religious Observances,
A Committee of Public Safety,
A Committee on Historical Research and Permanent Publication."

It was further voted:

" That each member of the General Committee pay the sum of one dollar, and each member of a sub-committee the additional sum of two dollars to the Bi-Centennial fund."

Subsequently the Executive Committee, acting for the General Committee, appointed from time to time other sub-committees found necessary in the progress of the work. These were:

A Loan Exhibit Committee,
A Committee on Vocal Music,
A Colonial Reception Committee.

The officers and members of the General Committee of Arrangements were as follows:

President, HENRY S. MYGATT;
Vice Presidents, ANDREW G. BARNES, FRANCES E. BALDWIN, STEPHEN C. BEACH;
Secretary, CHARLES N. HALL;

Members

John F. Addis.
Mrs. John F. Addis.
Geo. E. Ackley.
Mrs. Geo. E. Ackley.
W. H. Adams.
Victor L. Anderson.
Emil Anderson.

Geo. B. Ackley.
Mrs. Geo. B. Ackley.
Fred Anderson.
Mrs. Geo. W. Anthony.
Mrs. Phoebe L. Anderson.
Horace A. Allen.
Rev. J. J. Burke.

Dr. J. C. Barker.
Dr. B. E. Bostwick.
Chas M. Beach.
Alexander H. Barlow.
W. G. Brown.
Charles P. Bentley.
Reuben Booth.
*G. M. Breinig.
David E. Breinig.
Henry M. Baldwin.
Willis F. Bennett.
Willis G. Barton.
Dr. Charles P. Blinn.
Mrs. Wm. D. Black.
William H. Booth.
H. B. Bostwick.
Burton B. Booth.
Mrs. J. L. Buck.
Mrs. J. A. Bolles.
Mrs. Wm. Bostwick.
Miss Ruth T. Booth.
Frederick L. Bennett.
Andrew Buckingham.
Mrs. Chas. M. Beach.
Mrs. G. M. Breinig.
Mrs. A. M. Booth.
Mrs. H. E. Bostwick.
Miss C. B. Bennett.
Miss A. E. Bostwick.
Miss Helen M. Boardman.
Miss Kate T. Boardman.
Miss Grace Buckingham.
Miss May Brown.
Miss Adaline L. Buck.
Mrs. J. C. Barker.
Mrs. B. E. Bostwick.
Amos H. Bowers.

A. C. Bowers.
Andrew M. Booth.
Mrs. David A. Baldwin.
Mrs. Willis F. Bennett.
Lyman W. Brown.
Andrew J. Baldwin.
Noble Bennett.
E. Noble Bennett.
Mrs. Merritt Beach.
Mrs. I. B. Bristol.
Mrs. Edwin N. Bostwick.
Daniel B. Brewer.
Henry Booth.
Wiliam E. Bostwick.
Rev. T. J. Cronin.
Andrew C. Clark.
Mrs. Andrew C. Clark.
Daniel H. Canfield.
Lawrence C. Camp.
Robert B. Clark.
L. F. Curtis.
Mrs. L. F. Curtis.
P. M. Cassedy.
John D. Clark.
Alanson N. Canfield.
Mrs. Geo. N. Canfield.
Mrs. Lemira J. Carter.
Howard C. Clark.
Phineas E. Clark.
Warren S. Crossman.
John B. Cox.
Chas. B. Camp.
Salmon Couch.
A. L. Conkey.
Rev. Frank B. Draper.
Dr. J. A. Dolan.
Henry Donnelly.

* Deceased.

SEYMOUR S. GREEN
Chairman Executive Committee

STEPHEN C. BEACH
Vice-President

HONORABLE ANDREW G. BARNES
Vice-President

FRANCIS E. BALDWIN
Vice-President

SOME OFFICERS OF THE BI-CENTENNIAL CELEBRATION

INCEPTION AND ORGANIZATION 125

Robert L. Duncan.
Eben B. Dorwin.
Myron B. Disbrowe.
Edwin J. Emmons.
Mrs. Edwin J. Emmons.
Albert Evitts.
Rollin C. Emmons.
Chas. H. Evans.
Miss S. C. Erwin.
Thomas Fuller.
Munson Fairchild.
Alban G. Ferriss.
Samuel J. Ferriss.
Mrs. Albert Ferriss.
Henry Ferriss.
Miss Minnie A. Ferriss.
Miss Jane Fenn.
Dr. H. B. Griswold.
Minot S. Giddings.
Levi P. Giddings.
Wm. G. Green.
Seymour S. Green.
Henry Garvey.
Miss Jeanette L. Gaylord.
William F. Gaylord.
Fred R. Green.
* Ethiel S. Green.
William B. Green.
George W. Green.
William Green.
George H. Gaylord.
Mrs. James Giddings.
Rev. Marmaduke Hare.
Rev. Stephen Heacock.
J. E. Hungerford.
Mrs. J. E. Hungerford.
Walter C. Hine.

Mrs. Walter C. Hine.
Mrs. Charles N. Hall.
J. Stuart Halpine.
Wm. H. Hartwell.
Frederick C. Hoyt.
Henry D. Hine.
Oliver W. Hoyt.
Mrs. H. D. Hine.
Mrs. W. B. Hatch.
Virgil B. Hatch.
Merritt W. Hill.
Mrs. Mary H. Hunt.
Edson P. Hill.
Harvey B. Hoyt.
Martin L. Hungerford.
Arthur B. Hungerford.
Sheldon B. Hendricks.
Mrs. Sheldon B. Hendricks.
John H. Hall.
Edward Hendricks.
Merwin Hine.
G. W. Hatch.
G. L. Hamlin.
Oliver S. Hartwell.
Roger T. Hartwell.
Robert J. Hungerford.
E. D. Howland.
Minot L. Hartwell.
John T. Hepburn.
John M. Hine.
Frederick W. Hartwell.
Clark M. Hunt.
Samuel R. Hill.
Henry H. Hartwell.
* Albert S. Hill.
Allen S. Hill.
Edgar F. Hawley.

* Deceased.

E. F. Hartwell.
H. C. Ives.
Rev. Frank A. Johnson.
George H. Jackson.
L. N. Jennings.
Lucius Jackson.
Michael A. Kelly.
Dr. F. E. King.
Mrs. F. E. King.
W. F. Kinney.
Mrs. W. F. Kinney.
Nelson W. Kinney.
Arthur W. Knowles.
Henry Kinney.
Frederick W. Knowles.
Frederick Knapp.
Henry Kinney, 2d.
Joseph La Hait.
Geo. H. Lines.
Walter B. Leavenworth.
Carr S. Lyon.
Wm. P. Landon.
Frank W. Marsh.
A. H. McMahon.
Mrs. A. H. McMahon.
Daniel Marsh.
Chauncey B. Marsh.
J. B. Merwin.
Roland F. Mygatt.
Frederick Merwin.
Mrs. H. S. Mygatt.
Miss Grace H. Merwin.
John H. Morehouse.
James E. Mullins.
Miss Carrie H. Marsh.
Mrs. Margaret Moore.
Mrs. Carlos Merwin.

M. H. Mallett.
Amos H. Marsh.
James Marsh.
Miss Lottie Mallett.
Henry W. Murray.
Mrs. Henry W. Murray.
E. B. Marsh.
E. O. Marsh.
Mrs. E. O. Marsh.
Andrew J. McMahon.
Robert C. Mallory.
Wm. J. M. Miller.
* James H. McMahon.
George Newton.
Charles H. Noble.
Russell B. Noble.
Miss Ella F. Noble.
Wm. N. Noble.
Ithamer F. Northrop.
Jasper A. Northrop.
Alfred H. Noble.
Mrs. George Northrop.
Lawrence Northrop.
Charles Northrop.
J. H. Nettleton.
Charles H. Osborne.
Wilbur H. Osborne.
Abram Osborne.
Wallace W. Osborne.
Farley Osgood.
Robert A. Osborne.
Rev. John F. Plumb.
John Pettibone.
Henry H. Pomeroy.
Wm. B. Pell.
Mrs. Wm. B. Pell.
Mrs. Ivory Phillips.

* Deceased.

Inception and Organization

Mrs. Clayson S. Perry.
Charles Planz.
D. W. Pepper.
Wm. A. Parcells.
A. W. Peelstrom.
John Payne.
Edgar A. Peet.
Lewis A. Payne.
Lehman T. Peet.
Clinton H. Pomeroy.
H. Leroy Randall.
Mrs. H. Leroy Randall.
William J. Roberts.
Miss Sarah J. Roberts.
Mrs. C. E. Riddiford.
Charles Riley, Jr.
F. T. Richmond.
Seeley B. Richmond.
Mrs. Chas. Randall.
Mrs. Isaac Reynolds.
Wm. L. Richmond.
Levi S. Richmond.
Nathan H. Root.
C. E. Riddiford.
Orrin Roberts.
Rev. H. K. Smith.
Dr. Geo. E. Staub.
Verton P. Staub.
* Nicholas Staub.
Turney Soule.
Chas. H. Soule.
David E. Soule.
George T. Soule.
Frank E. Soule.
Henry S. Sanford.
Everett J. Sturges.
Frederick E. Starr.

Mrs. Verton P. Staub.
Vincent B. Sterling.
Geo. W. Squires.
Miss Caro S. Sanford.
Mrs. V. B. Sterling.
Carl F. Schoverling.
Henry A. Soule.
Walter D. Soule.
Mrs. Catherine Smith.
Mrs. C. R. M. B. Smith.
Albert Sterling.
Wm. W. Stillson.
Frederick M. Straight.
James S. Sullivan.
Israel B. Smith.
Mrs. Wm. Schoverling.
Lee Stone.
Mrs. C. C. Smith.
Miss Harriet V. Sherman.
Mrs. Ellen F. Shepard.
Mrs. Charles Taylor.
Frederick J. Turrill.
Arthur G. Todd.
Cyrus A. Todd.
Mrs. R. S. Todd.
Mrs. Henry R. Treadwell.
Mrs. Lucy Turrill.
Chas. A. Tappen.
Miss Martha Treadwell.
John T. Underhill.
Rev. S. D. Woods.
Dr. Geo. H. Wright.
F. M. Williams.
Mrs. F. M. Williams.
Philip Wells.
Stanley L. Warner.
Henry O. Warner.

* Deceased.

Wm. D. Wanzer.
A. C. Worley.
John E. Wells.
Charles A. Way.
Miss Edith Warner.
Mrs. C. E. Wright.
Miss Charlotte A. Wells.

Smith M. Waller.
E. M. Waller.
Frederick L. Wanzer.
Edward A. Wildman.
John F. Williams.
Newton B. Weaver.
Reuben M. Wilbur.

Miss Mary C. Wells.

The members of the special committees—appointed by the General Committee * to arrange for and carry out the plans for the Celebration—were:

Executive Committee: Seymour S. Green, chairman; J. B. Merwin, Everett Sturges, Verton P. Staub, Mrs. H. S. Mygatt, Mrs. C. M. Beach.

Finance Committee: H. Leroy Randall, chairman; Charles H. Noble, treasurer; Willis G. Barton, William G. Green, Turney Soule, Edwin J. Emmons.

Committee on Exercises: Charles M. Beach, chairman; John H. Morehouse, clerk; Willis F. Bennett, Frank E. Soule, D. W. Pepper, John Pettibone, Mrs. Verton P. Staub, Frederic M. Williams, Joseph La Hait, Samuel R. Hill, Chauncey B. Marsh, Miss Helen M. Boardman, Miss Ella F. Noble, and the selectmen of the town, *ex officio*.

The Committee on Exercises appointed the following marshals for the Civic and Military Parade, and the following subcommittees to arrange for Colonial features in the Parade and for an Automobile Carnival on Monday, June 17:

Marshals: Samuel R. Hill, chief marshal; David E. Soule, George E. Ackley, Henry O. Warner.

Committee on Colonial Features: Willis F. Bennett, chairman; Alfred H. Noble, clerk; William G. Green, Dr. Charles P. Blinn, Chauncey B. Marsh, Mrs. J. C. Barker, Miss Helen M. Boardman.

Committee on Automobile Parade: Roland F. Mygatt, chair-

* The President and Secretary of the General Committee were *ex officio* members of all committees.

H. LEROY RANDALL
Finance Committee

W. F. KINNEY
Invitation, Reception and Entertainment Committee

FREDERICK E. STARR
Music Committee

CHARLES P. BENTLEY
Decoration Committee

CHAIRMEN OF SOME BI-CENTENNIAL COMMITTEES

man; Henry D. Hine, Dr. B. E. Bostwick, Robert Dunlap, S. Woolsey Pepper, George T. Soule.

Committee on Refreshments: Miss Adaline L. Buck, chairman; J. Edwin Hungerford, clerk; H. C. Ives, Vincent B. Sterling, Mrs. Charles N. Hall, Mrs. Margaret Moore, Mrs. A. C. Clark, James E. Mullins, Wm. L. Richmond, Mrs. Walter C. Hine, George E. Ackley, P. M. Cassedy, Dr. B. E. Bostwick, Emil Anderson.

Committee on Decorations: Charles P. Bentley, chairman; Wm. B. Pell, Dr. Charles P. Blinn, John F. Addis, Geo. T. Soule, Frederick L. Bennett, Henry D. Hine, Mrs. F. E. King, W. H. Adams, A. W. Peelstrom, Levi P. Giddings.

Committee on Publicity: Charles N. Hall, chairman; W. G. Brown, Dr. Geo. H. Wright, A. C. Worley, David E. Breinig.

Committee on Invitation, Reception and Entertainment: W. F. Kinney, chairman; Miss Sarah J. Roberts, secretary; Russell B. Noble, Mrs. Frederic M. Williams, Mrs. H. S. Mygatt, Mrs. Albert H. McMahon, Henry S. Sanford, Andrew C. Clark, Stanley L. Warner, Mrs. Isaac Reynolds, Alexander H. Barlow, Andrew J. Baldwin, Charles Northrop, Mrs. George B. Ackley, Mrs. C. E. Wright, Miss Caro S. Sanford, Mrs. Chas. Taylor, Mrs. Wm. Bostwick, Mrs. Catherine Smith, Mrs. H. E. Bostwick, Orrin Roberts, Mrs. Merritt Beach, Alanson N. Canfield, Albert Evitts, George H. Jackson, Mrs. Wm. B. Pell, Miss A. E. Bostwick, Francis E. Baldwin, Oliver S. Hartwell, Mrs. E. O. Marsh, Henry Ferriss, Miss Jeannette L. Gaylord, Seeley B. Richmond, Mrs. Carlos Merwin, J. B. Merwin, Mrs. W. D. Black, Mrs. J. L. Buck, Mrs. Phœbe L. Anderson, Mrs. Henry R. Treadwell, Mrs. Wm. G. Green, Mrs. G. H. Jackson, Chas. B. Camp, Cyrus A. Todd, and the selectmen of the town, *ex-officio*.

The chairman of this committee appointed Albert Evitts, chairman of reception; Henry S. Sanford, chairman of entertainment.

Committee on Religious Observances: Rev. Frank A. Johnson, chairman; Rev. John F. Plumb, Rev. Frank B. Draper, Rev. T. J. Cronin, Rev. J. J. Burke, Rev. Marmaduke Hare, Rev.

Stephen Heacock, Rev. H. K. Smith, Rev. S. D. Woods, Rev. T. J. Lee.

Committee of Public Safety: Henry Donnelly, chairman; Charles Planz, Albert H. McMahon, L. N. Jennings, Charles Reilly, Chas. H. Osborne.

Committee on Historical Research and Permanent Publication: Minot S. Giddings, chairman; Russell B. Noble, Mrs. Henry E. Bostwick, Miss Charlotte B. Bennett, Miss Kate T. Boardman.

Committee on Loan Exhibit: Dr. George H. Wright, chairman; Wm. B. Pell, C. Andrew Humeston, Miss Flora G. Stillson, Herman C. Buckingham, Mrs. Clarissa R. M. Staples, Miss Jeanette L. Gaylord, Miss Mabelle Sanford.

Committee on Vocal Music: F. E. Starr, chairman; Prof. Edwin G. Clemence, director; Henry C. Harris, Mrs. H. S. Mygatt, Rev. H. K. Smith, Mrs. M. W. Hill.

Committee on Colonial Reception: Stephen C. Beach, chairman; W. F. Kinney, Wm. G. Green, J. Stuart Halpine, Charles M. Beach, Henry S. Sanford, Roland F. Mygatt, Frank W. Marsh.

All the committees worked nobly and in perfect harmony.

Upon the Finance Committee devolved the responsibility of raising the necessary funds, and the duty was splendidly performed. Solicitors were appointed in each district of the town, and furnished with books in which subscriptions were pledged to be paid on or before April 1, 1907. The solicitors, besides the members of the Committee, were: Henry W. Murray, Oliver W. Hoyt, Henry M. Baldwin, Nicholas Glennon, Nelson W. Kinney, Edgar A. Peet, John W. Pulver, John T. Underhill, Daniel Marsh, Walter C. Hine, Millard B. Dorwin, Charles H. Evans, Chauncey B. Marsh, Henry S. Mygatt, Charles N. Hall.

So successful was this canvass that the needed funds were all subscribed before May 15. The result speaks volumes for the enterprise and systematic work of the Finance Committee, as well as for the generosity and public spirit of New Milford's citizens.

The Executive Committee met frequently to authorize appropriations and receive reports, and, in May, opened an office in the Knapp Building on Bank Street, the second floor of that building having been very generously placed at their disposal by Mr. Frederic Knapp of Hartford.

Meetings of all the Chairmen of Committees were occasionally held, and were found very useful in promoting the work.

The Committee on Exercises had the greatest task to perform in arranging a suitable and comprehensive programme of exercises for the entire Celebration, co-operating as to Sunday's exercises with the Committee on Religious Observances. In order to secure full participation in the Parade, District Committees were appointed throughout the town, to look after Parade features in their respective localities.

These Committees were:

Lower Merryall: F. C. Merwin, H. W. Murray, S. B. Hendrix, W. D. Stone, John Pepper.

Waller: John T. Underhill, Smith Waller, Thomas Austin, Alexander H. Barlow.

Hunt: Nelson W. Kinney, M. W. Beers, Earle Morehouse, Chester Lyon.

Long Mountain: Henry M. Baldwin, H. H. Pomeroy, Wm. Pomeroy.

Gaylordsville: Chas. H. Evans, Wm. Gaylord, Chas. H. Soule, George Newton, Wm. J. Roberts.

Northville: Francis E. Baldwin, A. C. Bowers, E. B. Buckingham, Walter C. Hine.

Still River: Percy Collins, Fred P. Chase, Stanley L. Warner, Chas. H. Stevens.

Park Lane: N. H. Root, James S. Sullivan, W. B. Leavenworth.

Hill and Plain: Wm. D. Wanzer, Arthur E. Knowles, Merwin P. Hine, Geo. W. Hatch.

Second Hill: Robert Duncan, Robert J. Hungerford, Mrs. A. C. Clark, Mrs. J. A. Cowan, Mrs. T. Walsh, Wm. Hartwell, Millard B. Dorwin, Joshep Cowan, Miss Alice Beers, Mrs. Wm. Johnson, Mrs. Hans Ahlstrom.

Upper Merryall: V. B. Hatch, Israel B. Smith, A. H. Squires, Geo. W. Squires, Fred M. Straight.

Pickett: Nicholas Glennon, Mervin Andrews, Leslie Marsh.

Chestnut Land: Ivory Phillips, P. E. Clark, Howard C. Clark, Frank Erwin, Fred Anderson, E. F. Hartwell, Samuel Thompson.

Aspetuck: Daniel Marsh, Joseph Hill, E. Noble Bennett, Levi S. Richmond.

Boardman: Oliver W. Hoyt, Andrew G. Barnes, Sheldon Northrop.

The District Committee on refreshments were:

Upper Merryall: Mrs. Geo. B. Ackley, Geo. W. Squires; assisted by Mrs. Wm. Birkins, Mrs. Frederick Squires.

Lower Merryall: Mrs. Carlos P. Merwin, Mrs. Geo. N. Abbott, Mrs. H. W. Murray.

Hunt: Mrs. Myron W. Toohey.

Northville: Mrs. Walter C. Hine, Miss Elizabeth Baldwin.

Chestnut Land: Miss May Galvin, Edgar Phillips.

Second Hill: Mrs. Robert J. Hungerford, Mrs. Joseph A. Cowan.

Park Lane: Mrs. Mary D. Bostwick, Mrs. Wesley Northrop, Mrs. Edward C. Howland.

Boardman: Mrs. Oliver W. Hoyt, Mrs. Henry W. Kimlin; assisted by the Christian Endeavor Social Union.

Waller: Mrs. Thomas Austin, Mrs. Smith M. Waller.

Gaylordsville: Mrs. Arthur Hungerford, Mrs. J. A. Dolan.

Long Mountain: Mrs. Henry M. Baldwin, Miss Minnie Pomeroy.

Aspetuck: Mrs. Levi Richmond, J. Fred McEwan.

Hill and Plain: Mrs. Robert Osborne, Arthur E. Knowles.

Lanesville: Mrs. Laura Campbell, Mrs. Nora Dickey, Mrs. Horace A. Allen.

Pickett: Mrs. Edward O. Marsh, Mrs. Daniel B. Brewer, Miss Bessie Adams.

Center: Mrs. W. C. Beeman, Miss Kathleen Duncan, Mrs. Robert S. Todd, Mrs. Timothy Heacock, Miss Bessie I. Brown, Mrs. V. B. Sterling, Mrs. A. M. Booth, Mrs. P. M. Cassedy,

EDWIN G. CLEMENCE
Conductor of the Chorus

MISS ADALINE L. BUCK
Chairman Refreshment Committee

CHARLES J. RYDER, D. D.
One of the Speakers

HENRY DONNELLY
Chairman Public Safety Committee

Mrs. W. M. Keeler, Mrs. Albert Sterling, Mrs. Emil Anderson, Donald E. Hungerford, Francis Mulcahy, Clifford Castle, Mrs. James E. Mullens.

The Committee on Decorations furnished the town with a fine public flag pole and flag, to be used first at the opening exercises of the Celebration. The committee also carried out the beautiful plan of decoration and illumination on Main Street.

The Committee on Publicity kept the Celebration before the public in many ways. Printed envelopes of the Bi-Centennial were furnished to the citizens to the extent of several thousand. One thousand very attractive cards were sent throughout the State, and frequent items were published in all the newspapers of the State. This committee also published the official Programme of the Celebration.

The Committee of Invitation, Reception, and Entertainment devised, addressed, and sent out the official invitations; arranged for the official reception of all guests; and, in many ways, made all guests feel truly welcome. This committee arranged for Reception Headquarters and a Bureau of Information in Roger Sherman Hall during the Celebration.

The Committee on Religious Observances had charge of the exercises on Sunday, June 16, and arranged so well that this proved to be one of the most delightful days of the Celebration.

The Committee of Public Safety, co-operating with the selectmen of the town, provided most complete arrangements for the preservation of order and the safety of property throughout the days and nights of the Celebration.

The work of the Historical Committee was difficult and important in a high degree, and the task of collecting all the historical facts needed, and presenting the whole in attractive and interesting form, kept all the members extremely busy up to the opening of the Celebration. The committee received most practical and valuable assistance from The Grafton Press of New York City, which not only contracted to publish the book of the Bi-Centennial, but in many ways facilitated the preliminary work. This firm agreed to report, for the book, the entire proceedings of the four days, and, to this end, established a representative on the spot some days in advance, to remain throughout the Celebration. The reportorial work was under his direction.

The Loan Exhibit Committee were tendered the use of Grand Army Hall, through the kindness of Upton Post, and began early to look up all articles of historic value and interest. The amount of work involved was very great, but was most successfully accomplished.

The Committee on Colonial Features made preparations which contributed very greatly to the interest and success of the parade, spending a great deal of time and thought in representing the scenes of old Colonial days.

The Committee on Colonial Reception prepared the hall and made all arrangements for one of the most pleasurably anticipated events of the Celebration.

The Committee on Vocal Music, under the direction of Professor Edwin G. Clemence, prepared an elaborate musical programme and gave abundantly in time and efforts to perfect this most important portion of the exercises.

Rest Houses for women and children were established at various convenient places, in readiness for the crowds anticipated.

James C. Barker, M. D., and T. B. Merrin were appointed a Committee of Public Health and Comfort.

Owing to ill health, Mr. Henry O. Warner was unable to serve as Marshal, and Walter C. Hine was appointed in his stead.

The Marshal's aides appointed for the Parade were:

FIRST DIVISION

Perry Green.	Miss Madeline Todd.
Noble Booth.	Miss Louise Beeman.
Charles Pomeroy.	Miss Parthenia Todd.

SECOND DIVISION

Dr. C. B. Blackman.	George S. Dean.
	Spencer Welton.

THIRD DIVISION

Granville Breinig, W. M. Keeler.
Clifford A. Trowbridge.

FOURTH DIVISION

James Marsh. W. C. Beeman.
Clifford Marsh.

From January, 1907, up to the opening day on June 15, all the committees worked arduously and unceasingly to make the Bi-Centennial a success. Less opposition and discouragement were met than are usual in such enterprises, and to the public-spirited and loyal citizens of the town belongs the credit of all this work, so triumphantly accomplished.

THE OPENING EXERCISES

THERE never was a time and place, perhaps, in which a keener interest was taken in the weather than at New Milford during the days immediately preceding the Bi-Centennial Celebration. One of the most backward and inclement springs known to New England history seemed to have bequeathed all its inclemency to the summer month of June, and, on the afternoon of Friday, June 14, not only were the signs few and feeble that summer had come, but the sky was extremely threatening. The boldest prophet did not venture to predict fair weather for the following day with any approach to positiveness; and, under the besetting dread of a down-pour which would ruin the beautiful Bi-Centennial decorations already in place on "The Green," and interfere sadly with the Bi-Centennial exercises (most of which were to be in the open air) New Milford faces wore an expression of anxiety that was piteous to see. Saturday came without rain and without clouds, however, and, better still, brought with it that light, luminous haze, which, in this part of the world, presages a spell of dry weather—an augury that, happily, was to be fulfilled. The rows of white pillars with gilded capitals (typifying the Colonial architecture) and the clusters and festoons of national colors and navy signal flags (typifying our present national greatness), which constituted the official decoration of "The Green," assumed new splendor in this highly favorable light, while the private decorations, which had been delayed somewhat by the fear of rain, were brought to completion so rapidly that, by noon, the town was literally enveloped in flags and patriotic and Colonial bunting.

Promptly at four in the afternoon the Doxology pealed forth from the chimes of All Saints' (played by Prof. Clemence) and was quickly taken up by the voices of the large concourse gathered on "The Green" about the band-stand, on

CHARLES M. BEACH
Chairman Committee on Exercises

CHARLES N. HALL
Secretary of the Bi-Centennial Celebration

which the chairmen of the Bi-Centennial committees were seated. Rev. Frank A. Johnson invoked the blessing of God upon the coming Bi-Centennial ceremonies in an impressive prayer, after which "America" was played by the band (Gartland's of Albany) and sung by the audience. Charles N. Hall, Secretary of the General Bi-Centennial Committee, then stepped forward and delivered the following address of welcome:

"CITIZENS AND FRIENDS:

"For this seems the most comprehensive and fitting title by which to address such an assemblage as this; since many of you are citizens, and all of you are friends of New Milford. Citizens and friends then; to one and all; to those of you who are citizens; to those of you who were New Milford born, but have found other homes; to those of you whose forefathers were once New Milford's children; to each and every one of you, and to all guests yet to come, the General Committee of the Bi-Centennial, speaking for this entire community, extends a most heartfelt welcome.

"But our welcome is tinged with regret; regret that these words cannot be spoken to-day by the one man that is best fitted for, most entitled to, that honor. Those of you who have worked during these months of preparation, and all who know him, will bear witness that no man living has done more for this Celebration; no man living could have greeted you more gracefully or with greater sincerity than would our honored President, Henry S. Mygatt, were he present. But though not with us in person, we know that he is so in thought; that his hopes and best wishes are with us to-day.

"It is difficult to find words fitting for an occasion like this, for no occasion like this has ever before confronted us.

"For the first time in her history, New Milford fittingly celebrates a birthday anniversary. For the first time in her history, New Milford has planned a great general home-coming of all her scattered children. For the first time, we shall see, during these four days, all our own people gathered together in a common cause: and it is not likely that any now living will ever see them so gathered again.

"This then is The Event, not merely of the years, but of the centuries; an event which must occupy a place unique and unapproached in the history of our town; and words may well fail to express the sentiments which such an occasion must inspire.

"Since that day in the year 1707, when the pioneer, John Noble, first traversed the wilderness to this place, up to this day of June, 1907, every event and circumstance, toil and danger, hardship and prosperity, peace and war, all have been but successive steps leading to this Celebration, and making it possible. And, in this Celebration, we mark not this anniversary alone, but celebrate as well all that has gone before.

"We celebrate the founders of our town; the heroic men and women who, by their toil, their courage and their faith, not only made New Milford, but helped to lay the corner-stone of this nation. Every event in this, our Celebration; this flag-raising; the splendidly impressive service of Sunday; the historic addresses, and the reception of Monday; the imposing parade of Tuesday; all were planned, not only to afford pleasure and entertainment for our guests, and to glorify the New Milford of to-day, but also to commemorate and glorify the past.

"But while we celebrate New Milford, past and present, what shall we say of the New Milford to come? Shall not the civic pride, and energy, the patriotism, that have inspired this Celebration, continue to be moving forces toward a better New Milford? Shall not some of the thousands who visit us, impressed with the attractions of our town, remain and help us to make a greater New Milford?

"New Milford has done wisely and well to inaugurate this home coming, for such home comings are vitally essential to the right life and growth and prosperity of any community.

"New Milford is proud of her history; proud of her position among the hills and towns of old Litchfield County, in this blessed commonwealth of Connecticut; proud of her business enterprise, of her schools and churches; and proud of her children, whom she welcomes home to-day.

"You are here, not as chance visitors, or strangers, but as members of one great family. We ask you to be not only with us, but of us at this time; to become, for the time being, citizens of our town, and would be glad to have you become so in fact.

"New Milford and its Celebration are yours; be at home with us; survey the attractions of our town; visit and greet old friends; enjoy the Celebration to the utmost, and then if you must leave us, take with you the kindest thoughts, and happy memories of the Bi-Centennial."

At the close of this address, the band, playing "Auld Lang Syne," marched to the south end of "The Green" (the chairmen of the committees, the New Milford Cadets under command of Capt. Gifford Noble, and the audience falling in behind) to the new, white, eighty-foot flag pole, which had been erected there under the supervision of Grand Marshal, Samuel R. Hill. To the strains of the "Star Spangled Banner," Mr. Hill, assisted by Lewis W. Mosher, ran a new flag * up the pole, while the Cadets stood statue-like near its base. As the flag touched the peak, a cannon salute was fired by a firing squad under the direction of Samuel R. Hill, Jr. This was a signal for the playing of "We'll Rally Round the Flag, Boys," by the band, for the blowing of factory whistles, and the ringing of church bells; and, with this acclaim, the formal opening of the New Milford Bi-Centennial Celebration was ended.

* Presented by Charles P. Bentley of Booth, Bentley & Co.

THE LOAN EXHIBITION

THE LOAN EXHIBITION in Memorial Hall was opened to the public at ten o'clock Saturday morning, several hours in advance of the formal ceremonies of welcome described above, and was kept open during the entire four days of the Celebration. It proved an agreeable surprise, not only to the guests of the town, but to the townspeople themselves, who had no idea how rich their homes were in relics of the past until they were thus brought together for this Bi-Centennial occasion. Indeed, it was pronounced by competent judges one of the most interesting collections of antiquities ever seen in the State of Connecticut. By its aid, any person possessed of the slightest imagination could easily reconstruct the every-day existence (in-doors and out-of-doors) of the ancestors, and could even divine the intellectual, moral and religious ideas and ideals which governed them. Besides the local relics associated directly with the New Milford life of yore, were a number of curiosities from remote corners of the globe, which testified to the important rôle played by natives of New Milford in earlier times as merchants, ship-owners, travellers, and missionaries.

These various richly-stored heirlooms were a source of great joy to the aged, whose observations and reminiscences, as they moved about among the show-cases, were well-nigh as fascinating as the exhibits themselves; and a means of instruction for the young, to whom most of the objects displayed appeared as strange as if they had been brought from another planet.

The finest thing about this exhibition, however, was the public spirit it exemplified. The committee in charge met scarcely a refusal from the persons to whom they applied for loans, and, once the character of the undertaking was understood, volunteers came forward in such numbers that twice the space

The Loan Exhibition

afforded by the G. A. R. rooms might have been filled, had it been available.

Many of the visitors expressed regret that so remarkable a collection must be scattered so soon and a hope that New Milford would one day see its way clear to maintaining a permanent exhibition of the sort. And it would not be surprising if the ultimate outcome of this loan exhibition should be a museum of antiquities, since a large proportion of the exhibitors would gladly contribute their treasures to the common-weal, if a specially-constructed, fire-proof building should be provided for the conservation of them.

A complete list of the exhibits is given herewith:

Henry Kimlin:
1. Razor dated 1688.
2. Pair of spectacles.

Minot S. Giddings:
3. A deed to Jonathan Giddings of a tract of land on the Connecticut Reserve of Ohio, given by Elijah Boardman, Homer Boardman, David S. Boardman, Stanley Griswold, of New Milford, Ct., Elijah Wadsworth, Frederick Wolcott, Litchfield, Ct., and Zepheniah Briggs of New Fairfield, Ct. Dated 1800.
4. Razor. Portrait of Washington engraved on blade.
5. Sampler, Ruth Buck, date 1786.
6. Bible, Ruth Buck, date 1771.
7. Copy of "Washington's Political Legacy," 1800.
8. Copy of "Gertrude of Wyoming," date 1809.
9. Copy of "Life of Dr. Benjamin Franklin," by himself, date 1795.
10. "The Federal Calculator," 1802. Samuel Giddings.
11. The Prayer Book, 1795. Ebenezer Sanford.

Fred'k E. Starr:
12. Section of Pulpit of Meeting-house, 1754.

Mrs. Arthur Caldwell:
13. Grandmother's jewelry.
14. Pin, 1816.
15. Floral comb.

16. Candle tray and snuffer.
17. Fluid lamp.
18. Vase.
19. Bowl.

Dr. L. J. Pons:
20. Canteen, Civil War.

Lyman Caldwell:
21. Collection of arrow heads.

Wm. H. Marsh:
22. Pie platters, that the extra good pies of our grandmothers were baked in.
23. Churn. This churn is probably over a hundred years old.
24. A bottle of the Eighteenth Century.
25. A bottle of the Eighteenth Century.
26. A doll's cradle used fifty years ago.

Fred'k Berry:
27. Dress sword and sash. Presented to Capt. F. M. Berry, by Company H, 2d Conn. Artillery.

F. A. Johnson:
28. Tea pot, buried in the War of 1812, with other valuables, to prevent its falling into the hands of the British.
29. Rifle shot, picked out of the side of a Confederate fortification at Atlanta, Ga., where they had been fired in by General Sherman's troops.
30. French lancer's spear head, picked up on the battlefield of Waterloo, soon after the battle.
31. Arrow given by "Dave," one of the party of Modoc Indians who killed Gen. Canby. Secured in the Indian Territory.
32. Strip of Confederate flag, which was lowered from the Capitol at Richmond at the surrender, when the city was captured. Confederate money from Gen. Lee's treasure chest. Captured at Appomattox.

L. T. Peet:
33. Trencher and knife, used before the Revolution.
34. Candle-stick, used by Alba Peet 150 years ago, he being a shoemaker and working evenings.

THE LOAN EXHIBITION 143

35. Rock-salt pounder, used by my grandfather, Samuel W. Peet.

Henry E. Squires:
36. Green and white coverlet. Wool raised, spun, and woven in Merryall.
37. Plaid blanket. Wool raised, spun, and woven in Merryall.

Mrs. F. A. Mallory:
38. Flowered coverlet.

Mrs. G. B. Ackley:
39. Pair of silver candle-sticks, candle snuffers and tray.

G. B. Ackley:
40. Book, 1809, specimen of penmanship.

Mrs. G. B. Ackley:
41. Bible, 1806. Almanacs, 1803 to 1814.

L. E. Peet:
42. Water Yoke. Over 100 years old.

James H. Cole:
43. Collection of papers. Deed and other papers.

Mrs. E. J. Sturges:
44. Discharge paper.
45. Old paper, 1754.

Lottie A. Waldron:
46. Sugar-bowl.
47. Pair of glass candle-sticks.

May G. Brown:
48. Portraits of Dr. and Mrs. Thomas Holman, painted in Boston in 1819 by Prof. Morse, (inventor of the telegraph) just before they sailed as members of the *first* band of missionaries to the Sandwich Islands. They were great grandparents of May G. Brown.
49. Journal of Mrs. Thomas Holman, one of the first missionaries to the Sandwich Islands in 1819. Written on board the brig Thaddeus. Mrs. Holman's daughter was the first white child born in the Sandwich Islands, and Mrs. Holman was the first woman to go around the world. (See Nos. 50 & 114.)

50. Feather cape and wreath, red, yellow and black, worn by the native chiefs of the Sandwich Islands. Made from thousands of feathers of a rare bird, but one feather suitable being found on each. These articles were given by Kamahameha I. to the Holmans (missionaries). They are no longer made and there are few, if any, like them now in existence. They are, therefore, of great value. (See Nos. 49 & 114.)

Ruth T. Booth:
51. Casters, over 100 years old.
52. Coffee pot, over 100 years old.
53. Platter, over 100 years old.
54. Plate, over 100 years old.
55. Cup and saucer, over 100 years old.
56. Tea set, 11 pieces, 125 years old, formerly owned by my great-grandmother, Ruth T. Downes.

Harriet V. Sherman:
57. Sampler.

Mrs. Mary E. Stone:
58. Spectacles and goggles. Arrow head and bayonet.

D. C. Kilborne:
59. Lottery tickets. Sold by the first Cong'l Church Society of Bridgewater to raise money to build the church edifice.

Mrs. S. D. Woods:
60. Daily paper with the account of the funeral of George Washington. 1799.

Dr. L. J. Pons:
61. Rapier, used by Capt. Eli Booth, (1800) Milford, Ct.
62. Revolutionary sword.
63. Lantern from two-wheeled physician's chaise, used by Dr. Myron Downs, 1830-1860.
64. Bayonet and sheath, 1812.
65. Old English dagger. About 1790.
66. Lantern.
67. First glass lantern. About 1840.
68. Dragoon's helmet, 1775. Bearskin bush.

THE LOAN EXHIBITION 145

69. Dragoon's flint lock pistol. 1775.
70. Old English pistol.

Mrs. George Trieschmann:
71. Lutheran Bible, 1784.

Mrs. Chas. M. Beach:
72. Tea caddy. This was made at Read's Pottery in Lower Merryall, about the year 1780. It was part of a tea set which Mercy Sperry (who married Sylvester Wheaton) had when she went to housekeeping.
73. Invitations to assembly balls, one hundred years ago.
74. Grape shot, picked up on the battlefield of Waterloo, about the year 1820, by Rev. Nathaniel S. Wheaton, D. D.
75. Half-cent, American coin, 100 years old.
76. Brazilian dump, coin worth about 2½ cents.
77. Powder horn taken from the dead body of an Indian by Capt. Theophilus Baldwin, a volunteer in the French and Indian Wars, while Baldwin was on a scouting party. The Indian shot at him from ambush, and missed. Theophilus did not miss.

Mrs. H. H. Hartwell:
78. Flint lock gun. Carried through Revolution.
79. Gun. Carried by a French officer in the Revolutionary War. Afterwards changed from a flint lock to a percussion lock.
80. Cartridge belt and cartridges, used in Revolutionary War.
81. Autograph bond of Roger Sherman.
82. Brigade orders, Gen. Sedgwick.
83. Two commissions, Joseph Hartwell. As ensign. As lieutenant.

Geo. N. Canfield:
84. Cane, made from the hull of Old Ironsides. Inscription on head: "From the hull of the Constitution, first built in 1798, and dear to Americans for having successfully fought the Java, Guerrierre, Cyane, and Levant, the bombardment of Tripoli in 1812, and also

for her miraculous escape from the British Squadron. Presented to R. E. Canfield by S. Oaks, Esq., U. S. N."

Dr. G. Bragaw:
85. Flint lock gun with bayonet.

Edward H. Beach:
86. Indian battle axe.

Mrs. E. H. Austin:
87. War club, Sandwich Islands. Made from root of a tree.
88. Quilt, hand spun and woven.

Mrs. Hannah Fuller Austin:
89. Commission of Abraham Fuller. He was afterward Captain of Connecticut troops, most of his men being from Kent.

E. H. Austin:
90. Pewter flagon. Supposed to be 150 years old. Belonged to Mills family of Kent. Authentic record of age for more than 100 years. It was an old flagon when this record began.
91. English army belt clasps. Picked up on the field of Waterloo a few days after the battle. Forty-second Somerset.

Mrs. Thomas Austin:
92. Britannia tea pot. More than 100 years old.

A. H. Barlow:
93. An old deed, given to William Barnes of Haddam, by Samuel Barnes in 1734. Also some of the Continental money.
94. Daguerreotype, Gaylord's Bridge.

Mrs. A. H. Barlow:
95. Embroidered apron, 65 years old.
96. Collection of handkerchiefs and chemisette, over 65 years old.
97. Lace bonnet, worn in 1868.
98. Stockings knit by Mrs. Joseph Marsh for her eldest daughter, Mrs. Laura Bailey, and worn by each of her six children.

A. H. Barlow:
99. One spoon of a set given to the grandmother of A. H. Barlow as part of her " setting out." Made of silver dollars in 1799.

Mrs. A. H. Barlow:
100. Spoon, 1830.
101. Old jewelry, 2 lockets and 3 pins. Tortoise shell combs.
102. Three old lace veils.

Mrs. Edward Dakin:
103. Tea canister. Belonged to my great-grandmother, and used by her during her lifetime. Purchased in the year 1770.

Marion D. Underhill:
104. Netted lace, made from flax, raised by my great-great-grandfather on Kent Mountain; spun by my great-great-grandmother; and netted by my great-great-aunt, over eighty years ago.

Miss E. A. Bailey:
105. Cane, brought from England. Has been in the Bailey family for 209 years.

Mrs. A. B. Giddings:
106. Tea pot, brought to New Milford in 1707 by Zachariah Ferriss. Was the only tea pot in town.
107. Toddy tumbler and vinegar cruet, one hundred and fifty years old.

Harriet A. Taylor Lee:
108. Coat worn by Wm. Taylor as Colonel of Militia, 1789.
109. Colonel Wm. Taylor's duelling pistols, 1789.

Mrs. Chas. Taylor:
110. Pewter porringer, 200 years old.
111. Dr. George Taylor's wedding hat, 1825. (See No. 255.)
112. Pewter candle-stick, very old.

Bessie I. Brown:
113. Chinese chest, very old.
114. Calabash, very old. Used for carrying water. (Wicker work encloses a gourd.) This calabash and the Chinese chest were presents received in 1852 from

China by the Holmans, missionaries to the Sandwich Islands. (See Nos. 49 & 50.)

Chas. N. Hall:
  115. *New England Courant*, 1723. Published by Benjamin Franklin.

Elsie Cummings:
  116. Basket, used in Miss Cummings' family 125 years ago.

Mrs. Eli Clark:
  117. Ink stand and sand well. Has been in my family for 125 years.

Mrs. P. E. Clark:
  118. Hair brush, made by my grandmother, Lucinda Young, when a girl 12 years old, 96 years ago.
  119. A history, 108 years old, previously owned by Dr. Silas Castle of Roxbury, Conn., my great-grandfather.
  120. Iron mortar and pestle.
  121. Wooden water bottle.

Elsie Cummings:
  122. Foot stove.

Mrs. P. E. Clark:
  123. Barrel.

Mrs. Eli Clark:
  124. Warming pan.

Mrs. Carlos Merwin:
  125. Plate, Spanish bull fight, 1795.
  126. Brittania tea pot, 75 years old, " Muskmelon " pattern.

Fred C. Merwin:
  127. Constitution of Union Library, New Milford, 1796, the first in town. Sec. Elisha Bostwick, ancestor of owner.

Mrs. Carlos Merwin:
  128. Bead bag, 72 years old, hand made.
  129. Sampler, 76 years old.
  130. Knapsack.
  131. Bell that rang the " Minute Men " in, used by David Merwin in Merryall.
  132. Musket.

133. Plate, 75 years old.

Mrs. A. G. Barnes:
134. Sugar-bowl, 200 years old.
135. Cup and saucer, 150 years old.
136. Cup and saucer, 75 years old.

Mrs. C. T. Staples:
137. Seal of Wm. Penn, founder of Pennsylvania, public and private seal.
138. *London Post*, (1738).
139. Play bills.
140. Doll, 50 years old.

F. E. Baldwin:
141. Punch tumbler, from Isaac Stone Tavern, Park Lane.
142. Ancient lantern.
143. Powder horn, taken by Hezekiah Baldwin from body of Indian shot by him near Lake George in French and Indian War, about 1756.
144. Pitch pipe, used by Jeremiah Baldwin in giving the key to choir of Congregational Church, New Milford.

F. E. Baldwin:
145. Grain fan, fanning-mill of "Ye Olden Time."
146. Foot stove.
147. Warming pan.
148. Candle mould.

Frank H. Beach:
149. *Crêpe* cloth flowers (framed).

Mrs. Wm. E. Stone:
150. Masonic apron.

Flora G. Stillson:
151. "New England Primer," 150 years old.

Henry Harmon Noble:
152. Two discourses delivered at New Milford, December 14, 1800, by Rev. Stanley Griswold, it being the Sabbath next after the decease of Rev. Nathaniel Taylor.

Homer Wanzer:
153. Receipts (from 1796 to 1800).

Mary Bostwick Kelly:
154. Silver sugar tongs and six tablespoons. Sixteen teaspoons which belonged to Elisha and Betty Bostwick; over 100 years old.

Mrs. W. D. Black:
155. Portrait, Sally Northrop. Born June, 1776; died December, 1876.

Miss J. L. Gaylord:
156. Hand-made counterpane.

Mary Bostwick Kelly:
157. Portrait, Col. Elisha Bostwick, born Dec. 17, 1748.
158. Portrait, Betty Ferris Bostwick, born in 1768.
159. Portrait, Jared Bostwick, born May 24, 1787.
160. Portrait, Betsy Ann Bostwick, born July 11, 1792.
161. Picture, "The Old Bostwick Homestead." Has been in the family for 200 years.
162. Framed contract for house (1780). Cap and mitts worn by Elisha Bostwick, when he was baptized, in the year 1749.
163. Watch. Bull's-eye watch, carried by Colonel Elisha Bostwick through the Revolution.
164. Watch carried by Jared Bostwick. Over 100 years old.

Fred C. Merwin:
165. Indian hatchet and arrow-head, found on the farm of the late David Merwin, a "Minute Man."

Mary Bostwick Kelly:
166. Shawl, Betty Ferris Bostwick; 125 years.
167. Jackknife.

Mabel Marsh:
168. Ancient tea pot. Was brought over from Ireland about 100 years ago. At one time owned by Mrs. Mabel Baldwin.

Mrs. George Marsh:
169. Old-fashioned shade glasses. Worn by Col. Adolphus Hallock nearly 100 years ago, when driving cattle, travelling on foot and horseback from Ohio to New Milford.

THE LOAN EXHIBITION 151

Dr. B. E. Bostwick:
170. Old will and inventory, 1739.
171. Deed, 1720.
172. Certificate, survey by Roger Sherman, 1748.

J. B. Merwin:
173. Pine-tree shillings, 1652.
174. Hour-glass, used in the Revolution.
175. Six books, 1753, 1771, 1784, 1800, and 1805. New England Primer.

Mrs. Elizabeth Wells:
176. Bandanna handkerchief, owned by John Turrill, a soldier of the Revolution.
177. Parchment and bobbins, used by Roger Sherman's mother in lace-making.

Miss Catherine Wells:
178. Continental money.

Mrs. Elizabeth Wells:
179. Linen apron, 100 years old.

Miss Catherine Wells:
180. Paper dolls, 40 years old.
181. Linen skirt, 46 years old, hand-made.

Mrs. John D. Clark:
182. Candle stand, 100 years old.
183. Two sets silver spoons, one set 125 years old, the other set 100 years old.
184. After-dinner coffee cup, 125 years old.
185. Sugar-bowl with lid, 125 years old. Sugar-bowl without lid, 100 years old.
186. Work basket, over 100 years old.
187. Deed of land in New Milford, 117 years old. Deed of land on Long Mountain, 172 years old. Equation table, showing how much a clock should be faster or slower than a sun-dial, or the sun on the meridian.

George Thatcher:
188. Two knives and a fork. George Thatcher's grandfather, Michel Gould, used these 140 years ago.
189. Pocketbook, 1790.

Mrs. Chas. Taylor:
190. Fireplace griddle; fireplace waffle iron; skillet for baking hoe cake (coals put underneath and on top); fireplace gridiron; fireplace chop broiler; fireplace toaster; fireplace baking-kitchen; fireplace iron fork; fireplace frying-pan; fireplace roasting-kitchen, 100 years old. These and the other fireplace fittings were so grouped as to form a most realistic picture of the fireplace of ye olden time.
191. Old foot stove.

E. J. Sturges:
192. Rapier, carried by Ebenezer Perry, of Col. Andrew Burr's regiment, of Fairfield, at the fall of Louisburg, June 17, 1745.
193. Portrait, Mrs. Mary Sturges, who witnessed the burning of her home in Fairfield, by the British, July 9, 1779.

Minot S. Giddings:
194. Silver spoon. A spoon or a set of spoons, made from silver dollars, was presented by Mary (Baldwin) Giddings to each of her children, with her initials engraved on them. Jonathan Giddings and Mary Baldwin were married Jan. 2, 1766.

W. O. Corning:
195. Bassoon, over 100 years old.
196. Serpent, over 100 years old.

Mrs. Salmon Couch:
197. Flannel dress goods, 1844, colored and woven by Mrs. Sarah Peet and Mrs. Goodsell.
198. Tin-baker, over 100 years old.

Mrs. F. M. Williams:
199. Pewter tankard, 100 years old.
200. Child's linen skirt, over 100 years old.
201. *Connecticut Courant*, 1799, containing account of death of George Washington.

Mrs. Dan. Clark:
202. Hand-made wedding veil (100 years).

THE LOAN EXHIBITION 153

Mrs. T. T. Marsh:
  203. Portrait, Dr. Jehiel Williams, one of the first doctors of New Milford (1815), and grandfather of the late T. T. Marsh and of Edward W. Marsh of Bridgeport, Ct.

Mrs. Chas. Taylor:
  204. Early Colonial pewter basin.
  205. Early Colonial pewter tea set.
  206. Pewter platters.
  207. Pewter platters.
  208. Fluid lamp, one of the first sperm-oil lanterns, carried by Dr. Geo. Taylor.

Flora Geer Stillson:
  209. White satin wedding slippers and sash. Rachel Ann Bostwick and John Stillson, married in June, 1774. These articles loaned by their great-granddaughter.
  210. *Crêpe* shawl, figured with nasturtiums, worn by Mrs. John Stillson on trip of the first train run on the Housatonic Railroad, 1840. Loaned by her granddaughter.
  211. Bead bag on linen, worked by Loretta Geer in 1823, when she was ten years old. Loaned by her granddaughter.
  212. Bead bag, worn by Mrs. John Stillson. About 75 years old.
  213. Sampler worked by Almira Turrill in 1824. Loaned by her grandniece.

L. T. Peet:
  214. Sickle, used for cutting grain, 125 years old.
  215. Toby jug, made in Jersey City pottery, 60 years ago.

Miss Helen M. Boardman:
  216. Miniature of Major Lawrence, of the British Army, a nephew of Mrs. Wm. Taylor of this town.

Miss Kate T. Boardman:
  217. Locket, owned by Mrs. Wm. Taylor. She was the daughter of the second minister of this town.

The Misses Boardman:
  218. Candle-sticks, brought from Warwick, England, and used in the days of Queen Anne.
  219. Japanese tray and cups, brought from Japan in 1854 by Frederic A. Boardman, who was in Commodore Perry's expedition to that country.
  220. Bas-relief of George Washington, owned by Judge David Sherman Boardman in 1820.

Miss Rose Murdoch:
  221. Decanter and glasses, presented by the Marquis de Lafayette to David C. Porter, in Paris, in the year 1825.

Mrs. C. A. Smith:
  222. Chair, 150 years old.

Peter Peterson:
  223. Pitcher.
  224. Bottle.
  225. Two pictures and silver spoons made in 1600.
  226. Brass scenes, brought from Denmark.

Harriet A. Taylor Lee:
  227. Stamp, Greek word, meaning " Quit yourself like a man." Belonged to Rev. Nathaniel Taylor, 1748.
  228. Baby stocking of Harriet D. Allen (1806), afterwards Mrs. George Taylor.

Mrs. C. N. Hall:
  229. Picture, old Canfield Homestead, 150 years.

Mrs. Mary D. Bostwick:
  230. Bible, Thomas Wells, 100 years.

Mrs. H. R. Treadwell:
  231. Box made of a fragment of the old ship " Constitution."
  232. Sampler worked by Ruth Taylor, afterwards Mrs. Elijah Downes. Loaned by her granddaughter.
  233. Autograph of John Hancock.
  234. Cut from a bill of fare of a banquet given to Henry Clay, printed on satin. His autograph added.
  235. Seal of completion of Erie Canal, 1825.

Mrs. H. R. Treadwell:
   236. Portrait of Roger Sherman.
Charles B. Camp:
   237. Silver pipe, smoked during Revolutionary War. Over 100 years old.
   238. Bible, published in 1639.
Mrs. Chas. B. Camp:
   239. Patch box, from estate of Alex. Rosseguie, a Huguenot of France. Loaned by his great-great-granddaughter. (See No. 287.)
   240. Towel, 200 years old. From estate of Alex. Resseguie.
   241. Candle-stick, from estate of Alex. Rosseguie.
Charles B. Camp:
   242. Fife, used in Revolutionary War by John Camp. Loaned by his grandson.
Jay Cogshall:
   243. Silver spoon, 1787.
   244. Spoon mould and spoon, 200 years old.
The Misses Wells:
   245. Samplers worked by Mary G. Sherman, afterwards Mrs. Stephen Wells.
L. N. Jennings:
   246. Piece of gun picked up on battlefield of Antietam a few days after the battle.
Mrs. Eli S. Roberts:
   247. Cup and saucer formerly owned by Mrs. Eunice Clark Morris. Over 100 years old.
   248. Mrs. Cornelia Morris Young's baby shoes, 86 years old.
Mr. E. P. Hill:
   249. Basin, platter, and plate, used by Capt. James Buck, who was married to Roger Sherman's sister.
   250. Documents: Raising recruits for Continental Army. Tax List, 1781.
Elizabeth H. Noble:
   251. "Old London Penny Postman." Accurate portrait

brought from England by Mrs. Henrietta Burritt about 1800. Loaned by her great-granddaughter.

252. "Wife of Old London Penny Postman." Portrait.

Mrs. Helen B. Carr:

253. Portrait. Mrs. Susan Masters Blackman, granddaughter of Rev. Nathaniel Taylor.
254. Picture, "Old Masters House."

Mrs. T. E. Stewart:

255. Trousers. Dr. Geo. Taylor's, worn when he was two years of age, and first calico brought to New Milford (1804). The man who wore the hat (No. 111) wore the trousers twenty-one years earlier.
256. Baby's dress. Embroidered by Mrs. Nathaniel Taylor for her son, Dr. Geo. Taylor, in 1802.
257. Slippers, worn by Dr. Geo. Taylor.
258. Collar, made by Harriet Allen (afterward Mrs. Geo. Taylor) while attending the Moravian School.

Mrs. H. S. Mygatt:

259. Portrait, Colonel Samuel Canfield, of the Revolutionary Army.
260. Wood from Roger Sherman's house.
261. Old English pewter cup.
262. Whale oil lamps, from Stonington, Conn. Over 100 years old.
263. Fluid lamp.
264. Silver tea set, belonged to Tamar Boardman Taylor, daughter of Rev. Daniel Boardman, and wife of Rev. Nathaniel Taylor.
265. Silver spoons, used by Noadiah and Clarissa Mygatt.
266. Silver spoon, marked T. M. (T. Mygatt).
267. Pewter dish, French pewter, dated 1777.
268. Old pewter lamp.

D. K. Crofut:

269. Quilt, warming pan, and ancient hoe.
270. Flint lock musket.

May G. Brown:

271. "Tapa" cloth, made from bark by natives of the Sandwich Islands.

Mrs. H. S. Mygatt:
272. Cane. Belonged to Philo Canfield, son of Col. Samuel Canfield.

Roger Sherman Chapter, D. A. R.:
273. Warming pan.
274. Foot stove, used in the Congregational Church, New Milford, 1812.

Mrs. G. W. Wright:
275. Picture of New Milford.

A. E. Taylor:
276. Piano, age unknown.

Lehman T. Peet:
277. Indian work basket, made by Rachel Mauwehu, a squaw of the Schaghticoke tribe, about 1847.
278. Thread stand, about 125 years old.

Congregational Church:
279. Chair, belonging to Rev. Nathaniel Taylor, second pastor of the Congregational Church, from 1748 to 1800.

Mrs. B. F. Humeston:
280. Fireplace cooker. Used in 1775.
281. Cuff buttons, made in 1797 from ore found in Roxbury.

Mrs. S. E. Bristol:
282. Pitcher, Staffordshire, 175 years old.

Mrs. S. E. Bristol:
283. Silhouette, 90 years old. William Bristol, father of Isaac B. Bristol.
284. Miniature, 80 years old, Heman Crane.
285. Cake basket, 100 years old.

Mrs. H. R. Treadwell:
286. *Massachusetts Gazette* and *Boston News Letter* of 1775.
287. Patch box, as used by fashionable ladies of the 17th and 18th centuries, to contain black patches, cut in various shapes and sizes, to stick on the face, supposedly to heighten the brilliancy of the complexion by contrast.

Bessie Kennedy:
  288. Shears, hand wrought, date unknown.
Annie Kennedy:
  289. Ink well, hollowed out of a solid piece of soapstone.
E. Kennedy:
  290. Skillet.
Jeannette L. Gaylord:
  291. Old Honiton and point lace.
  292. Old embroideries.
  293. Portraits, Mr. and Mrs. Ebenezer Gaylord, about 1798.
  294. Shell cameo. Portrait of owner's uncle, W. L. Jewitt, 1840.
  295. Old rum bottles and liquor jug, the latter being used in olden times to carry to the hayfields.
  296. Indian needle-case and horn spoons.
W. F. Gaylord:
  297. Three Indian implements.
Mrs. Theodore Carlson:
  298. Swedish bracelet. Wood and iron watch chain, Swedish.
Jeannette L. Gaylord:
  299. Lace evening cloak. 1850.
Mrs. Henry Hine:
  300. Articles from Martinique: Lava; tile from old cathedral; goblets which went through fire; pictures of Martinique after the eruption.
  301. Pottery vase from Equador, between 400 and 500 years old.
  302. Asphalt, from Asphalt Lake, La Brea, Trinidad.
  303. Pottery from Fort de France, Martinique.
  304. Tea pot from Cuba.
  305. Chocolate bean and picture, Trinidad.
  306. Two photos, Kingston, Jamaica.
Mrs. Charles Taylor:
  307. Miniature of Mrs. Margaret Craft. Painted just before her marriage in 1832. She is now 97 years old.

THE LOAN EXHIBITION 159

308. Miniature of Mr. James Craft in 1832.

Harriet A. Taylor Lee:
309. Badge of Israel Putnam in a Greek Society at Yale College, 1776. Given by him to Wm. Taylor.
310. Prayer Book, English, published during the reign of King George and Queen Caroline. Belonging to Colonel Wm. Taylor.

Mrs. E. A. Wildman:
311. Pewter platter, 130 years old.

Mrs. Henry Hine:
312. Anklet, or Hindoo bracelet.
313. Alligator.
314. Candle-stick, Trinidad.
315. Poinsettia bean, Martinique. Nutmeg, Puerto Cabello. Betel nut (natives chew to blacken teeth).

Miss A. E. Bostwick:
316. Sampler, 1831, made by Lucy M. Sanford (afterwards Mrs. William Bostwick), when nine years old.

Mrs. C. A. Smith:
317. Brass candle-stick, made by hand in 1767.
318. Legal document bearing signature of Roger Sherman.
319. Pocketbook made by Kent Wright, the first white child born in Kent, Conn.

Mrs. Lily Traver:
320. China, 18 pieces, very old.
321. Cuff buttons, hand-made, Chinese.
322. Indian implements and bead bag.
323. Silver spoons, very old.
324. Candle-stick.
325. Coins and bill (Confederate).
326. Breastpin and ribbon, 100 years.
327. Book and old documents. Account of third and last voyage of Capt. Cook, in 1776.
328. Salt-cellar.
329. Map, drawn by Sarah Northrop (afterwards married to Col. Starr) in 1822.

Mrs. J. Leroy Buck:
330. Tea caddy. Owned by Mrs. Ithamar Canfield, born Jan. 2, 1770. Loaned by her great-granddaughter.
331. Dressing case, owned by Ithamar Canfield, born Feb. 19, 1764; died Apr. 11, 1848.
332. Document. Share in Toll Bridge Co.

Lawrence Northrop:
333. Sword, carried in War of 1812.

Willis F. Bennett:
334. Powder horn, used in Revolutionary War by Sam Bennett.
335. Snuff box, used by Isaac Baldwin, soldier in the Revolutionary War.

Flora G. Stillson:
336. Invitation to opening ball at the New England House, Dec. 11, 1856.

J. H. Nettleton:
337. Indian relics, found in New Milford.

Helen M. Boardman:
338. Chinese idols, brought from China in 1854 by Frederic A. Boardman.

The Misses Boardman:
339. Gondola hook, used in Venice by the nobility in the early part of the 17th century.

Miss Rose Murdoch:
340. English miniature, mother of Mrs. David Murdoch.
341. Mexican ivory, very old.

Albert Evitts:
342. Vegetable dish, used by Dr. Williams. Old willow ware.

Mrs. H. S. Mygatt:
343. Bull's-eye watch, over 100 years of age.
344. Bouquet holder, 75 years old.

Helen M. Boardman:
345. Compass, made from tree sent by Thomas Jefferson to Mount Vernon, and planted by General Lafayette.

Martha D. Treadwell:
346. Watch, 75 years old.

347. Jewelry, very old.

J. H. Nettleton:

348. Flint lock pistol.

Mrs. Nettleton:

349. Hand-made collar, 60 years old.

Congregational Church:

350. Picture of Rev. Noah Porter, D. D., LL. D., pastor of the Congregational Church 1836-1843. Afterwards President of Yale College.

Russell B. Noble:

351. Picture of house (now standing) on the plains about two miles south of the village of New Milford, with the deed, dated 30th day of May, in the 12th year of his Majesty's reign, A. D. 1772, conveying it to his son, Ezra Dibble Noble, by Zadok Noble, grandson of John Noble, the first settler.
352. Silhouette picture of Charles Clement Noble, son of Ichabod, son of Ezra Dibble, son of Zadok, son of David, son of *John Noble*, who settled in New Milford, A. D. 1707.
353. Three commissions signed by Governors: Jonathan Trumbull, John Treadwell, John Cotton Smith.
354. Dr. William Gordon's " History of the Rise, Progress, and Establishment of the Independence of the United States of America," in 4 volumes. Published in London, 1788.
355. Map of New Milford, published by Richard Clark, 1853.

Mrs. Henry Brinsmade:

356. Picture, Mrs. George N. Mallory, born in New Milford, Sept. 17, 1808. Now living in New Haven. This picture was taken at the age of 97.

Geo. B. Ackley:

357. Bellows, over 100 years.

Mrs. Charles E. Marsh:

358. Bible, leather-covered. printed 1696. From my grandfather, Allen Marsh.

Chas. E. Marsh:
- 359. A reel.
- 360. Double linen wheel.
- 361. Foot stove.
- 362. Single linen wheel.
- 363. A spinning wheel, for wool.

Mr. E. P. Hill:
- 364. Iron fire dogs.

Miss Sarah J. Roberts:
- 365. A Pilgrim staff, brought to New Milford in 1750 by Mr. Eli Roberts.

Mrs. Arza Morris:
- 366. Ancient gridiron.
- 367. Reel.
- 368. Swift.
- 369. Linen wheel.
- 370. Wheel for spinning wool.
- 371. Blue and white blanket (Phebe Velie).
- 372. Blue and white blanket.
- 373. Hatchel for flax.

Mrs. Eli Welton:
- 374. Old mirror.
- 375. Sunrise quilt, home spun and woven.
- 376. Tulip quilt.

Mrs. Carson B. Mead:
- 377. Map of original thirteen States. About 1785.
- 378. Gun used in Revolutionary War.
- 379. Indian hatchet and pistol.

Mrs. Grace C. Wellwood:
- 380. Hanging iron lamp.

David Barnum:
- 381. Button-hole cutter.

Mrs. Hannah More Jessup:
- 382. Candle-stick, used in Platt's Tavern in Bridgewater, in 1820.
- 383. Whale-oil lamp.

THE LOAN EXHIBITION 163

384. Geography, 1807.
385. Tent lantern of Gen. Burgoyne, taken by a Bridgewater soldier at the time of his surrender, at Saratoga, 1777. Gen. Burgoyne's own lantern.
386. Lantern belonging to one of the first settlers of New Milford (Bostwick) and used in the War of 1812.
387. Tripod wooden candle-stick.

Mrs. Dora K. Sanford:
388. Glass lamp, 1850 or earlier.
389. Pewter lamps, about 1800.
390. Lard lamp, about 1770.

Mrs. Horace Allen:
391. Masonic pitcher.

Boardman Wright:
392. Autograph letter of Daniel Webster.
393. *New England Weekly Journal,* April 8, 1728, an early number of one of the first newspapers published in this country, the first number of the *Boston News Letter* (the first newspaper) having appeared Apr. 24, 1704.
394. *Country Journal and Poughkeepsie Advertiser,* 1787 to 1789. Contemporary account of Washington's first inauguration.

George W. Murphy:
395. Iron tea-kettle, over 100 years old.

Mrs. Henry Ives:
396. Silver spoon, made from silver coin earned by spinning (1799), by the grandmother of Deacon Henry Ives.

H. C. Ives:
397. Silver tea-pot, about 100 years old. Owned by the grandfather of H. C. Ives.

Mrs. H. C. Ives:
398. Sugar-tongs, made from silver dollars in 1825, at the silversmith establishment of Stanley Sanford Baldwin, for his bride, Harriet Stevens. Grandparents of Mrs. H. C. Ives.

399. Brass candle-sticks, over 100 years old.

F. J. Turrill:
400. Deed, from Daniel Boardman, 1729.
401. Plow, used by John Turrill, a Revolutionary soldier.

William B. Pell:
402. Collection of Continental currency.
403. Pewter mug, part of the camp outfit of the 24th regiment of Napoleon's *cuirassiers*. From the room which the Duke of Wellington occupied after the battle, and known to have been used by him.
404. Club, made from a part of the ram "Merrimac" of the Confederate Navy. Sunk at the engagement at Hampton Roads, Va., by U. S. S. "Monitor."

W. F. Gaylord:
405. Gun, used in three old wars. Carried by Zephaniah Briggs, when 24 years old, in French and Indian War; in the Revolutionary War by the same man at 46 years of age; and in the War of 1812 by the same man at 78. He lived to be 103.

Mrs. S. E. Bristol:
406. Old China, 100 and 150 years old.

Mrs. H. C. Ives:
407. Collection of old china, 97 pieces, all very old.

Mrs. P. L. Anderson:
408. Roman mosaic jewelry, 60 or 70 years old.

Mrs. Henry R. Treadwell:
409. Autograph letter of Gen. Washington.

Mrs. W. H. Percy:
410. Silhouettes, Stanley Sanford Baldwin and wife, 1825. Mexican medal, presented by State of Louisiana to Zachary Taylor, Major General.

Miss M. E. Hine:
411. Sampler, worked by Alta Eliza Gaylord, 1829.

Mrs. G. W. Wright:
412. The idol of the royal family of the Sandwich Islands. Presented to a missionary by Kamehameha I.
413. Taper for reading, age unknown.

414. Spoon, formerly the property of Daniel Boardman, who was ordained the first pastor of the Congregational Church, then called the "Church of Christ," Nov. 21, 1716. The spoon is marked:

B
D I

B is for Boardman, D is for Daniel, I is for Jerusha, his wife.
415. Latin Psalter, 1509.
416. Prayer Book. Changed from the English ritual to American P. E. ritual in handwriting of Bishop Provost. It lay on the altar of Trinity Church, New York, for many years previous to the Revolution. When the church burned down during the occupancy of New York by the British, the cinders from the burning roof left their marks on the cover.

Boardman Wright and Rev. F. A. Wright:
417. Pictorial German Bible, 1692. Formerly property of Rev. J. Friedrich Schröder, minister in the German Lutheran Church, in Mecklenburg.

Mrs. Boardman Wright:
418. Silver chatelaine.
419. Scarf.
420. Scarf.
421. Sandalwood fan.
422. Hand-painted fan, sticks, mother-of-pearl, gold inlaid.
423. Fan, sticks, mother-of-pearl, silver inlaid.
424. Lace, Rose Point and Duchesse.
425. Old lady's cap.

Boardman Wright:
426. Invitation, Dance Programme and Menu. Ball given in honor of Prince of Wales (now King Edward VII.), in 1860.
427. Silver tankard, property of Daniel Boardman, the first minister of New Milford. Probably brought from England by Samuel Boardman in 1633.

Mrs. Florence Buck Loonan:
  428. Clock, more than 150 years old. Wooden works, made with a knife.
Raymond Goodsell:
  429. Indian arrow-heads in case.
Mrs. C. H. Allen:
  430. Lustre pitcher, about 150 years old.
  431. Sugar-bowl, over 100 years of age.
  432. Lafayette Cup.
Mrs. G. W. Wright:
  433. Chair, property of Madame Boardman (Mrs. Daniel Boardman), wife of the first minister of New Milford.
Boardman Wright:
  434. Hat badge (U. S. Engineers). Worn by Gen. Robert E. Lee through the Mexican War.
Dr. G. H. Wright:
  435. Old wooden fireplace, frame and mantel. Old fireplace crane.
Mrs. Henry E. Bostwick:
  436. Commission, William Gaylord, 1723.
  437. Two commissions, Benjamin Gaylord, 1760 and 1762.
  438. Sword captured during the Revolutionary War from the Tory leader, Wade Vaughn, by the Gaylord Band.
  439. Silver, over 100 years old, showing style of engraving at that time. Initial of both husband and wife, D. T. M.—David and Tamasin Merwin.
  440. Pitch-pipe used in the old Congregational " Meeting House."
  441. Powder horn, carried through the Revolutionary War.
  442. Piece of the wedding dress of Mrs. Abel Seeley, married before the Revolutionary War. It is homespun linen and hand-woven, in imitation of French muslin.
Mrs. Henry E. Bostwick:
  443. Pewter porringer.

THE LOAN EXHIBITION 167

444. China.

Mrs. G. W. Wright:
445. Tea pot, cup and saucer, imported from China by Hon. Elijah Boardman, about 1790.
446. Holster and flint lock pistols.

Mrs. S. E. Bristol:
447. Gold watch and chain, 150 years old.

E. J. Emmons:
448. Newspaper, *Ulster County Gazette*, 1800. Account of funeral of George Washington.

Mrs. C. H. Allen:
449. Medicine chest, over 100 years old.

Sadie Strong:
450. Knitted counterpane, about 40 years old.

A. H. McMahon:
451. Millennium plate, over 160 years old.

Mrs. Henry E. Bostwick:
452. Engraving of Roger Sherman.

Mrs. Willis F. Bennett:
453. Iron peel, nearly 100 years old. Used for placing and withdrawing food from the brick oven.

Dr. G. H. Wright:
454. White satin suit, worn by Senator Elijah Boardman.

Dr. H. H. Hartwell:
455. Trooper's coat.

Mrs. Helen B. Carr:
456. Dress, made in style shown in London Fashion Book of 1799.

Mrs. Salmon and Fred Buck:
457. Silver spoon, 150 years old. Cup and saucer used by Roger Sherman's sister.

Mrs. Helen B. Carr:
458. Sermons of Rev. Daniel Boardman.
459. Sampler, 1804.
460. Locket and ring, worn by the grandmother of Mrs. Helen B. Carr.

Will Cogswell:
  461. Dagger found during Revolutionary War. Indian Hammer Head.

Mrs. F. W. Knowles:
  462. China, over 100 years old; 11 pieces.
  463. Flax grown in New Milford by John Caldwell, in 1800.
  464. Tailor's shears, over 150 years old. With these shears the lady represented in the daguerreotype of No. 465 earned by tailoring the gold beads of No. 465.
  465. Gold beads and daguerreotype, very old.
  466. Dress worn by Harriet Beard when married to Charles Knowles.

The Misses Boardman:
  467. Two brooches; one, tomb of Washington, the other, made from the Charter Oak.

Clarissa T. Staples:
  468. Queen Anne knife and fork, Sheffield plate, made in 1690.

Mrs. Ellen Lamson:
  469. Tea pot, 200 years old, brought over from England.

G. G. Bray:
  470. Tray, 150 years old.

C. Andrew Humeston:
  471. Wedgewood pitcher; lustre pitcher, very old; cup and saucer, 80 years old.

Mrs. F. E. Starr:
  472. Apron, home-spun linen, worked with crewels. Very old.

Clarissa T. Staples:
  473. Candle-stick, formerly used by Samuel Treadwell.

Ormida Northrop Pratt:
  474. Brewster Cup, 150 years old, belonging to Mrs. Mary Brewster Beach, whose father was William Brewster, second son of Elder Brewster, of the *Mayflower*.
  475. Sampler, 90 years old, embroidered by Mary Brewster Beach, great-great-granddaughter of Elder Brewster, of the *Mayflower*.

476. Fan of Mrs. Jane (Mills) Bordwell, wife of Rev. Joel Bordwell, pastor of Kent Congregational Church, 1758-1811.
477. Purse, 75 years old.

Mrs. Seymour C. Loomis:
478. Ring dropped by Lafayette in the house of my great-great-great-grandmother, Abigail Starr Taylor, in Danbury, during the Revolutionary War.
479. Brooch. Belonged to Mrs. Ithamar Canfield, worn during 1700.
480. Book, used by Abigail Starr, wife of Major Daniel Starr, 1750.
481. Letter of Abigail Starr, 1756.
482. Slipper worn by Abigail Starr, 1765.

Helen M. Boardman:
483. Brooch (Italian), about 75 years old.

Miss M. D. Porter:
484. Door-handle from back door of Rev. Nathaniel Taylor's house in New Milford, probably made for the front door by the old blacksmith, Daniel Burritt, whose initials are on it, 1759. When repairs were made in the house, in the summer of 1880 or 1881, this old latch was taken off and given to Mrs. Mary Taylor Porter.
485. Powder horn (Abel Hine, 1758).
486. Pulpit Bible, used by Rev. Nathaniel Taylor, who was settled in New Milford in 1748, and died after a pastorate of 52 years. This Bible was given to him by his father, Daniel Taylor, of Danbury.
487. Silhouette, Rev. Nathaniel William Taylor, D. D. (grandson of Rev. Nathaniel Taylor), made by Samuel Metford, New Haven, in 1842.

Mrs. Chas. Taylor:
488. Hand-made counterpane. Made for large four-post bedstead, of linen, with pattern done in candle wicking, drawn through.

THE OLD HOME GATHERING

THE "Old Home Gathering" in Roger Sherman Hall, at 8:30 o'clock Saturday evening, was presided over by W. Frank Kinney, Chairman of the Committee on Invitation, Reception, and Entertainment. Mr. Kinney, by way of welcome, spoke as follows:

"You do not know how hard it is for me to come to-night into a place like this. I was asked by the committee to take charge of these exercises for reasons that you well know. I am asked to give you a welcome to our town. 'Surely, the love of home is interwoven with all that is pure, deep, and lasting in earthly affection. Let us wander where we may, the heart turns back with secret longing to the paternal roof. There all the scattered rays of affection concentrate. Time may enfeeble them, distance overshadow them, and the storms of life obscure them for a season, but they will at length break through the clouds and gloom, and glow, and burn, and brighten, around the peaceful threshold of home.' Thus wrote the poet Longfellow, and I repeat those lines because they express in so much better language than it is possible for me to do, the thoughts that are uppermost in your hearts to-night.

"We welcome you to-night to these grand old hills, among which your ancestors were born and bred, and where they drew the inspiration that made them the men of mark and note of their day; over whose wooded heights you tramped with the old gun on your shoulder, looking for the gray squirrel, watching for the rise of the partridge, or listening to the distant baying of the hound, as he chased the fox along the trail.

"We welcome you back to these beautiful valleys, where, in your earlier days, you bent your back, and, by the sweat of your brow, earned your daily bread. We welcome you back to the

ROGER SHERMAN HALL AND CHURCH STREET

noble old river, where you swam and bathed in its clear, bright waters, or sailed so smoothly upon its bosom, or skated over it, in its winter coat, or, perhaps, studied astronomy by counting the stars as you lay prone upon your back.

"We welcome you back to these beautiful mountain streams that come tumbling down the hills, and through the valleys to the river, which many a day you followed with hook and line, trying to entice the speckled beauty from some favorite haunt. Welcome back to the little red school house at the corner, where you learned your A, B, C's, and to the historic old birch tree that stands near by, and of whose branches you still have tender memories. Welcome back to the dear old church, within whose sacred walls you spent so many hallowed hours, and from which you took many of the sweetest, as well as the saddest, memories of the old town.

"Welcome back to the old homesteads, 'Sacred to all that can gladden, or sadden, the heart of man, over whose thresholds of oak and stone, life and death has come and gone.' We leave you there, we cannot cross those thresholds; but when you come forth again, we welcome you to our beautiful village, to the festivities of this Bi-Centennial occasion. And to those who have come back after a few years of absence, and to those who have come to the homes of their ancestors for the first time, you will find we have hearts warm enough, and homes large enough, to welcome you all. Again I say, welcome, thrice welcome to our grand old town."

Brief speeches, replete with sentiment and reminiscence, were made by Rev. George S. Bennitt, D. D., of Jersey City; Hon. Henry C. Sanford, of Bridgewater (formerly a part of New Milford); Boardman Wright and Timothy Dwight Merwin, New York lawyers; Rev. John T. Huntington, of Hartford, and Edwin W. Marsh, a Bridgeport banker—all members of families which have been closely identified with New Milford interests for several generations.

The Chairman read the following poem, written for the occasion by Mary Murdoch Mason, daughter of a former pastor of the Congregational Church:

"HOME

"Born on these hills, or in this happy vale,
  Our feet turn swiftly toward the well-known trail:
  At all great moments, when the heart is stirred,
  The exile's soul spreads wings like homing bird.

" 'Tis in this village church our knees are bent,
  When, 'neath cathedral dome or tropic tent,
  We hear the burial service for the dead,
  'Tis in the old home pew our prayers are said.

"No brilliant light in bold, bright city street
  Can dazzle eyes accustom-ed to greet
  That golden splash and sparkle where the sun
  Kisses our River's curve ere day is done.
  You know the spot. We see it from Town-Hill;
  It stirs our hearts and makes old memories thrill.

"In Switzerland, the snow-capped heights grow dim,
  Mt. Tom appears, and Guardian Mount with him.
  Rigi's a dream, and even Jungfrau pales,
  While Alpine glow lights up New England dales.

"Old Ocean's storms and winds for us grow calm,
  The while we dream of Housatonic's charm:
  And we forget the harbor at Trieste
  To float upon Lake Waramaug's dear breast.

"No bells that ring from far-famed distant towers
  Are half so sweet as those 'First Bells' of ours.
  And songs that thrill the world were never sung
  As noble as those hymns we loved when young.

"On London 'bus, or in Pall-Mall's vast crowd,
  Sudden we're walking through a field fresh plowed:
  Upon the steamer's deck far out at sea,
  We hear a robin sing in Main Street tree.

"In wind-swept wastes, we're filled with joy, not gloom,
Because at home th' arbutus is in bloom.
And when June comes, and roses blow, we say:
'Oh, for those roses round our porch to-day!'

"But 'tis at night beneath the heavens we cry:
'These same kind stars with ever-friendly eye
Upon our well-beloved graves look down,
Far, far away, in dear New Milford town.'"

Charles N. Hall, Secretary of the General Bi-Centennial Committee, read the following cablegram:

"London, England, June 15, 1907.

"Success to the Bi-Centennial and best wishes for the dear old town! Deeply regret my absence. FRANK HINE."

He also read the following letter, explaining that, although addressed to the Committee, it belonged to all New Milford, since it came straight from the heart of one whom all New Milford loves:

"New York, June 11, 1907.

"CHARLES N. HALL, Esq., Secretary of the Bi-Centennial Association of New Milford,

"*Dear Sir:*—

"Owing to a severe and unexpected attack of illness I am reluctantly compelled, acting under the imperative orders of my physician, Dr. Allan McLane Hamilton, of New York, to relinquish any participation in the Bi-Centennial ceremonies, and I, therefore, request that arrangements be made to have my duties assumed by the officers upon whom they will devolve.

"It is impossible for me to express my deep regret at the necessity of giving up any part in these exercises, to which I have looked forward with so much pleasure and pride, and my profound appreciation of the high honor conferred on me by the people of New Milford in electing me President of this Association.

"I desire to extend to them all, through you, my sincere and heartfelt thanks; and to all guests and friends who honor us with their presence on this glad and memorable occasion, and whom I hoped to meet personally, I extend a warm welcome and a hearty greeting.

"Very truly yours,
"HENRY S. MYGATT."

Before and after the exercises of the evening, much informal sociability was indulged in, in the course of which many stories of old times were exchanged and many old friendships renewed. The occasion was a highly enjoyable one, especially to those who had come from a distance after an absence of many years. It was an " old home gathering " in the best and fullest acceptation of the term.

OUR FOREFATHERS

Written for Bi-Centennial Sunday by Charles N. Hall

Lord of the Pilgrims; they who came
Far over-seas to praise Thy name;
Braving the wave, the wilderness,
Firm in their faith that Thou wouldst bless;
Planting upon a new world's shore
Thy name, their faith, forevermore—
Grant us, their children, thus to be
Persistent in our faith in Thee.

Dark seemed the way; grim forests frowned,
Hunger and cold crouched close around
That Pilgrim band; while wintry seas
Rolled wide, 'twixt English homes and these,
Who, faithful still, to doubt unknown,
Laid here the Nation's cornerstone.
Grant us, their children, thus to be
Unfaltering in our faith in Thee.

Bitter their sufferings and tears;
Hardship and toil marked all the years;
But through it all Thy saving hand
Guided and held the chosen band;
Leading them safely home at last,
All hardship done, all trials passed.
Grant us, their children, thus to be
Guided, sustained, brought home, by Thee.

THE SUNDAY EXERCISES

SERMONS appropriate to the occasion were preached to large congregations in all the churches Sunday morning. These sermons, in so far as they were historical, are reproduced herewith:

BY REV. FRANK A. JOHNSON
IN THE FIRST CONGREGATIONAL CHURCH

". . . In the summer of 1707, an eagle, poised on extended pinions over the Housatonic Valley, would have looked down upon a scene of singular beauty. He would have beheld a wilderness; but has not a wilderness a beauty unsurpassed by the artificial works of man? Mountain, hill and valley were clothed with magnificent forests of oak, chestnut and ash. The river, then a clear mountain stream, weaving its way among the hills, added to the sylvan beauty of the scene. There was no sign of the presence, or even existence of man, save possibly the thin smoke from the camp-fire of some peaceful Indian, who loved these hills, the home of his fathers.

"Into this trackless wilderness, from the then far-away northland of Massachusetts, came John Noble and his little eight-year-old daughter. Do we, who know this lovely valley so well, wonder that he built his simple home here, and that his descendants have remained here ever since? His house was for some time the last house this side of Albany.

"After a short time, a company from Milford, on Long Island Sound, took up much of the land here, and naturally gave the name New Milford to the new settlement. These men were of a sturdy race, strong in body, courageous, believers in God and His righteousness. Just think of the task that confronted them! The great forests, which would be a better possession than a gold mine now, were an encumbrance then. The traditions of these fathers tell us nothing of enervating club life, or midday siestas; the daily rule of life for man

SOME NEW MILFORD CHURCHES
Methodist Episcopal Methodist, Gaylordsville
Baptist, Northville Saint Francis Xavier

and woman then was work, work, work, that we might enter into the goodly heritage we now enjoy. Among the early settlers was Mr. John Read, who built a primitive house at the upper end of "The Green," near Mr. Frederic Knapp's house. Mr. Read, at one time, intended to enter the ministry. He preached the first sermon here in his own house. The founders of our State and town believed in God, and delighted in his worship. They were assured that God could manifest himself in the wild woods, or in some log cabin as well as in a stately cathedral. And so, before their families were fairly settled, they provided some place for the stated worship of Almighty God.

"So, here, after Mr. Read left the town, the people continued to use his simple home as their place of worship. I quote from our church manual: 'These people held their religious services in what was called Mr. Read's house, which has been described as probably built of logs, one story high, and had but one window, and was not very commodious nor an ornamental place of worship. The first vote to build a regular meeting-house was passed in 1716, and, then, so many difficulties were encountered, and so limited were the resources of the people, that the building does not seem to have been completely finished and furnished till 1731—though it was probably occupied for worship in its unfinished condition as early as 1720. This building stood on Town Hill, on the upper side of the present "Green." In 1754 a new and more commodious meeting-house was erected upon the village "Green," nearly opposite the present residence of Mrs. Henry E. Bostwick. This building was used as a house of worship for seventy-nine years, during the pastorates of Revs. Taylor, Griswold and Elliot. During the pastorate of the Rev. Mr. Rood in 1833, the present edifice was erected. In 1860, it was completely renovated.'

"In 1892 it was again renovated and a considerable addition made to this audience room, and the chapel, parlor and class rooms were added to the main building. In 1902 the present parsonage was built, and the ample grounds about it were laid out. In 1904 the organ was presented by one of our members. . . .

"They were a godly people who settled in this valley; a people who believed in the Sabbath as a day of rest and worship, and we may be sure that some kind of religious service was held here from the beginning of the settlement, but a regular church was not organized until 1716. Eight female and five male members were formally recognized as a church by council on November 21 of that year. It was a Congregational Church of the 'Standing Order,' and all the early inhabitants seem to have been in sympathy with it. It has continued an unbroken organization to this day. It has always been influential in the moral and religious movements of the community; and we are proud of its history, and are glad that we are members of it in this later day.

"We are so firmly convinced of the wisdom of the separation of Church and State, that is it hard for us to appreciate that our own church, through much of its history, was rigidly united with the State. For thirty-four years after the organization of the church, the Ecclesiastical Society and the town were practically the same thing. The larger part of the business of town meetings was the consideration of religious affairs. The town called the minister, provided for the expenses of the church, cared for the building; in fact did about everything that the church and society would do now. It was a town meeting that voted the size of the shingles and clapboards to be placed on the church building. Some of you, not very old, can remember when the town voted in the basement of this building. If there is any virtue in a union of Church and State, this church must have received the full measure. Until 1819 this Society had the legal right to tax all the inhabitants for its own support; but naturally, other denominations, which had arisen within the town, would object to this, and, as a matter of fact, this right was not insisted upon. The only relic of this incongruous relation of Church and State, according to American standards, is the Ecclesiastical Society; and, in the formation of new churches, this is generally done away with, the church feeling abundantly able to take care of its own affairs.

"During the one hundred and ninety-one years of its history this church has been served by ten settled pastors, and by several ministers who acted as pastors for limited periods. All of these ministers were men of power and influence, and have left their mark upon both church and town. From the organization of the church in 1716 to the end of the eighteenth century the church was served by only two pastors—the Rev. Daniel Boardman, and the Rev. Nathaniel Taylor. They were strong men and did much for the religious development of western Connecticut. Their descendants are still influential residents of our town. The third pastor was the Rev. Stanley Griswold, a man of strong personality and pronounced ability. After leaving New Milford he retired from the ministry, and, entering upon political life, became Secretary of Michigan Territory, and afterwards one of the first United States Senators from the State of Michigan. Later, he was Chief Justice of the Northwest Territory. The Revs. Andrew Elliot and Herman Rood were strong men, leaving the impress of their labors upon the life of the church. The sixth pastor was the Rev. Noah Porter. He was a faithful worker here, and his work was greatly blessed. He afterwards became known to all the world of scholars as the distinguished President, for many years, of Yale College. The Rev. John Greenwood was a pastor greatly beloved. After a period of absence from the town, he returned to spend his latter days with the church he loved. The eighth pastor was the Rev. David Murdock, Jr. He was a forcible preacher, and many of the present membership were received into the church during his fruitful ministry. He was pastor during the exciting days of the Civil War, and his stirring, patriotic addresses never left any doubt of the position of this church in the days which tried men's souls. The last three ministers, the Revs. James B. Bonar, George S. Thrall, and Timothy J. Lee, were the friends and pastors of a large part of the present congregation. Many of the older members were welcomed into the fellowship of the church during their ministries. Not only here, but in other fields of labor, they gave good proof of their ministry. Of all this list of former ministers, only one is living to-day, the Rev. Timothy J. Lee, the immediate predecessor of the present pastor.

"These ministers were advised and assisted by a consecrated band of deacons; men chosen for their piety and interest in the affairs of the church. The New England Congregational deacon has always filled a large place in the moral development of a community; and so these men have done their part in promoting the better life of this town. It would be impossible to write a true history of the town without giving their names a prominent place. The name of one of their number, also sometime clerk of our Society, is written high in the annals of his country, the distinguished patriot and statesman, Roger Sherman, associate of Thomas Jefferson, John Adams, Benjamin Franklin, and Robert R. Livingston, on the committee of five which prepared the immortal Declaration of Independence. His colleague, Thomas Jefferson, said of him, he was 'a man who never said a foolish thing'; and the noted Senator Macon declared, 'He had more common sense than any man I have ever known.' At this anniversary time, we are happy to recall the name of such a man as a citizen of our town, and a member and officer in our church. . . .

The following hymn, written for the occasion by Charlotte B. Bennett, was sung in the Congregational Church in the course of the service at which the above sermon was preached.

BI-CENTENNIAL HYMN

"God of our fathers, in whose sight
  The centuries are but as days,
We ask, as those of old, Thy light;
  We bring, like them, our gift of praise.

"We bless Thee for the fathers' love;
  They made the rough way smooth, that we
Might safer walk. O, may it prove
  The path of peace that leads to Thee.

"We reach across the vanished years
  And touch their holy lives to-day,
They kept the faith through toils and fears;
  Grant healing in the touch, we pray.

"If mists of time have dimmed our sight,
  And faith has faltered on the way,
May clearer vision in the light
  Of holy memories, crown this day.

"Alike to Thee are new and old;
  Thy care through ages is the same;
Thy love links with a chain of gold
  The centuries, in one dear Name.

"Keep in the hollow of Thy hand
  This hallowed place, while years shall last;
For righteousness still may it stand,
  Till days and ages are all past."

BY REV. SAMUEL HART, D. D.

OF MIDDLETOWN, CONNECTICUT, IN SAINT JOHN'S CHURCH, ALL SAINTS' CONGREGATION UNITING

"It happened, as men say, that the beginning of the settlement of this town fell in the year which saw the organization of the first parish of the Church of England in Connecticut; the bi-centenary of New Milford is also the bi-centenary of the Diocese of Connecticut. It is but natural, therefore, that one who is called to speak to-day as to that part which this parish has borne in the history of the town, should recur to the origin of the Church in this Colony, and should have in his mind the inspiration of last week's commemoration in Stratford; we cannot but look back from the time when the Church's ministrations were first held here, to the earlier ministrations on the shores of the Sound. But we have a stronger reason to-day for turning to the beginnings; for the two clergymen who first officiated here, at the request of a few adherents of the Church of England, were Dr. Johnson, missionary and rector at Stratford, 'the father of the Church in Connecticut,' and Mr. John Beach, of Stratford birth, Dr. Johnson's pupil in theology, in charge of congregations in Redding and Newtown. But, as it appears, we can go still further back; for one of the first settlers here, of whom indeed it is said that he claimed the land by title from the Indians, was John Read, who, at the time when the church services were first held by a clergyman in Stratford, was ministering to the Congregational society there, and presently connected himself with the newly formed congregation of Churchmen; indeed, we are told that at one time he had it in mind to go to England and ask for ordination at the hands of a bishop. Whatever his plans in this matter, they were not carried out; for he removed to this place, granted the use of a house which he built as a place of meeting for public worship, and occasionally preached to those who assembled there. He became a lawyer and Queen's attorney, and removed to Boston, where he was a communicant in King's Chapel. His son John was one of the first settlers of Reading (Redding) and named the town for his father. Thus there was here, from the very first, a little Church of England leaven.

"But we are told of no formal church services here for twenty-two years, and of no separate congregation until 1748. At this time, Dr. Johnson, that man of great learning and prudence and missionary zeal, had been ministering for twenty years in Stratford, extending his journeys to places adjacent and remote in the Colony, and exercising a strong and healthful influence on behalf of the Church. Among the young men whom he trained in the Church's ways and in her theology, his pupils and members of his family, was John Beach, for eight years Congregational minister at Newtown, 'a popular and insinuating young man,' as was testified of him, who after ordination in England came back to his former field of labor and began a wonderful work there and in Redding, with a small congregation of five families. These two men came hither at

ST. JOHN'S CHURCH

the request of a few Church people, of whom Mr. Beach wrote in 1743 there were about twenty families in New Milford and New Fairfield, who frequently attended church at Newtown, and to whom he ministered at their homes as he was able, but rarely on the Lord's Day. The town, presently, on the petition of twelve men, granted them a piece of land in the street at its south end, 'near where the old pound used to stand,' forty feet by sixty, 'in order to build a Church of England upon;' and the building seems to have been erected in 1744. . . .

"Under Mr. Beach's care many in this part of the colony—for he had a wide circuit for visitations and services—accepted the Church's ways; and thus was the Church established in the faith and increasing in number, as in the primitive times. When at last he asked to be relieved from the care of the congregations and scattered communicants in Litchfield County, the Rev. Solomon Palmer took charge of the Churchmen in this neighborhood, and became the first clergyman resident here. After five years he removed to Litchfield; and to him succeeded, in 1762, as by a kind of exchange, the Rev. Thomas Davies, whose grandfather and father, faithful laymen, had founded the parishes in Litchfield and Washington. His whole span of life was but thirty years, and he ministered here but four years; but he left a record for untiring labor, constant pastoral labor, persuasive eloquence, and godly living, which has not been effaced by time, and the results of which, we cannot but believe, still remain in this community. Even when there was talk of a division of his work, he proposed to retain the towns of New Milford, Woodbury, Kent, and New Fairfield as his mission, leaving Litchfield, Cornwall and Sharon, with a few Churchmen in nine other towns, to the care of another clergyman. During his ministry, a second house of worship was built, the old church being too small for the congregation; it stood in part on the street, some twenty or thirty rods north of the former site. After Mr. Davies, followed the Rev. Richard (or Richard Samuel) Clarke, the twenty years of whose ministry included the cloudy days that preceded the Revolution and the stormy times of the Revolution itself. He was a Tory in political convictions and, after the war, removed to Nova Scotia, where he died in 1824 at the age of 87, the oldest missionary in the Colonies.

"It would be ungracious to dwell now on the opposition, for the most part conscientious, and nearly always quite in accordance with law, which the early Churchmen experienced. It is pleasanter to note that their neighbors and the Colonial authorities extended to them what was for the times, a generous toleration as to 'sober dissenters,' and allowed them, if they actually attended church, to turn their 'church rates' to the support of their own clergymen. And this parish had the special favor, shared with but two others, of a special act of the General Assembly, which practically put it before the law in the full status of a society of the standing Congregational order. Even the hard feelings of Revolutionary days, almost excusable at the time, soon passed away. The Church of England in Connecticut, under the nominal care of the Bishop of London, became the Church of the Diocese of Connecticut, under the care of her own Bishop, and presently a constituent part of the Church in the United States, loyally maintaining the Commonwealth and the Republic, actually guiding the organization of the State, and moulding a large part of the people in the ways of soberness, righteousness, and godliness.

"In all this time, the parish of St. John's, New Milford, was a true center of missionary work. We wonder when we read of Dr. Johnson from Stratford extending his journeys to Newtown and Middletown and New London; of Mr. Beach from Newtown visiting New Milford and other places, really caring for a whole county with 'parts adjacent'; of Mr. Davies from New Milford going about in circuit, preaching and baptizing in Roxbury, and New Preston, and Salisbury, and Litchfield, and Sharon, and divers other places in the Colony, and crossing the line into Great Barrington, where he found difficulties incident to another government, but where a church was built under his care; and how he, in his turn, directed to that place the steps of Gideon Bostwick, who ministered for more than twenty years in Berkshire, in the southern part of

Vermont, and in the eastern part of New York. Moreover, there came in 1769, to the clergy of Connecticut, assembled in Convocation in New Milford, a memorial from the few Churchmen in the new settlement of Claremont, in New Hampshire, asking that their case might be presented to the Venerable Society in England, with the hope that they would be allowed at least a catechist and schoolteacher, until (as they said) they should have passed 'the first difficulties and hardships of a wild, uncultivated country.' Such a man was commissioned, and did good work as an unordained missionary; while a clergyman was presently sent to make a personal exploration of the northern provinces. It is apart from our immediate topic; but we can never think of the religious history of New Milford without being reminded of that remarkable man, Count Zinzendorf, who held the episcopate among the Moravians, and for a while ministered to the aborigines in this very place—one of the few places in which the Indians remained, and in which they were affected by the preaching of Christianity. There were others also here whose very presence was a challenge to the teaching of the Church at one time or another—Separatists, and Quakers, and Jemimaites, and Glassites. Among them all, the Church held her place, and guided the life of no small part of the whole community.

"For the last ten years of the eighteenth century the Rev. Truman Marsh was rector of New Milford, with New Preston and Roxbury. In 1793 the Church, already occupied for eight and twenty years, was formally consecrated by Bishop Seabury, eight of the clergy being present for a Convocation. It had been long in an unfinished state, as we gather from the frequent entries in the parish records, which refer to the work yet to be done. Only two years before the consecration it was voted, 'To go on and finish the Pulpit, Reading Desk, Clark's pew, and Gallery'; and in the next year a vote was passed as to the assignment of seats; and, the front seat in the gallery being reserved for singers, and the back seat there for blacks, it was commendably voted, 'That People of any Denomination that Wish a Seat Shall have one.' This edifice, repaired from time to time, served the purposes of the congregation until 1837; and the third Church was in turn replaced by the present beautiful and enduring building, on a new but adjacent site, twenty-four years ago, in 1883. There must have been of old a glebe lot here, though we do not find early notice of it; it lay on the west side of the Main Street, and, in Mr. Marsh's day, it had a house and barn upon it; there is a tradition that it was secured in part from the sale of a piece of land which the parish owned at a still earlier day and in part from the parish's share of the avails from undivided land in the highway; at any rate, it was sold long ago.

"The history of post-Revolutionary times must be rapidly passed over. Mr. Benjamin Benham began here as a lay-reader, and, having been ordained in 1808, was rector for nearly twenty years, having duties also at New Preston, Roxbury, Bridgewater, and Brookfield; then, for another score of years the Rev. Enoch Huntington ministered to the congregation, and, after an interval, another twenty years of your records is covered by the rectorship of the Rev. Charles G. Acly, in whose time a rectory was secured.

"This brings us down to a date but little more than thirty years ago, well within the memory of many in this congregation; and the last twelve of these years belong to the present rectorship, as to which we may well hope, both for the rector's sake and for the people's, that it is much nearer its beginning than its end.

"A few figures will show the remarkable growth of the parish, noticeable even among the thriving country parishes of Connecticut. A hundred years ago, already a century after the first settlement, there were seventy-four communicants in the cure of New Milford, New Preston, and Roxbury; fifty years ago, St. John's Church, New Milford, reported one hundred and twenty-five communicants and one hundred Sunday scholars; in 1885, not quite thirty years later, the number of communicants had increased to two hundred and eighty-nine, and the number of Sunday scholars was one hundred sixty-four. In the last named year, the new congregation of All Saints' Memorial Church was canonically organized, its beautiful place of worship being consecrated in a subsequent year, and a rectory being added some twelve years ago. The result of this increase of the provision for the worship of the Church and for its varied ministrations in this town has been a growth, under all the circumstances, more remarkable than that of former times; in twenty-one years the number of communicants has increased from two hundred eighty-nine to five hundred forty-nine—four hundred five in the older parish and one hundred forty-four in the younger; and where there were one hundred sixty-four scholars in one Sunday school, there are now two hundred fifty-eight in two schools, of which the mother parish has two hundred nine. . . ."

BY REV. S. D. WOODS

IN THE BAPTIST CHURCH AT NORTHVILLE

"Our best authority tells us that while Baptists were not very numerous in the early days of the town's history, yet a decade or more before the close of its first century there was a sufficient number to warrant the carrying on of services at varying places—Bridgewater, Warren, and Gaylord's Bridge. These were kept up for twenty-five years, when, on Jan. 7, 1814, a meeting was held at the residence of Asahel Baldwin, at which time it was voted: '1st, To organize ourselves into a society to be known as the "New Milford Baptist Church." 2d, To invite a council from sister churches to meet with us on Feb. 9, to consider the propriety of recognizing us as a regular Baptist Church.' This council met as planned, and after a proper examination of 'their Articles of Faith and their Covenant,' voted, unanimously, 'to recognize them as a sister church in the Lord.'

"By this act twenty-two believers became a recognized body of worshipers, who, ten days later, voted to license Eleazer Beecher as pastor. He was ordained Sept. 15, 1814, at the residence of Abel Canfield on Long Mountain. The services were conducted in the open air.

"This first pastorate continued for seven years, when Rev. Seth Higby assumed charge for one momentous year, as it witnessed the beginning of this present house of worship; and the following year, 1822, saw its completion, when Elder Higby resigned, and Elder Beecher was again installed, serving the church for ten years more. He was succeeded by Rev. Nathan Benedict in a two years' pastorate, and he, in turn, by Rev. Elijah Baldwin, who remained until 1840. For ten years the church was without a settled pastor, though the pulpit was supplied by various non-resident clergymen.

"From 1850 to 1866 but little growth is recorded; they were years of struggles and trials. There was a succession of pastors, Revs. H. M. Barlow, J. F. Jones, and J. Hepburn, serving as under shepherds.

"In 1868 the Rev. C. W. Potter was called, and his three years of service witnessed a gracious revival and added ten to the church roll. With the resignation of Elder Potter, the church experienced five years of pastorless existence, though being supplied occasionally by Rev. Arthur Day. With the settlement of Rev. Edwin Beardsley, in 1875, the church entered upon a new era of growth and activity. The records show that two are still members who came in during that time. The succeeding pastor was Rev. J. P. Cotney, who remained about three years, adding two by baptism. He was succeeded by Rev. F. P. Braman, in 1887, who remained two years, baptizing six into fellowship. In 1889 the Rev. Frederick Kratz was installed, to be succeeded within two years by Rev. John Scott, during whose ministry of two years the parsonage was well-nigh completed and three members added to the church roll. This pastorate also saw the church made a corporate body. In 1893 Rev. F. D. Luddington was called, and remained three years, baptizing twenty-eight into church fellowship. In July, 1896, Rev. Charles I. Ramsey assumed the pastorate, and for nearly five years continued the good work already begun, by adding ten by baptism. The Rev. A. H. Manee began his pastoral labors in August, 1901, closing his labors in October, 1904, baptizing one into fellowship.

"From November, 1904, until April, 1905, the pulpit was supplied by various clergymen, when Rev. S. D. Woods became pastor, and continues in that office at the present time. Thus far there have been nineteen baptisms, and the church shows the largest membership in its history.

"All told, there have been two hundred and sixty-nine baptisms. The present membership is seventy. . . .

BY REV. HARRIS K. SMITH

IN THE METHODIST EPISCOPAL CHURCH

"*Text—Proverbs 22: 28. 'Remove not the ancient landmark, which thy fathers have set.'*

"A burning desire to deliver a living message is one landmark in the evangelism of the fathers of our church. The age of our town is nearly four times as great as the years of Methodism's church edifice in our village; more than twice the years of Methodism in the present confines of our town; one hundred twenty-seven years greater than Methodism in the State; thirty-seven years greater than Methodism's first Conference. Indeed, John Wesley, its founder, was but four years old, in June of the year, when John Noble, New Milford's first settler, penetrated these forests primeval. Our fathers came not as a colony, but as evangelists, impelled by a vital experience. They believed that sin separated from God, that only by salvation, through the atonement of the Redeemer, could sinners be in harmony with the Father, that personal righteousness and the witness of God's indwelling Spirit were results of redemption, and that the redeemed were to go on unto the likeness of Jesus. Without ignoring other elements in their belief, the stress laid upon personal experience and its intensity led them far and wide. That they did not thrust an alien graft upon New England religious stock is seen in one instance, at least, by the demands of Jonathan Edwards for personal righteousness, and for conversion as a requirement for all seeking the communion of the Lord's Supper;

and the sad rejection from his pulpit. Infidelity, imported with the teaching of the French revolutionists, was alarmingly on the increase. The custom of discussing metaphysical subjects and of weaving fine-spun doctrines was spreading more or less throughout Christendom; to so large an extent had London been infected, that Blackstone, the famous law commentator, in visiting every church of note in that city, said he did not hear one sermon that had more of Christianity than had the writings of Cicero, and that they could not have been called Christian sermons. The revival-stirring sermons of Wesley and Whitefield were permeating through and upward from the masses of the people. And the reception given to this message, so ardently delivered, assures conclusively the need that had been unsatisfied. So, then, the fathers of our Church entered this field with the ringing word of God in their hearts as their warrant.

"Faithful sowing and careful husbanding of the harvest constituted another landmark. When, in 1789, Jesse Lee was appointed to Stamford, he had neither preaching place nor congregation as a rallying point; not even a member in all New England to greet him. He entered with a 'roving commission.' True enough, Methodism had been presented by some of the most prominent evangelical preachers since the visit of Charles Wesley, nearly sixty years prior to Lee, and including Whitefield, Boardman, and Garretson, within a short time of the more concentrated mission in 1789. Lee's fine appearance, his massive frame, his weight being about three hundred pounds, his wit and good humor, his wisdom and judgment of human nature, his knowledge of the Bible, and his depth of consecration gave him an entry. The labors of Lee extended, during his first year, from Norwalk along the Sound coast, and upward to Ridgefield and Danbury. These pioneers approached our town from the south, reaching the part now separated into the town of Bridgewater, about 1800; they came from the Hudson River in the north to Gaylordsville in 1813, and to Northville in 1816; from the southwest to Lanesville, then called Pleasant Valley, in 1815. These activities from all directions soon resulted in the erection of church buildings at all of these points. The care of the preachers was constant to train the converts enlisted. They visited and revisited, at heavy privations and difficulties, to make sure of the standing of even one or two new members.

"The essential coworking of the laymen is another landmark. Methodism, from its inception, would have been incomplete without the largest degree of co-operation on the part of the laity. It has been a layman's movement, under the direction of ordained leaders. As soon as two or more were converted at a place, one of the number was delegated as leader for the others, thus forming classes for religious culture. Awaiting the visits of the preacher in charge, these classes were hives of industry, and seminaries of learning, and communions for worship in charge of one of their own number, the class leader. Those more qualified by nature and grace were called for special activity as local preachers, and they went from place to place, preaching to other congregations, alternating with the ordained preachers and under their direction. These meetings were in homes, at times the choicest in the center of the town, or at others, far in the fastness of the forest within the rude log cabin, or at others, in God's open temple with the swaying branches of the trees as their rafters. The time of worship might be at any hour from sunrise until midnight, and on any day during the week. The congregation was called from the home, the shop, the store, and the field, not by the chime of the church bell, but by the volume of hearty singing; the numbers might be confined to one beside the preacher, or mount upwards to more than twenty thousand. The immediate results of these preaching visits were to be cultivated by the resident laymen. And nobly did they keep the faith. Exhortation, rebuke, counsel, encouragement, forbearance, and brotherly love must come by means of fellow laymen, in many cases but little older in the faith than the new recruits.

"Zeal in building up the local church was another landmark. Within a few years after the introduction of Methodism, church buildings were erected at Gaylordsville, at a cost of eight hundred dollars; at Northville, on ground of Harvey Benson, at a cost of six hundred dollars, beside labor and material contributed; and at Lanesville, at a cost of three thousand dollars. This indicates considerable sacrifice on the part of the members, and interest in the community. In 1849, after considerable discussion, the members of the different churches, so close in location, agreed upon the village as a central point, and our present edifice was built. Since 1833, when its name had first appeared in the conference minutes, it has been known as the New Milford charge. Before that it had been part of the Stratford circuit, which, in 1822, when our town first had a permanent preaching place on the circuit, had only three church edifices; while to-day this range contains church property, including parsonages, worth nearly a million dollars, has several thousand members, and gives for benevolent purposes, outside its own borders, more money every year by far than the total amount contributed for all causes at that time.

"Within a few years of the building of the present edifice a parsonage was erected. Every year additional money was laid out on the property; principally in 1869 in the pastorate of the Rev. W. R. Webster, and in 1891, when the church was remodeled and enlarged, at a cost of several thousand dollars, in the pastorate of the Rev. R. T. Cooper. . . . In the long line of preachers, whose counsel and administration have cheered and molded many lives, was the Rev. William T. Gilbert, one of a great class graduated from Yale University, who, with earnest manner and finely wrought sermon, built deeply and broad; and, after laying aside his pastoral duties, he re-entered the ranks, working faithfully along different ways in the activities of the laymen. The Rev. George Lansing Taylor, D. D., L. H. D., ended a life of great intellectual power and moral grandeur, while your pastor. For breadth in learning, strength of thought, independence for truth, tenacity to purpose, and conscientious following after his Master, he was notable. His pastorate will long be memorable in the history of this church, and be felt in the lives of its members, among the younger especially, as they were marked by his striking personality."

BY REV. ORVILLE VAN KEUREN

IN THE GAYLORDSVILLE METHODIST EPISCOPAL CHURCH

"Methodism was established in Gaylordsville in 1825, under the following circumstances:

"Rev. Cyrus Silliman, of the New York Conference, came to visit a cousin, Mrs. David Sterling, who lived one and a half miles below the village, in the town of Sherman. While there, he made an appointment for a week-evening service at the Strait district schoolhouse. The attendance was so large and the interest so marked that he continued the meetings four evenings, and then returned to his charge in the State of New York.

"The people, however, continued the meetings for several weeks, holding them in private houses. Rev. Andrew Elliot, the pastor of the Congregational Church at New Milford, learning of the revival, came up several times and visited the families.

"The following year, as a result of these meetings, twenty-six persons joined the Congregational Church, nineteen formed a Methodist class at Gaylordsville, and others joined the Baptist Church. A subscription was started to build a union church at Gaylordsville, which was built in 1826. Rev. Aaron Hunt, a Methodist preacher from the State of New York, preached the first sermon in the new church, which was used jointly by the Methodists, Congregationalists, and Baptists up to about 1854. This church stood on the east side of the river, just back of the store now occupied by A. H. Barlow. It was afterward sold to Peter Gaylord, who removed it to his premises and converted it into a barn. At a quarterly meeting, held in that church, Rev. Edmund Storer Janes, D. D., LL. D., afterward a bishop of the Methodist Episcopal Church, received his license as a local preacher.

"In 1854, under the pastorate of Rev. David Nash, the present church edifice was erected, upon a site given by the Rev. John Henry Gaylord, who also raised by subscription about $2800 toward the cost of the new church. The parsonage, which adjoins the church, was purchased in 1884, during the pastorate of Rev. M. M. Curtis.

"In 1827 Rev. Josiah L. Dickerson settled here, built a house, and engaged in making brick. As a local preacher, he filled some of the appointments on the circuit up to about 1834, when he joined the New York Conference, and continued in the regular work of the ministry until retired by reason of age. He died in 1862, and is buried in the Gaylordsville cemetery.

"Methodism was introduced into Sherman Center, under the pastorate of Rev. Alonzo Selleck, in 1838, under the following circumstances:

"A few years before the Congregational Church of Sherman became divided over the building of a new house of worship, or, rather, the location of the building. A majority of the society decided it should be built about a mile north of the Center, where the present church stands. A minority, living at the Center and in the southern part of the town, built a church at the Center, and called it a union church. Rev. Selleck was preacher in charge of New Milford circuit, which, at that time, included the following appointments: Pleasant Plains, Iron Works, Newtown, Merryall, Hawleyville, Northville, Kent Mountain, Gaylordsville, Bull's Bridge, and Long Mountain. There were but three churches on the circuit. The other preaching places were schoolhouses or private dwellings.

"Following a revival service held at the Leach Hollow schoolhouse in the fall of 1837, the Center people invited Rev. Selleck to come up and preach in the new church, which was not entirely furnished at that time. The first service was held on New Year's Eve, as a watch night service. The church was filled to overflowing, and, at that service, seventy-five persons came forward as seekers of religion. The meetings were

THE SUNDAY EXERCISES

continued several weeks, Rev. H. Ames, a retired preacher residing in the town, assisting much in the work. About two hundred fifty persons professed religion during this revival. Of that number, seventy joined the Methodist Church, while many joined the Congregational Church, of which Rev. Mr. Gilson was then pastor.

"A few years later Sherman was made the center of a circuit, separate from New Milford, taking in the appointments in the northern part of the town. From 1826 to 1848 this circuit was connected with the New York Conference. At the session of the General Conference in 1872 it was again transferred to the New York Conference, where it still remains. When the transfer was made in 1872, the records for the charge showed a membership of seventy-three, the Sherman Society having at that time but thirteen members.

"The church has had a long list of pastors, who served in the following order: Revs. John Reynolds, William Jewett, Fitch Reed, Samuel Cochran, Seth W. Scofield, A. S. Hill, Francis Donelly, the exact dates of whose pastorates we cannot give; 1837, Alonzo Selleck and Asahel Brownson; 1838, Alonzo Selleck and Samuel Weeks; 1844-5, Gad S. Gilbert; 1846-7, Elias Gilbert; 1848-9, Justus O. Worth; 1850, Thomas B. Treadwell; 1851, William Wake; 1852, Alexander McAllester; 1853, Gilbert Hubbell; 1854-5, David Nash; 1856-7, William H. Stebbins; 1858-9, Thomas D. Littlewood; 1860-2, John H. Gaylord; 1863, William Ross; 1864, John Henry Gaylord (during his pastorate the church sheds were built); 1865-6, Benjamin A. Gilman; 1867-8, F. W. Lockwood; 1869-70, Sherman D. Barnes; 1871, Frank F. Jordan; 1872-3, B. M. Genung; 1874-5, Uriah Symonds; 1876, W. A. Dalton; 1877-9, R. F. Elsden; 1880-1, Robert Kay; 1882-4, M. M. Curtis (during his pastorate twenty-six joined the church, two of whom entered the ministry—Rev. Henry Hoag, a member of the Conference, and Mark B. Howland, a local preacher); 1885, Gustave Lass; 1886-7, E. H. Powell; 1888-92, W. H. Peters (under whose pastorate the church was thoroughly repaired and refurnished); 1893-4, I. H. Keep; 1895-7, John Henry Lane; 1899, C. B. Conro; 1900-1, E. H. Roys; 1902, Robert F. Elsden; 1903-6, Edmund T. Byles; 1907, O. Van Keuren, the present pastor.

"In 1898 the charge was left to be supplied. The Rev. M. M. Curtis, then superannuated, filled the pulpit for a few weeks. When, by reason of failing health, he was obliged to discontinue the work, the Rev. James A. Hurn, who has since united with the Conference, supplied for the rest of the year.

"During the pastorate of E. T. Byles the church property was greatly improved by the addition of well-appointed church parlors, equipped with all modern conveniences, the entire expense being provided for before the work was begun.

"The membership, though small, is thoroughly united and intensely loyal.

"Others have labored, and we have entered into their labors, while they, in continuous procession, have passed on to receive the reward of the faithful.

"The present membership of the church is eighty-eight."

BY REV. ELISHA J. ELLIS, OF DANBURY

IN THE ADVENT CHRISTIAN CHURCH

"Early in the history of the movement which resulted in the formation of the Advent Christian denomination, the seed of the doctrines which distinguished this people were sown here by pioneer hands. So far as ascertained, the first preachers to arrive on the field were Elders Ira Morgan and Samuel G. Mathewson, about 1844. Quite a number of conversions followed, and Elder Mathewson baptized quite a number in the stream which flows near the present church site. Rufus Way, Horace Gregory, and Richard Heacock were converts about this time—also A. S. Calkins, who afterwards became a talented preacher in the West.

"Joshua V. Hines preached here in 1846 or 1847. Afterwards, in the sixties and seventies, representative men like

ADVENT CHRISTIAN CHURCH

Miles Grant, Horace L. Hastings, I. B. Potter, Peter and Samuel Patro labored here; also H. K. and A. D. Flagg.

"Under the labors of Rev. A. D. Flagg, in 1870, the pastor of this church, at the age of eighteen, found Christ in personal salvation, and, with his grandfather, was immersed in Still River near Lanesville. Over thirty-five years ago, Stephen Heacock first commenced to publicly work for the Master, and for years conducted a mission in the Town Hall building.

"Between eleven and twelve years ago the speaker had the pleasure of introducing him to the Advent Christian Connecticut Conference, and on November 11th, 1897, in the Town Hall, Stephen Heacock was publicly ordained to the gospel ministry, by the speaker and his associates of the Ministerial Board of the Conference. While others have labored hard toward the spread of the Adventual faith in this section, I think, all present—yea, the entire community—will agree that largely to the self-sacrificing, heroic efforts of this man, and his wife, the success of our cause is due in this section. . . .

"Not fulsome eulogy, but well-deserved words of praise, have I spoken here, because, from personal observation and connection, I have closely followed, and have been somewhat conversant with its history. On February 20, 1900, while President of the State Conference, I was summoned here to set this church apart in gospel order. On March 6, 1900 (in the hall on Bank Street), the church organization was duly incorporated, and, on August 6, 1901, we were present, with other clergymen, at the laying of the cornerstone. On November 14, 1901, the church was formally dedicated to the worship of God and the work of soul-winning, Rev. Henry Stone, of Wallingford, preaching the dedication sermon. . . .

"It will, doubtless, be interesting to present a few statistics furnished us by the pastor in charge: The Advent Christian Church of New Milford was organized February 20, 1900, with thirty-two charter members. Forty members have been received since organization to date. Four deaths and two withdrawals leave the present membership sixty-six persons. The pastor, since his ordination, has celebrated nine marriages, officiated at thirty-six funerals, and baptized forty-eight persons. The total number of baptisms in this faith by various clergymen in this vicinity would aggregate one hundred fifty. Elder Heacock has preached in seventy-five different places during his ministry here, and has spoken, by invitation, in Baptist, Methodist, Congregational, and in union churches, in this vicinity. As a result of this outside work, fifty or more conversions have resulted; and, during the years in which he labored in the Gospel temperance work, prior to the establishment of the Advent Christian Mission, many people were induced to abandon the drink habit, and stand for God and the right. Only eternity will rightfully exhibit the definite results of this work in and about this village.

"Before we close the historical part of this discourse, let me call your attention to a highly interesting feature of this edifice—the church bell.

"Not only the church people, who worship here, but all the citizens of New Milford must be specially interested in the bell, which swings in this church tower, and whose presentation to this church is designed to perpetuate some facts of general interest. . . . Partridge Thatcher, of New Milford, was moderator of an assembly of landed proprietors, who, with himself, had been granted lands in the wilderness of Vermont. These proprietors held their first meeting in this town on May 10, 1770, at the home of Colonel Samuel Canfield, and Thatcher, acting for these men, made the first survey of Waterbury, Vt., in 1782. A lineal descendant of Samuel Canfield—in the person of Lawrence Northrop—belongs to the present membership of this church. Waterbury, Vt., stands on the banks of the Winooski River, and, on a branch of that river, named (after the original surveyor) 'Thatcher's Branch,' stands the Advent Christian Church of Waterbury. In this town of Waterbury, lives an Indian gentleman, Agamenticus, or Joshua Merimam by name. . . . The blood of the aboriginal inhabitants—the North American Indians—flows in the veins of this beloved pastor and his wife (the former descended from the tribe of the Narragansetts, and the wife, from the warlike clan of the Pequots), and also in the veins of many of the church members who worship here. These facts came in some way to the knowledge of this Mr. Merimam, and he, in connection and with the aid of the town clerks of Waterbury, Duxbury, Middlesex, and Moretown, Vt. (adjacent communities on the banks of the Winooski River), and a Mr. Shonio, conceived the idea of presenting this church in New Milford a bell, which should not only keep green in memory the fact I have already stated, but also the memory of a historic and tragic incident of the old French and Indian War . . . times, which I will now narrate.

"Over two hundred years ago, the French Catholics of Montreal erected a church for their Indian converts, and imported a bell from France, which they hung in this church tower. Soon after this, the English Colonists raided Montreal, plundered the church, seized the bell, and carried it, with many French and Indian prisoners, down the St. Lawrence River, thence *via* the ocean to the mouth of the Connecticut River to Deerfield, Mass., where the Indians were sold into slavery, and the bell hung in Rev. John Williams' local church. At a point of the Winooski Valley, where are now located the four towns I have just mentioned, there was a neutral council-ground, called the Moheagans, where the Indians of the New Milford section, the Indians of Massachusetts, and the Northern tribes met annually to discuss matters of mutual interest. At one of these gatherings, the Northern Indians learned the fate of their comrades, and laid plans for a rescue. Early in 1704 three hundred Indians and a few Frenchmen, under the noted French priest, Hextel de Rouville, as leader, made a raid on Deerfield—going and coming through Waterbury, Vt. Those familiar with early Colonial history will recall what followed: the burning of Deerfield, Mass., the massacre of many of the whites, the rescue of the old bell and of the Indian captives, and the capture of more than a hundred prisoners of war. On the return march, at the junction of the Winooski River with Lake Champlain, they hid the bell till a more favorable moment. Returning in May, with one black ox, driven by a negro, one white ox, driven by a white man, and one red ox, driven by an Indian, the drivers and oxen garlanded with festoons of wild flowers, they carried the bell home to Montreal with great rejoicing, where yet it swings, so far as we know, in the same old tower as of yore. In memory of this incident, and of the friendship of the New Milford Indians, to their Northern brethren in the old Colonial days, Agamenticus of Waterbury, Vt., with his friends, the white town fathers of the old Vermont towns surveyed by the New Milford Thatcher, gave this bell to the Advent Christian church of New Milford, Conn., and christened it '*Sansaman*' in honor of the first Indian Christian Missionary of New England, killed by King Philip of the Wampanoags in 1675. . . ."

BY REV. JOSEPH RYAN

IN ST. FRANCIS XAVIER'S CHURCH

"To-day, my dear friends, the celebration of an important and certainly noteworthy event is taking place in this town of New Milford. With pageantry and music and speech, in gayety and festivity, with reunions of old friends and neighbors, the historic happening is receiving ample recognition and celebration. And they do well, the people of New Milford, proud of their town and its history, to recognize on such a splendid scale its two hundredth birthday. With all their ceremonies of civic and social celebration, the religious side of their town's history has been given equal attention. Almighty God has not been forgotten—He who is the Creator and Supreme Ruler of the Universe, from whom comes all that we are and all that we have, who holds in the palm of His hand the destiny of the world and the fate of its people.

"To-day, in her different houses of worship, special religious exercises appropriate to the occasion are being held. This morning, in particular, sermons are preached of the history of her different churches.

"I need not tell you the history of your church; you all know it. It is the common history of the Roman Catholic Church the world over. It cannot well or easily be separated from that magnificent general history stretching back through the ages nineteen hundred seven years to that ever memorable first Christmas morn when Jesus Christ, the Son of God, taking flesh of the Virgin Mary, was born in Bethlehem's stable. And, in that wonderful stretch of history, two hundred years are as a drop in the bucket, as a sand on the seashore. From the days when the Holy Sacrifice of the mass was first offered up in the home of Matthew Dunn near the railroad station, or in Wright's Hall on Main Street, or in the residence of Edmond Finn, to this very day, Roman Catholic history in New Milford has been the same as it has been the world over—a history of early trials and sufferings and labor, all of which have gradually and surely melted away before the grand old faith of the ages. The loyal Catholics first in New Milford, though their future looked dark and stormy, clung to the faith richly planted in their noble hearts, and put their trust in the words of Him who first established their Church upon this earth, 'Thou art Peter and on this rock I will build my church and the gates of Hell shall not prevail against it.' And they did well to put their trust in Him who had also promised, 'Behold I am with you all days even to the consummation of the world.' In the language of St. Paul, those pioneers of the Roman Catholic Church in New Milford have fought the good fight, they have saved the faith, and they have gone to receive from their Divine Master the crown of eternal glory. . . .

"They knew well the truth of their Holy Religion, yes, and its value. No mess of pottage, however alluring, be it greater position in society, or greater financial considerations, could tempt them to part with their Divinely given birthright of Catholic faith. They were in Peter's boat and well they knew it, and, better still, they showed it by their lives of rugged righteousness.

"The fair name and fame of the Divinely built ship that has ridden over the waves and through the storms of nineteen centuries was safe in their keeping, for not only did they love their religion, but they also lived it. You, their descendants and successors, to-day, I would say to you, in the words of your Divine Master, 'Go you and do likewise.'"

THE UNION MEETING

At three o'clock in the afternoon, a union open-air service of all the churches in the town was held upon "The Green." Three thousand people, it is estimated, were present. A chorus of one hundred voices, conducted by Prof. Clemence and accompanied by the band, rendered the "Gloria in Excelsis" and "The Heavens Are Telling" in a highly effective manner, and led the audience in a number of familiar hymns. Rev. F. A. Johnson of the First Congregational Church presided. Rev. J. F. Plumb of St. John's Church, Rev. S. D. Woods of the Baptist Church, and Rev. H. K. Smith of the Methodist Church offered prayer, and Rev. Stephen Heacock of the Advent Christian Church read the Scripture. The addresses were by Rev. Frederick A. Wright, D. D., of New York City, a former New Milford boy, and by Rev. Charles J. Ryder, D. D., of New York City, Corresponding Secretary of the American Missionary Association, who, although not himself a native of New Milford, is connected with a family formerly prominent in the affairs of the town.

Dr. Wright said:

"It is a pleasure to me to address you, both because I count it an honor to speak to this audience, and because I feel it a privilege to speak on this occasion, and in this place. My ancestors, both on my mother's side and on my father's, have been identified with this town for six generations, so that I feel a sort of intimate kinship with the very fields and mountains; and this soil is in a double sense my 'mother earth.' And, just as Antæus, the child of earth, gained tenfold strength every time he stretched his length upon the grass, so, wearied with the rush and crowding of the city, and the sorrows of its poor,

NEW MILFORD PASTORS

Rev. Frank B. Draper
Professor of Mathematics and Chaplain, Ingleside School

Rev. Marmaduke Hare
Rector All Saints Memorial Church

Rev. Father John J. Burke
Curate of Roman Catholic Church

Rev. Timothy J. Lee
Former Pastor of First Congregational Church

Rev. Frank A. Johnson
Pastor of First Congregational Church and the Chairman of Religious Committee of the Bi-Centennial

Rev. Solomon D. Woods
Pastor Baptist Church Northville Society

Rev. Harris K. Smith
Pastor of the Methodist Episcopal Church

Rev. John F. Plumb
Arch Deacon and Rector of St. John's Episcopal Church

Rev. Stephen Heacock
Pastor of Advent Christian Church

and the 'weighing of fate and the sad discussion of sin,' I come here and find refreshment and repose. The large city has certain great attractions, and, in some respects, life in it is far broader and greater than it can be elsewhere. That is the reason I went to New York. But the town, and the *small city*, have other advantages, and it is by those that my love of this place is kindled. And so, on this birthday of New Milford, I want to speak of those qualities which I prize so highly in this place.

"And, first on the list, comes personal freedom. Thackeray said that England had fifty million people in it, mostly fools. Well, when you have an enormously big city, there are so many fools gathered together there, that it is not feasible and practicable for the sensible people to be free. You must not carry a pistol, because there are so many 'gumps' that cannot be trusted with firearms. You cannot let people walk on the grass, or they will destroy the foliage. It is all paternalism. The law is taking care of you. You cannot let people take their children into the park on a sled. They might get hurt. A cordon of police guard the ice on the part of the lake that is not safe. If they did not, some idiot would skate into the water. Now, I resent being protected from myself. I feel like Ben. Franklin, 'Where freedom is, there is my country.'

"Another good treasure you have is simplicity. Life here is less complex. There are so many things in city life that demand attention that our energies get scattered, and our attention diverted, and our ways conventional and artificial. It is hard to express just what I mean; but life up here is less confused and more elemental and natural and real. That is a good thing. Then, you have the sunshine and the air and the open fields. You have what people who come up here from the Bowery call '*loneliness*.' It is aloofness. One can withdraw here, can get away, can get out of sight, can hear that still small voice which speaks only through the peace of nature— can 'flee as a bird to the mountains.' One idea of holiness is that which is set apart. Your landscape has a holiness which is not shared by shaven lawns punctuated by statuary. Our national emblem is the eagle, and there is an eagle spirit in the American people which likes the cliffs and the forests better than the boulevards and the parks.

" Then, there are not so many of you but that you can know each other and be interested in each other and help each other. The so-called philanthropy, which is more interested in institutions than it is in individuals, is a bad thing. What this world, with its suffering and sin and error, needs, is not more brown-stone laboratories and patent book-shelves and institutes for the uplift of the masses and the glorification of the millionaire rascals that endowed them; what the world needs is men that are interested in the individuals that surround them. I have not twenty-five thousand dollars to give away; but, if I had, I would pick out a worthy family that needed it and give it to them. I would endow a tradesman and not a trade *school*. Now, conditions here are good, because of the human interest you take in each other. If there were five hundred thousand of you, such personal interest would be impossible. Try to take a *personal* interest in one hundred thousand people. You cannot do it. The personal relations of employer and employed, of neighbors and friends, in a village are a priceless blessing.

" All these things are characteristics of this place.

" Besides this, it has its own history, its beautiful street, its scenery so exceptionally sweet and lovely—it is for these things that we celebrate its birthday."

Dr. Ryder's address was entitled " THE VILLAGE AND THE NATION." He spoke as follows:

" In this picturesque, beautiful and impressive Celebration, the Bi-Centennial of the settlement of this region, thought is naturally turned to the village of New Milford and the community life gradually developed here. There were certain fundamental characteristics of this village life which you, who were a part of it in later days, appreciate much better than your speaker. And yet even a superficial knowledge of what was here begun and has been gradually developed impresses these fundamental characteristics.

"This was a simple and natural life. The speaker preceding me has developed eloquently this fact. Artificiality had not yet crept into the social conditions of this life. The value of a man was not estimated by his heredity nor his wealth. It was a pure, clean democracy where every man was a man in privilege and opportunity 'for a' that, and a' that.'

"But another element of this village life was also evident from the first. This was the articulation of the community. Every one knew every other one within the confines of the settlement, although stretching along the edges of the beautiful rivers, down the valleys and plains, and up the slope of the stately old mountains. When Mary Jones' husband died and left her with a brood of little children, every man and woman in the community knew it, and most of them called upon Mary Jones with their burden of food or clothing or wood-shed supplies. It was the articulation of one life into another life, and of each life into the whole, that made the village of New Milford and every village in New England so strong and safe and efficient.

"But, little by little, these villagers in New Milford and other communities round about felt the need of the articulation of community interest into a larger whole. And so the community of associated responsibility and help took in Waterbury, Norwalk, Bridgeport, Hartford, and New Haven and other villages and towns scattered over this general region. This articulated the separate communities into a larger whole and the commonwealth was created. It was not a formal government so much as a community of interest and sympathy and love and organized efficiency. These several communities became a commonwealth for protection and development. Self-control was the basis of governmental control. The village was strong and vigorous in so far as the individual man and woman were strong and vigorous. The commonwealth developed these qualities of influence and strength only as the village developed them. And so this simple, this articulate life of the village became the life of the commonwealth.

"Then a new condition arose. King George came across the

water, established his forts, anchored his fleet in the harbor of another community that began as a village in the neighboring colony of Massachusetts. There was need of protection and safeguard in a larger way than the group of communities or villages furnished. So there came the articulation of the commonwealth with that of other commonwealths, and the united colonial power came into being. This afterwards became, as we all know so well, the United States.

"So, in constructive analysis, beginning with the unit of governmental power and influence, we find the village. No fairer or better or cleaner or more dignified than this village of New Milford existed in all the group of villages amid all the clustered commonwealths. A son of some Pilgrims from New Milford, who drifted into northern Ohio, who is your speaker at this moment, rejoices with you who have dwelt here in the East, in this magnificent and imposing Celebration of the founding of New Milford.

"But a larger view than this must be taken if we would estimate the importance and meaning of this village Celebration. The articulation of interests in the life of our nation as it exists to-day is much more difficult than it was when these villages grew by natural processes into the early national life. Multitudinous and heterogeneous masses are mingled in our body politic to-day, coming from nations that know nothing about the traditions of Puritan, or Pilgrim, or Dutch, or Cavalier. In many of these nations from which these peoples come and mingle in our life, the only thought of government is that of power, of police force, or suppression. Danger threatens us as we attempt to assimilate into our own national life these heterogeneous masses. It is not that they are bad, but that they come to us with no such conceptions of the simplicity and articulation of life and government as our fathers possessed who established the villages of New England. Our responsibility is to spread everywhere the great principles that lay at the foundations of village life in early New England. It is not from northern Europe that immigrants come who are a menace to these institutions that have made the United States what they are to-day. The real problem is the assimilation of unassociated races who are making a large portion of our body politic. Twenty million of the eighty million who are citizens of the United States are of the brown-skinned, undeveloped races. They represent fundamentally different ideals from those that made New England and the southern colonial States the power they were. It is for us in this generation to stimulate in these brown-skinned people the higher conceptions and loftier ideals represented in these villages that furnished the unit of development in the early years of the nation. There are two United States to-day, and we cannot neglect either of them with safety. There is Continental United States, the familiar old stretch of territory from ocean to ocean and from gulf to northern Alaska. This furnishes problems enough for the children of the Pilgrims to meet and solve. But another United States has been added in these later years, and that is Insular United States. They were brought to us through the arbitrament of war. We did not seek them; we perhaps are the poorer for their possession. But the great problem that God in His providence has put upon us to-day is the elevation and redemption of the masses of these island peoples. They have no village traditions or life to look back to. They have no intelligent conception of freedom. Morality is almost an unknown quality as we use the term. One great problem before Americans to-day, therefore, is the Americanizing and Christianizing of these masses that have become a part of our body politic, and whose future will largely determine the future of our entire nation.

" The village ideal, the simple, natural life that the smaller communities illustrated, the articulation of interests into one common and homogeneous whole, is what is demanded to-day, and what we must struggle for and achieve if the nation remains in its integrity and strength and dignity.

" When we analyze back to the village, we only go a part of the way. The unit after all was the home. One home articulated with other homes was the final analysis of strength and safety. It is the home, and not the church or the school, that holds men and women to that which is best and noblest. It was the home in the villages of New England, it was the home in New Milford, that determined its value and contributed to its beauty of community life. We have got to create in these masses that are coming among us the desire for the best, purest, noblest Christian home, or our entire civilization is in danger. If this Bi-Centennial of New Milford shall stir the hearts of the descendants of the brave men and women who established this village with a great passionate desire and an overmastering determination to perpetuate these great ideals and visions which the fathers held and nourished in their homes and united in their community life, then this Bi-Centennial were indeed an occasion of deepest rejoicing and abiding value."

SUNDAY EVENING

At five o'clock a service was held in All Saints' Memorial Church (St. John's Congregation uniting), which was attended by pastors of the churches of several denominations—another illustration of that fine Christian fellowship prevailing in New Milford which the Union Meeting on "The Green" had signally exemplified. The rector, Rev. Marmaduke Hare, preached an eloquent and profound sermon, in which he claimed that the master-force in the growth of mankind in all the higher qualities has been the truth and hope of the Gospel, and protested against imputing to nature, reason, science, philosophy, commerce, and politics what belongs to Christianity. "Ethical societies," he said, "may preach ideals, parliaments prescribe methods, literature describe the movements and processes of civilization, but the Church of the living God supplies the moral dynamic which makes possible all the rest."

At seven o'clock historical addresses were delivered at the Congregational Church and Saint John's Church, by Rev. Charles J. Ryder, D. D., of New York, and Rev. George S. Bennitt, D. D., of Jersey City, respectively. Dr. Ryder's subject was "PILGRIMS FROM NEW MILFORD." He said:

"Western Connecticut and Massachusetts contributed more

MEMORIAL BUILDING AND PUBLIC LIBRARY

ALL SAINTS' MEMORIAL CHURCH

to the early settlement of northern Ohio probably than any other section of the country. Pilgrims from this portion of New England began early to find their way westward. Along the fertile valley of the Mohawk, on the edge of the great inland seas, these settlers planted their homes. You can easily trace the line of their march in the intelligence and dignity of character that their descendants possess to-day in these regions. New Milford contributed to this body of Pilgrims that followed the sun toward its setting. As they went out, they left that which has been so eloquently set forth in various public addresses during the progress of this Bi-Centennial of New Milford. The beautiful valleys and imposing mountains, the clear rivers and foaming brooks, the marvelous, picturesque beauty of New Milford and its environment, they left behind them. They did not find these, as they planted their tents in the great forests of northern Ohio. How often have I heard one of these Pilgrims from New Milford describe her homesickness as she looked out upon the almost flat country, which the local clearing had revealed, into the dense forests that shut down upon the edge of this clearing on every side! Turbid streams, muddy roads, wooden sidewalks, the plain and unattractive natural scenery, and the rough conditions of pioneer life were vastly different from the beautiful landscape and refined conditions of this home town from which they went out.

"But they did not leave all, nor the best, of that which they had gathered in the life in New Milford, as they left its borders and went overland by their own conveyance into Ohio. They took with them three fundamental conceptions of life. First, that of the Christian home; second, that of the public school; third, that of the Christian church. To these ideals, planted in the hearts of these early Pilgrims, may be traced the fruitage of the strong intellectual and moral life which has developed in the citizenship of northern Ohio.

"These Pilgrims from New England found chiefly an opportunity. The physical conditions were depressing and hard. The problem of life was serious and difficult, the hardships encountered were rigorous and persistent; but wherever these Pilgrims planted a colony in the Western Reserve, or New Connecticut, as it was called, they established the Christian home, the public school, and the Christian church.

"Philo Penfield Stewart, a Pilgrim from the neighboring town of Sherman, illustrates the character and purposes of these early settlers. He went into Ohio in 1832, and, even before his weary body could have rested from the long and tedious journey, he began at once, in connection with Rev. J. R. Shipherd of Elyria, plans for the establishment of a college and colony at Oberlin. It is possible, as history hints, that the first white pioneer into Ohio was Ferdinand De Soto, who possibly pushed his way into the region of this great central State as early as 1539. It is most fortunate, however, that not the descendants of De Soto, but the Pilgrims from New England and their descendants, gave the ideals and formative influences to this new commonwealth. That there should be the least percentage of illiteracy in the northern counties of Ohio, known still as the Western Reserve, of any part of the tabulated world, is not an accident. The schoolhouse was as much a part of their essential requirements as the barn or the shop. When in the height of his wide-reaching influence, Dr. Joseph Cook went once to Cleveland; he carefully studied the conditions of the public schools of the Forest City. He afterwards bore testimony that 'in coming from Boston, Massachusetts, to Cleveland, Ohio, he came *up* in the character of the appointments and work in the public schools, and not down'; that 'the educational system of Cleveland was better than the educational system of Boston.' Your speaker having had somewhat intimate acquaintance with both systems, would speak an humble word of endorsement to this testimony of Dr. Cook. These Pilgrims from New Milford found mud, homeliness, forest, hardships, toil and privation. But they found opportunity. This opportunity they improved to the best of their ability or of any ability that human beings could command. They planted churches and worshiped within their sacred precincts with loving reverence; they built their schoolhouses and had no lack of teachers, for many of their wives and daughters had been teachers in Old Connecticut.

They sent their children to school, sparing them from needed work on the farm or in the shop or store. They did this, because they were building life, character; were establishing a Christian civilization to outlast them and their immediate descendants. They did it, because they believed in God and man and in making the most of life. Better than all, they gathered in their homes around the clear-swept hearth of their open fireplaces, in love, peace, and confidence. Often the crackling fire on the open hearth was the only light that the home possessed for the evening. Sometimes, as we learn from their records, they put melted tallow in a tin basin and hung a bit of cotton wicking over the side to light their humble homes. 'Two such lanterns,' they tell us, 'were sufficient to light up the church for evening service.' It was almost reverting to the type of the lamp used in early Jewish history, and quite to the profound Hebrew reverence. But whatever artificial light these Pilgrims had, they saw clearly the great purposes of existence, and read with undimmed vision 'their title clear' to the best that devotion and energy and faith and courage could achieve.

"When the great agitation came in favor of freedom, as against chattel slavery, the descendants of the New Milford Pilgrims in northern Ohio did not flinch nor hesitate. Professor Hart, in his recent volume on 'Slavery and Abolition,' says:* 'One reason for the force which abolition early acquired in Ohio was the fallow field waiting for it in the Western Reserve. This region, settled by Connecticut people between 1790 and 1820, was still a little New England, its churches, schools, and local government closely modeled on those of Connecticut.' Nor did this 'fallow field' among the Pilgrims from New Milford prove unproductive. Rustic lads, whom Dr. James Harris Fairchild, President of Oberlin College for many potential years, represented, bearing his testimony to these hard, early conditions, waded through the snow barefooted in order to attend school. Such lads could not be kept away from the privileges of higher training. Colleges were immediately necessary. Such institutions were established, buildings erected, faculties gathered, lecture and class rooms crowded with eager pupils, as

* Page 196

by the magic wand of some scholastic magician. Within a few months of its establishment, Oberlin College had hundreds of pupils. They had brought together a faculty perhaps unequaled, man for man, in the faculty of any institution ever founded. They were giants, intellectually and morally. Their names to-day are wrought not alone in the intellectual and educational history, but into the very warp and woof of our national life. Ohio, the great West, the South, and the nation could hardly have been the great, united nation that it is, had it not been for these Pilgrims from New Milford and their descendants, who stood with heroic courage for the highest ideals, and strove to attain them at tremendous sacrifice and suffering.

"Professor Hart is responsible for the following bit of history: 'When Harriet Martineau attended an anti-slavery meeting, she found that she had given offense to the best society in Boston. Theodore Parker found his clerical brethren refusing to exchange pulpits with him; "My life seems to me a complete failure socially; here I am as much an outcast from society as though I were a convicted pirate." The eastern colleges, almost without exception, were strongholds of pro-slavery feeling. . . . In 1848, Charles Sumner, a graduate of Harvard, spoke to the students of the college. Longfellow said: "The shouts and the hisses and the vulgar interruptions grated on our ears. I was glad to get away!"'

"But such a spirit of cowardice and weak surrender to the financial and social influence of the South as was manifested by many eastern colleges, was not that of the western colleges planted in the clearing of the great forests of the New Connecticut largely by the Pilgrims of New Milford. They spoke out steady and strong against the 'twin relic of barbarism.' Professor Seabert, in his history of the 'underground railway,' bears testimony that through the Western Reserve almost every line of secret escape for the slave running toward the north star passed. At Oberlin, where the Pilgrims in whom your speaker is most profoundly interested had their home, eleven underground railroads passed. They radiated as many as the ten fingers of the two hands, and one hand had an extra finger.

It was the boast of these brave men and women, and the boast was proven by the fact, that no negro was ever taken back to slavery who reached the Western Reserve. How well I remember those early incidents in my boyhood home! The Oberlin-Wellington rescue case is written in the history of the nation. How the excitement and agitation of that New England village in Ohio come to me as I think of it! It was but a few months after the death of my father, Oliver Roberts Ryder, a Pilgrim from Danbury to this same Western Reserve. A negro boy, John Price by name, had escaped from slavery. He had been a resident for some time in Oberlin. Through the intrigue of a pro-slavery countryman near the village, he was waylaid, captured by a band of slave-holders, bound and gagged, thrown into a wagon, and hurried off to a railroad station on the railroad leading into the South. The descendants of our Connecticut Pilgrims of the town heard of it. Prayer was offered first, for faith in God was the very threshold over which they passed to the accomplishment of any brave purpose. Wagons were hastily gathered, firearms piled into them, and away the Oberlin rescuers went to win this black boy, rather worthless fellow in himself, to personal freedom. This was his constitutional right under the Declaration of Independence, for he surely was born to be 'free and equal' in privilege. He was rescued from the slave-holders, although they were armed to the teeth and displayed their guns, but did not dare to use them. The faculty, the Sunday school superintendent, the leading business men were in this band of rescuers, and were afterwards thrown into prison for the technical crime of their acts. Here again the splendid traditions which these Pilgrims brought from their eastern home came in play. Obey the law they must. They could do it by not breaking it, or by submitting to the penalty. They chose the latter, and no one made the slightest effort to escape, but submitted without a moment's hesitation to the processes of the law, and stood before the jury. They were not subpæna jumpers, and in this showed that they were not criminal in intent, as those who seek to escape the processes of the law always are.

"No, be it said to the glorious memory of the Pilgrims of New Milford and Western New England, they did not follow in the wake of many of the larger institutions in the East, and cringe and whimper and grovel under the crack of the whip of the slave-holding aristocracy. Open and free and manly, they stood out for the defense of freedom, whether applied to the person of black man or white man. It was the highest type of educational training which any institution can furnish. It was not tamely to learn axioms or to demonstrate mathematical problems, but to know, to believe, to defend that which was best and truest. These worthy Pilgrims who went out in the early part of the nineteenth century into this western forest, stood for this with all the sturdy strength of these mighty trees that shadowed their homes. It is because they went, and others like them, that the Buckeye State has risen to and maintained her dominant influence in the nation's life. It is due to these Pilgrims, more than to any other one force, that the whole Northwest was from the first saved the disgrace of slavery. Institutions of learning in which women as well as men had the right to the best education were planted. They maintained the school, the church, the home in every hamlet and city and village; and, to-day, this region they settled presents the finest, largest, and most comprehensive type of Christian civilization that the earth affords. All glory, then, to these Pilgrims from New Milford! They, like one of old, 'went out not knowing whither they went.' They dared and suffered and died, but always achieved. Well may this village, a beautiful gem set in the midst of these rolling hills, rejoice in its own noble development and progress and prosperity. Your life here is almost ideal. The conditions are as fine as the world affords. But, as you rejoice in this Bi-Centennial of your own founding, forget not, O brave and true men and women of this generation; forget not, O Christians of these churches; forget not, O patrons of this redeemed nation, that the Pilgrims that went out from your firesides and homes into the great West inaugurated the tremendous forces that have moved on in increasing power and breadth until the whole nation has been made the rihcer by their mighty power."

Dr. Bennitt's address at Saint John's Church was as follows:
". . . Religious matters, during our beginnings, did not run very smoothly. The desire for greater religious freedom caused a considerable falling away of sundry church members to Quakerism in 1731 and 1732. There were also families who had come into the town, and brought with them an affection for their old Church in England; and, as the English Church had been established in Stratford in 1707, and in Newtown in 1732, only fifteen miles away, the influence of this Church began to exert itself here. When the Rev. John Beach . . . established the services of the Church of England in Newtown, the Churchmen of New Milford journeyed on Saturdays to Newtown, carrying their own provisions, and the Churchmen there gave them their lodgings. He baptized their children, and came here to officiate at a marriage in 1739. He began services here about 1742. He sent Mr. Barzilla Dean here as a lay reader, services being rendered in one of the houses of a Church family.

"It is stated that certain Churchmen in New Milford were fined for refusing to attend the meetings of the Established Church. These fines were, by recommendation of the Rev. Mr. Beach, paid, and copies of the proceedings taken to be forwarded to the King and Council. The fact becoming known, the authorities refunded the money, and granted permission to build a church which before had been refused. . . . In 1745-6 materials were gathered, and the English Church in New Milford erected.

"Let us glance for a few moments at the village street at this time. The early settlers had laid out their town plot, because of a beautiful spring of water, at the head of the street, nearly in front of Ingleside School, and about under the present sidewalk. The water from this spring meandered its way down through the village street, *bowing* from the spring to the south end of the street, where it formed a small pond, which was called 'The Goose Pond.' This accounts for the east side of Main Street *bowing*, while the west side is straight, and the street opening out considerably wider at the south end, on account of 'The Goose Pond.' This spring was there in my boyhood days, although an open ditch had been constructed through the middle of 'The Green,' in which the stream flowed. Since the construction of the water works, however, and the laying of pipes through the street, both the spring and the stream have disappeared.

"The First Established Church stood near the head of Main Street, near the spring, and the land granted for the Church of England was in the street, east of Mr. Samuel Prindle's house, near where the old pound used to stand, at the south end of Main Street, therefore, and in the middle of the street. Here they built the first Church of England in New Milford. . . . It was a frame building, forty feet by thirty. It had two rows of windows, one above the other, and presented the appearance of a two-story house, and the door was in the side. It was surmounted by a turret in the center of the building, and stood ends to the east and west. The door was on the south side, and within, on the north side, stood the pulpit. It was not until 1756 that the building was finished, when, upon the building of the second meeting-house, it was voted to give three-quarters of the body seats and two pews in the old meeting-house to the Church of England. Then, the church was furnished with the square box seats, and the pulpit stood aloft, beneath which was the reading desk for the prayers, and, beneath that, the pew for the clerk, to lead in the responses, and to tune the Psalms. A curtain across the corner served as a robing-room for the vesting of the clergymen, and, around little tables which were placed in the middle of the square box seats, gathered the families of the Churchmen of that early time. And on account of the love and affection they bore to the Rev. John Beach, of Newtown, who first planted the church in their midst, they named it 'Saint John's Church'; and it has borne that name ever since,

"The Rev. Solomon Palmer, a Congregational minister of Cornwall, dissatisfied with his orders, conformed to the Church, and went to England for ordination. After that, he returned here, and became the first Church of England minister who resided here, from 1754 to 1760. . . . He was succeeded by the Rev. Thomas Davies in 1761. He was a missionary sent by the 'Venerable Society for the Propagation of the Gospel in Foreign Parts.' . . . a graduate of Yale College, a man who had become a minister of the church from conviction, a gentleman and a scholar, a reader of the service, and preacher of the highest order. . . . Under this man of God the Church outgrew its small building, and entered upon the construction of a new, more commodious, and churchly edifice.

"I have a copy of the diary of the Rev. Thomas Davies, containing most of his ministerial acts, and some of these shed considerable light on the old times. He records, on November 15, 1764: 'On St. Pumpion's (Pumpkin's) Day, I baptized at Ethel Stone's, Martha, Ester and Edmond, children of Ethel Stone, Hannah of Gad Sperry, Joseph and Hulda of Samuel Peet, and David Smith of David Smith.'

"He alludes to St. Pumpion's Day in other records, which leads us to suppose that this was a colloquial term in those days for designating the annual New England Thanksgiving, which was celebrated by an abundance of pumpkin pies.

"I have a manuscript sermon of the Rev. Thomas Davies, preached at New Milford, written in the finest hand, showing clearness of thought, a fine choice of language, and rising to eloquence, in pressing home to the hearts of his hearers the word of God.

"The Rev. Mr. Davies was succeeded by the Rev. Richard Clark from Milford, who remained here until 1787. He was here during the Revolution. The church begun by Mr. Davies was completed sufficiently to begin services therein, and the old church was sold to the town for a town house. This was removed to the head of Main Street and used for several years.

"The second Church of England, begun under Rev. Mr. Davies, had Partridge Thatcher for its architect, but was modeled after the church at Stratford, but somewhat plainer in its ornamentation.

"It stood, facing the road towards Butter Brook, a few rods north of the first church, had a steeple which projected out in front of the building, and long windows round at the top. Within, it had the high pulpit with circular stairs; its reading desk and clerk's pew beneath, making what was called a three-decker. A communion table was in front of all, and the whole was surrounded by a communion rail. A gallery was across the south end; and a curtain across the corner, served again as a robing-room. The service of that day had its peculiar features. The clergyman was robed in a long surplice and black scarf. He wore a white wig, to give age and dignity to his ministrations. The surplice was exchanged for a black silk gown and bands before the sermon, the congregation all knelt for the prayers, and, in doing so, turned around and knelt to the seats. The clerk (or clark, as the people called him) doled out a line of the old Metrical Psalms, and the congregation sang it, and waited for another line. There was no fire in the church, and, in winter, the women carried their foot stoves to keep their feet warm.

"The Revolution, however, gave great discouragement to the Church of England people, for everything English was hated by the inhabitants, and the Rev. Mr. Clark, after ten years of struggle, gave up and fled to Nova Scotia in 1787, and the church was closed.

"The kind of Church people that were made in the Colonial days of the Church in Connecticut may be illustrated by the name of Samuel Peet, a devout Churchman from Stratford, who came to settle in the New Milford North Purchase, in the vicinity of Rock Cobble, west of Peet Hill. He selected a site for his future home near a great rock, which, by some convulsion of nature, had been rent asunder, leaving a portion like an altar between, with two natural steps to ascend it. Here, Samuel Peet, the Hermit, knelt day by day to worship his God, and the holes he chiseled out for his knees on the top of that altar are to be seen to this day. He erected his house just west of the altar, and here reared his family, desiring to be buried between the rocks, but, as it was found they came together just below the surface of the ground, he was buried on the east side of the altar rocks, in one of the most romantic burying-places of this town. Now, in 1789, when the Rev. Mr. Clark had fled to Nova Scotia, and the church in New Preston was boarded up to save its windows from being destroyed, Samuel Peet was on his death-bed, desiring to receive the Holy Communion. He sent a messenger away down to one of the churches nearer the Sound, for a priest. It was in March, and the roads were very heavy, and a prolonged time was required.

"Meanwhile, Samuel Peet was nearing his end. He asked that bread and wine be prepared and placed on a table beside his bed, that no time be lost when the priest of the Church arrived. Again and again, he sent out to see if the messenger and the priest might be seen coming in the distance; and, as the end grew nearer, and the priest had not arrived, Samuel Peet said, 'Let us pray,' and, when all had knelt around his bed, he prayed: 'O Blessed Jesus, Our great High Priest, come down and consecrate this Bread and this Wine to be Thy Body and Blood.' And, after silence had been kept for a space, he reached out his trembling hand and communicated himself, after which he soon fell asleep in Jesus. Who shall say that was not a valid consecration!

"The priest of the Church arrived that night, and remained to commit his body to the earth, looking for the general resurrection in the Last Day. . . .

"It is a tradition that some of the rectors of the Church of England had a habit of talking to themselves, and, behind the curtain while they were robing, would often repeat over the notices to be given out, the most interesting being the publishing of the banns of matrimony, which was the custom in those days. On one occasion the banns were published between Orin Marsh and Maria Hill, who lived upon the plains. Now, there were in the Church, Orman Marsh of Boardman's Bridge, and Maria Hill, of Aspetuck, whom the congregation thought were the parties published, greatly to their confusion. That day, the second-named began their acquaintance, suggested by the banns, and, in due time, their banns were likewise published.

"The Rev. Enoch Huntington, who entered upon the rectorship in 1827, began parish records, and, upon the first page, states that there was a congregation of about thirty. No Sunday school, and no music. Also the church was in need of repair, but he concluded not to spend much upon it, but later to build a new church, the third one of the society. The new rector soon gained the love and esteem of the people in general, and the attendance of young people became a prominent feature in his ministry. So devoted were his people, that they are spoken of, when the church roof was old and leaky, as sitting in their pews during a shower, with their umbrellas up, listening to the preaching of the word of God. A bell was placed in this old church steeple, the first one the church possessed. In 1837 a new church was erected on the east side of Main Street at the corner of what is now called Church Street. This church was a frame building, with long windows, square at the top. It had a square tower upon it, and, within, a gallery around three sides, a massive mahogany pulpit, reading desk below, and a small mahogany communion table in front, with two mahogany chairs on either side, a communion rail enclosing them. A vestry-room was built in the rear, and the rector entered the pulpit from stairs in the vestry-room, and appeared through a door cut in the wall behind the pulpit.

"The pulpit and reading desk were covered with cushions of black silk velvet, with heavy silk-corded fringe across the front, and large silk tassels suspended at the corners. There was a sofa seat behind the reading desk attached to the pulpit.

"The pews had doors with large black tin plates attached with numbers on. This church was considered very handsome in its furnishings, and was the pride of both rector and people. It was furnished with a new bell, and into this came the first organ owned by Saint John's Church. Rev. Mr. Huntington resigned in 1848, and, after his decease several years later, was brought here and buried in the village cemetery, having this honorable record—of being the rector of Saint John's Parish longer than any other clergyman from its beginning to the present day. . . .

"During the incumbency of Rev. William H. Reese, I was baptized in that old church, out of the silver bowl placed on the communion table. When I was a little child, I well remember how Bishop Brownell catechised the children, standing about the chancel rail, but, perhaps, as I grew older, the most vivid impression made upon me was the preparation for, and attendance upon, the old-time Christmas Eve service. Evergreens were gathered upon the Plains, and the people assembled at Mr. George McMahon's to tie them. They were gathered in Aspetuck, and the people assembled at Mr. Marshall Hill's or Mr. Stephen Morehouse's. They were gathered at the village, and the people assembled at the house of my father, Noble S. Bennitt, on Bennitt Street. The refreshments consisted of a pan of doughnuts, round and sugared. The cracking fire on the hearth consumed the broken branches, and the young people remained for a social time after their elders had departed. Such large ropes of evergreens were tied, and afterwards suspended from corner to corner of the church, and all around the walls, and in front of the gallery!

"White covers of bleached muslin covered the pulpit and reading desk, to which were attached fringes made of the needles of the pine, by Miss Bostwick, afterwards Mrs. Leroy Buck. Mottoes of evergreen on white cloth were put up on the walls, and candelabra, of five candles each, across the ends of the pulpit and desk cushions. Miss Cornelia Boardman brought a large fluid lamp with a glass globe and put it on the communion table. The people reserved their whitest and purest tallow to make dipped candles to hang up in tin back candlesticks under the gallery, while Edgar and Henry Wells made a great star of five points, covered it with evergreens, and suspended it from the ceiling in the middle of the church, containing as many candles as it was the year of the century. This was the only time in the year that the church was lighted up, and the people of the town turned out and filled the church and its galleries to overflowing. The good old Christmas

Eve service of the old times, who that was then alive shall ever forget it!

"But the solemnity of the old-time Sunday comes up with all its hallowed associations. The Sunday church bells, with the orderly ringing and tolling of their first bells and last bells; with their solemn tolling for a death—nine for a man, seven for a woman, five for a boy, three for a girl!

"The sleigh bells, too, bass ones and tenor ones, jingling all the week in the winter time, but no sleigh bells on Sunday! I well remember when two young men, in their want of respect for the traditions of Sunday, drove through the village street with sleigh bells on their horse on the Lord's Day, thereby shocking the sober-minded people of the churches and the town.

"The social gatherings of the people come back to one, as he recalls the old times, also. The annual donation parties given by the parishioners to their parsons, when, it used to be said, 'The people would bring all kinds of good things to the parsonage, and then remain for a good social time, spread all the good things brought for a feast, and then largely consume them before they departed.'

"Other social gatherings had their attractions for the people, but I recall *one* which was to occur, but never took place.

"It was on the coldest day of February, 1860, when, in large sleighs, a company of people set out for a dinner party to be given upon the Plains. As they passed down the Main Street, the bell of Saint John's Church was tolling for a funeral about to be held within it. It was thereupon agreed to stop and attend the services, warm themselves by the fire, and then proceed on their journey. . . . The clergyman took for the text of his funeral sermon, which in those days was a very dignified discourse, 'It is better to go to the house of mourning, than to go to the house of feasting: for this is the end of all men, and the living will lay it to heart.' Consternation filled the hearts of all. The women and the children remained in the church by the fire, and the men went to the village cemetery to assist in the burial; after which all returned to their homes. The effect of the sermon had been marvelous, and the living had laid it to heart. The funeral was that of the widow of Dr. Amaziah Wright.

"Rev. Charles G. Acly, who became the rector in 1856, wrought a good work here, and, under him, the church was enlarged in the summer of 1860, by the nave being extended nearly twice its length. A recess chancel was added, and a stained-glass chancel window given, as a memorial of the Hon. Elijah and Mary Anna Boardman—the first stained-glass window in the town. The old mahogany pulpit was made into an altar. There was an altar cloth of red which served for the whole year, a beautiful reading desk and pulpit combined, which stood outside the chancel rail, and, in the center, before the altar, given by Mr. Solomon E. Bostwick, a pedestal with a marble bowl for a font. . . .

"In this church I began my first work in the Church of God by blowing the first organ the church ever owned, and Miss Schroder, now Mrs. George W. Wright, was the organist at that time. We sang the Metrical Psalms and the few hymns then bound up with the Prayer Book. The *Te Deum* was generally read, but on high occasions we rendered Jackson's *Te Deum*. The old *Gloria in Excelsis* was always sung at the end of the Psalm for the Day in the afternoon, and sometimes Greatore's *Bonum est* and *Benedicite* after the Lesson. On Communion Day, once a month, after sermon, the choir came down in the body of the church, and there was no music. But Easter was distinguished by the choir remaining in the gallery and singing the *Sanctus*. In that church, I was confirmed and ordained to the holy ministry by Bishop John Williams, and, to that church, I came afterwards to preach my first sermon in my native town. One can hardly imagine my feelings, as I came to stand for the first time before my elders, teachers, kindred, and those to whom I had looked up from childhood. It was a trying moment. I preached a written sermon, for fear I might be embarrassed. When it was all over, and some one in the churchyard, during the noon hour, ventured to call it a good sermon, one of the men spoke up and said, '*Yes, if he wrote it!*' Surely, 'A prophet is not without honor, save in his own country, and among his own kin.' Stirred by this remark, which came to my knowledge, I preached without notes that afternoon, and did the same upon every visit to New Milford for many years following. . . .

"The Rev. Mr. Acly was a good man, and a conscientious priest of the Church of God; painstaking in his sermon preparation, a good reader and preacher, while as a pastor he went in and out among his people for twenty years beloved by them. He resigned in 1876, but continued to reside here until his death in 1880, and he was buried in the village cemetery, awaiting the resurrection of the just.

"He was succeeded by the Rev. Alfred S. Clark, who was rector from 1876 to 1879. While his stay was only four years, yet he is remembered with much affection. The Rev. Edward L. Wells, D. D., became the next rector, whose eloquence can never be forgotten, and by him was started the project of building a new stone church for Saint John's Parish. Plans were drawn and accepted, but, in less than a year, he was removed by death, in 1880.

"Rev. Edwin R. Browne succeeded him, and, as the contract for the new church had already been made, he carefully attended to its erection. This was carried forward for two years, and entirely paid for by the congregation, so that on Thursday, the fifteenth day of March, 1883, we all assembled to take part in its consecration.

"The Rt. Rev. John Williams, D. D., Bishop of Connecticut, the Rt. Rev. Charles Quintard, D. D., Bishop of Tennessee, and thirty of the clergy of this and other dioceses, met to put on their vestments in the old church, before proceeding to the new. The emotions which filled my soul on that day were many and varied. It was the last act to be performed in the old Saint John's Church. I went into our old family pew, where I had grown up to manhood, and, *there*, I put on my vestments. I went up to the chancel rail and, kneeling down, offered the last prayer in that old church—where I had first heard the service of the Book of Common Prayer, first listened to the preaching of the word of God,—whose walls had witnessed my baptism, my confirmation, and my ordination to the holy ministry—and I said, ' Oh, to have enduring churches of stone, where the holy associations of a lifetime may never be disturbed!' It was this thought which led me forth to assist in the services of the consecration of the new Saint John's Church of *stone*, where the services might hereafter continue, undisturbed, from generation to generation. The vested procession of bishops and clergy walked from the old church to the new. The day was full of sunlight, and even the March winds seemed to cease, so as to give us Heaven's own benediction. We entered this beautiful stone church, filled with a congregation which occupied its whole capacity. Bishop Williams then consecrated this new Saint John's Church, and called upon me to read the sentence of consecration.

" That day was the greatest red letter day this parish ever saw—twenty-five years ago, on the fifteenth day of March next!

" The Rev. Mr. ·Browne continued his ministry here until 1890. He was a most indefatigable parish visitor, and the sympathy of his people and their prayers followed him, in the affliction which afterward came upon him.

" He was followed by the Rev. E. T. Sanford, who was the rector from 1891 to 1895, a man of exceedingly lovable character, who endeared himself to all.

" He was succeeded by the Rev. John F. Plumb in 1896, who after eleven years still continues in the rectorship. His character and ability are so well known among his people, that it would not become me to enter into them here. Suffice it, then, to say, that he is held in such honor and respect by his brethren of the clergy of his Diocese, that they elected him Archdeacon of Litchfield County some years ago, which position he now holds with honor to himself, and with appreciation by his parish and friends. May he long continue to go in and out among you as your rector, pastor, friend, and long continue to occupy his high and honorable position, as the venerable Archdeacon of Litchfield County."

THE AUTOMOBILE PARADE

No feature of the whole Bi-Centennial Celebration partook so much of the nature of an experiment, perhaps, as the Automobile Parade of Monday, which took place a little before noon. It was the first event of the kind that had ever occurred in New Milford, and there were consequently no precedents to go by. It was, however, an unqualified success. Fifteen decorated autos, followed by nearly a score without decorations, were in line. The owners of the decorated autos were:

Henry D. Hine, New Milford, Conn.
Geo. T. Soule, New Milford, Conn.
A. N. Trott, Waterbury, Conn.
H. L. Randall, New Milford, Conn.
Edward S. Hine, New Rochelle, N. Y.
Mrs. Isaac B. Bristol, New Milford, Conn.
Jas. S. Robertson, Pittsfield, Mass.
John Bauman, New Haven, Conn.
E. M. Watson, Sr., Jersey City.
C. F. Long, Jersey City.
Peter Peterson, New Milford, Conn.
C. W. Lines, New Britain, Conn.
J. E. Murphy, Southbury, Conn.
H. Lake, Brookfield, Conn.
Robert Dunlap, New Milford, Conn.

The judges were George B. Noble of Northampton, Mass., Mrs. Dr. Wallace of Glen Ridge, N. J., and Miss Beatrice Fisher of Montreal, Canada.

The three prizes (silver cups) were awarded as follows: Henry D. Hine, New Milford, first; A. N. Trott, Waterbury, Conn., second; Mrs. Isaac B. Bristol, New Milford, third. Robert Dunlap was given a special honorable mention.

The decoration of Mr. Henry Hine's car was very dainty and elaborate. It was done in white, pink, and purple. In front of the chauffeur was a Cupid, driving three white doves with white and purple ribbons. Before the machine were banners inscribed with the figures 1707-1907. The tonneau was banked with evergreens and wild flowers. The rear tire on the tonneau was covered with a wreath of evergreens, in the center of which was suspended a Cupid with bow and arrow. The chauffeur and the lady passengers wore white and pink.

Mr. Trott's car bore a canopy of salmon pink, olive green, and white *crêpe* paper flowers, and carried as passengers Dr. and Mrs. Bragaw in Colonial attire. The wheels and the back of the tonneau were similarly decorated with *crêpe* paper.

Mrs. Bristol's car was decorated with laurel, ferns, and white daisies, supplemented by yellow and white bunting, and carried several passengers in white, with daisies in their hair.

Mr. Dunlap's car was literally covered with grass-green and white draperies and bore an arch of these colors. Its lady passengers wore white gowns and white picture hats trimmed with green.

Mr. Peterson's car, with a colossal figure of Uncle Sam, and Mr. Randall's with festoons of lemons, gave rise to much merriment. The other cars were decorated with flags and bunting; Colonial blue and yellow bunting; white and pale-green bunting; daisies and flags; peonies and daisies. The party-colored cars presented a brilliant and beautiful picture, as they coursed rapidly round and round "The Green," and evoked many outbursts of hearty applause.

THE HISTORICAL MEETING

The Historical Meeting of Monday afternoon, the next important event in the Bi-Centennial Celebration, was presided over by Frederic M. Williams. Mr. Williams, after a few genial words of greeting, introduced, as the first speaker, Dr. Samuel Hart, President of the Connecticut Historical Society, explaining, as he did so, that New Milford welcomes her guests, not only with the best that she has, but with the best that there is.

.Dr. Hart spoke as follows:

" The recurring anniversaries of the towns of our ancient State are bringing before us, as in a series of living pictures, the history of the whole commonwealth and of all its parts. Beginning, within the easy memory of many now living, with the quarter-millennials of the first settled towns, Hartford and its sister towns on the Great River, Saybrook at its mouth, New Haven on its fair harbor at the mouth of the Quinnipiac, and then its allied towns, Guilford to the east and Milford, your mother-city, to the west, we are passing now to the bi-centennials of those, the history of which begins in the opening years of the eighteenth century. Our origins have been brought before us, and we have studied again the men and the times, the founders of our first colonies and the foundations which they laid, the early history of two differently ordered federations or groups of organized communities, and their union into one government under a charter from the English king which made them almost independent of his authority. We are passing on now to another period, when, under varied influences and in changed circumstances, many of our most beautiful and prosperous towns were founded. Two years ago Newtown, which once had part of its boundary-line in common with you, observed its bi-centennial; and the two-hundredth anniversaries of Derby and Woodbury and Waterbury and Danbury—to mention only those in this neighborhood—were earlier than that.

"There was a movement of life into this part of Connecticut, the meaning and result of which will be brought before you by those who have studied it in its details, and can describe it with local color. Without repeating or anticipating their words, I may venture to ask you to think of the difference which a little more than seventy years had made in the motives that swayed men's minds, and the impressions that were made on them by the new lands which they occupied. One thinks of the stern resolve, both political and ecclesiastical, which sent Hooker and his company on their long walk through the wilderness till they came to the river and crossed it into a strange land, with a determination like that of the father of the faithful when he crossed the great river of the eastern world; and then one questions whether they admired the beauty of the meadows, and one feels sure that when they climbed the hills and looked down into the more beautiful valley of the Tunxis, they were drawn by it to travel still further west. One follows in mind the military instinct which saw the importance of the control of the Connecticut River, and built a fort at its mouth, and levied dues on traffic and transportation, and laid out streets for the houses of people of quality who were expected to come to dwell there. And one thinks of the surprises which befell those who sailed slowly along the shore of the Sound, looking into inlet and bay, and finding at the Fair Haven a place where they might build a city after the pattern of the heavenly Jerusalem, and in it dwell and get gain.

"In each of these early instances there was an element of romance, of strong conviction of duty, mingled with an appreciation alike of the beautiful and the practical, that combination which, as Horace told us long ago, 'carries every vote.' To some extent this had passed away two hundred years ago, when possession was taken of the farming lands, and the fair, though rugged, hillsides enclosing the river valley in which we now stand. The settlers, who came up into the high grounds from the shores of the Sound, did not leave, for the most part, on account of disagreement with their neighbors in matters civil or ecclesiastical, nor with a special sense of divine calling or mission. They were rather led by the Anglo-Saxon spirit of colonization to settle on new soil, to extend former industries or to undertake new ones, and to organize new units of life in the body politic. Still, we cannot doubt that when they, too, looked over the fields they saw more than the possibility of gathering harvests and crops from them, and that when they followed the water-courses they did more than estimate the use which they might make of the force of the falling stream. They had something of the enthusiasm of discovery, and something of the joy of those who first turn nature's forces to man's account. It is worth our while, as we go back in mind to these beginnings, to try to think as they thought, who first looked upon the natural features of the landscape, which it takes much more than two centuries materially to change, and to see why they chose as they did, who fixed on this spot as their home.

"In this regard, there is in all our settlements, early and late, something that they have in common, which appeals more, I am inclined to think, to the philosopher than to the historian. Perhaps the student of history delights rather in noting the differences in the plans and purposes of those who settled our early towns, and in finding in each, as he readily may, some detail of character or event which marks it with a special interest, and almost always brings in the suggestion of a special romance. As your early history is read before you to-day in detail, you are reminded how it differs from the history of every other town in Connecticut. At its beginning you hear of names which give it a stamp peculiarly its own: that of the first minister, continued by an honorable succession through all the generations to this day; that of the early settler who lived here in a log hut on land which he had bought of the Indians and lived to be Attorney General of Massachusetts; somewhat later, that of the man who came here as a shoemaker and removed hence as a judge, to become one of the few leaders in the constitutional history of the land; and with them the names of others which shed a special luster on your annals. Again, the importance of the Indians in this neighborhood, both in numbers and (as it would seem) in influence and character, suggests an almost unique chapter of history, especially when we note that it led to the sojourn of the remarkable man who led hither his band of Moravian missionaries and labored not in vain among the aborigines before he withdrew to make a permanent settlement in another province, and later to return to his home·in Europe. And, if you care to boast of it, you share with but one or two other towns the honor of having had congregations of the Glassites—who under their name of Sandemanians will always be remembered for having had in their eldership one of the greatest men of science of a generation ago—and you have the exclusive honor of having been the home of the Jemimaites. Certainly, no two communities are exactly alike, and it is in the study of their differences that much of our pleasure in the reading of their history consists.

"While I bring to you to-day, Mr. President, a greeting on behalf of the Historical Society of the State, I venture to ask you and all the citizens of this venerable town, and all who are interested in her annals already written, and in the record which she is to make in years to come, not to allow the interest of these memorial days to pass away with the days themselves. This week is bringing to the memory of some of you that which you have already heard with your ears and your fathers have declared unto you, while it is teaching many others, and in particular the youths and maidens, their first lessons in the history of the community in which their lot is cast. The story of the founders and those who carried on their work, who they were and what they did, what New Milford was in itself and what part it played in the State and the Republic, told again now in greater detail than it has ever been told before—do not let it be soon or readily forgotten. See to it that the whole town becomes a sort of historical society, for the appreciation and preservation of that which is old, for the lending of a proper perspective to that which belongs to our own day, for preparation rightly to understand and rightly to value and use that which is coming. They best do the duties of the present, they best provide for the future, who read and value the lessons of the past."

The second speaker, Chief Justice Baldwin, was presented to the audience by Mr. Williams with these words: "New Milford has had many notable and useful citizens during her two centuries of existence, but she has had none as illustrious as Roger Sherman. We have with us to-day one of his descendants, Simeon E. Baldwin, LL. D., Ex-President of the American Bar Association, Ex-President of the American Historical Society, Ex-President of the International Law Association, and Chief Justice of Connecticut, who will now address you.

Chief Justice Baldwin then delivered the following address on "ROGER SHERMAN":

"The rarest and most ill-defined class of human beings is that of great men. Only those belong to it who have done a great work in a great way. The 'mute, inglorious Milton' is not to be reckoned among them. They number none, however great their natural gifts or acquired attainments, who have not made for themselves, by their own merits, a place in the history of their times. It is from their lives, indeed, that history gains its color and its inspiration.

"It was the good fortune of New Milford to be the home of such a man in the middle of her first century of existence.

"It was a hundred and sixty-four years ago, this very month that a tall and well-set young fellow of two and twenty ended in this town a toilsome journey, taken on foot from the neighborhood of Boston. He had come to make New Milford his home, bringing on his back the tools of his trade—that of a shoemaker—and with their aid he here gained for a year or two an honest livelihood.

"A shoemaker and the son of a shoemaker, he had, and felt he had, capabilities for a larger work. His mind was already

HONORABLE SIMEON E. BALDWIN
Chief Justice of the Supreme Court of Connecticut

set on that of a surveyor. For this, too, he fitted himself well; but there was that before him of which he did not think. He was to fill a long succession of official trusts, affecting all the Colonies and the States which succeeded them, to be bestowed upon him at a time of great events, and to be so well discharged as to make him one of the great figures of American history.

"When Connecticut, a few years ago, was called upon by the nation to choose the two of her sons whose statues should be set in the Capitol at Washington, there could be no question as to one. The land of steady habits must, at all events, be represented in that place by Jonathan Trumbull, the War Governor of the Revolution,—the Brother Jonathan who typified to the nation the rugged virtues and hard good sense of the New England character.

"The other statue also must belong to the same great era, the era which began with the struggle for independence, and closed with the attainment of settled constitutional government. Our heroes must be taken from that which above all others was our heroic age. Should we thus commemorate the impetuous gallantry of Putnam, the noble death of Hale, the courtly eloquence of Johnson, the judicial power of Ellsworth? All these were sons of Connecticut, born upon her soil. No. She chose one born and bred to manhood in another State; not trained at her college, nor at her schools; not at any schools. She sought to put the form and features of Roger Sherman into marble, to show to all time what qualities and achievements the people of Connecticut hold in most honor. This man, without eloquence, with no advantages of education, with no grace of manner, was her choice—taken from many, for solid qualities, not shining ones; for a life-long love of liberty, but only as it was regulated by law; for steadfast devotion to duty; for practical sagacity; for calm, and sound judgment in things both small and great. Such a character wears well. It is men of this stamp that have made Connecticut what she is.

"Roger Sherman was born to a great opportunity. So was every child born in the American colonies during the years between 1720 and 1760. Those colonies were then assuming proportions inconsistent with the long maintenance of British dominion over a territory so distant and a people so enterprising and intelligent. The day was soon to come when they would strike for liberty. Who were to be the leaders, then?

"Massachusetts was to furnish her full share, and two of them grew up, in neighboring towns, to begin life as apprentices and end it as statesmen.

"Franklin was already at work in a Boston printing office, when Sherman, in 1721, was born in Newton. Neither had any advantages of education. Franklin's schooling ended when he was about ten, and Sherman was apprenticed to a shoemaker and began to learn his trade at an age not much greater. He had hardly acquired it when his father, then living at Stoughton, Massachusetts, died, and he found, at the age of nineteen, that the main charge of a numerous family of younger brothers and sisters, as well as of his mother, must thenceforward rest upon his shoulders. Three years of struggle upon the small farm, which his father left, satisfied him that to support this load he must seek some more remunerative employment.

"An elder brother had previously removed to this town, then a frontier settlement. Connecticut was the West of that day to the towns of eastern Massachusetts. It was the place for more than century where many of the most active and enterprising sons of the older colony had gone to found new homes and breathe a freer air. Connecticut, it will be recollected, had preserved her charter and elected her own governors. Massachusetts, for half a century, had received hers from the crown.

"Sherman resolved to join his brother, and the whole family were united in New Milford in 1743. From the early years of his apprenticeship he had been in the habit, as he bent over his last, of keeping a book open on his bench, to the study of which he gave what moments he could occasionally snatch from his work. In this way, and in his hours of leisure, he had been able to pick up the elements of a good English education, and to make considerable attainments in mathematics and plane geometry. One object of his removal to Connecticut had been to put this knowledge to practical use by engaging in the business of a surveyor.

"Those were days when the quick division of land, from the great blocks included in colonial patents granted for the formation of a new township, into numerous small farms, called far more frequently than now for the services of men who could run a line with precision and describe it in the proper terms of art. Within two years from his arrival at New Milford, he had fitted himself to engage in this business, and received from the General Assembly the appointment of a Surveyor of Lands for the County of New Haven; for New Milford was then a part of that county, Litchfield County not having been created until 1751.

"This office of County Surveyor was a responsible one. Whoever held it took an oath, prescribed by statute, to discharge its duties 'without Favour or Respect to Persons,' and, if he had occasion to employ chainmen for his assistance, was to administer to each of them an oath, adjuring them 'by the ever living God' to keep and render a true account of whatever lines and measures they might take.*

"That there is an ever living God, who is the supreme authority on earth as in heaven, has always been the faith of Connecticut, and shines through all her statute books. From 1640 down to the present hour it has been part of the solemn ceremonial—solemn to those who stop to think of what it is and what it means—of admission to the privileges of a freeman or elector, that every man shall with uplifted hand swear that with God's help, whenever he shall be called to give his vote, he will give it as he shall judge will conduce to the best good of the commonwealth, without respect of persons or favor of any man. How many of us, on each election day, bethink ourselves of the high obligation to which we have thus pledged ourselves, and ask the help we have invoked to act our part as voters 'without respect of persons or favor of any man'?

"I doubt if Roger Sherman, as a County Surveyor, needed

* Conn. Stat., Revision of 1715, pp. 110, 234.

the weight of an official oath to bind him to his duty, but I doubt not that his sense of duty was bottomed on a sense of God, and that honesty and Christianity were to him, from boyhood on, one and inseparable.

"He had joined the Stoughton church a few weeks before he came of age. It was a time, in the year 1742, in which were gathered in the fruits of religious awakening in New England. Our churches had lapsed into formalism; and dogmatic belief had been accorded a prominence which threw Christian conduct into the background. Seventeen hundred forty-two was a marked year in the course of the returning tide towards better things.

"In 1749 Sherman used his mathematical attainments for a new purpose. He prepared an almanac for 1750, which was published in New York, and was the first of a series which he put out during a considerable period of years.

"By this time he had saved some money, and, in 1750, we find him putting part of his capital, in partnership with his elder brother, into a country store. This was a business in which he was interested first at New Milford, and then at New Haven, with a branch at Wallingford, for more than twenty years.

"The country store then, as now in the more thinly settled communities, was in miniature the department store of our modern cities. There were few of them, and their customers came from a wide circuit of country. The trade was largely one of barter. The farmer's wife drove in with her cheese and butter, and might go back with stuff for a dress, a box of needles, a new coffee-pot, a bottle of salts, a loaf of sugar, a quintal of codfish, and perhaps a volume of sermons. The store was not daily visited by drummers. The proprietor went himself every few months to Boston or Newport, New York or Philadelphia, to replenish his stock, and with every such journey found his mental horizon broadened, and felt better acquainted with the great world of men and things that lay beyond the limits of his own neighborhood.

"Sherman, from the first, made the most of these glimpses

of a larger life. If he rode down to New Haven to buy West India molasses, he would visit the college to ask President Clap's opinion about the probable course of an expected comet.* If he went to New York to correct the proofs of his almanac, he would take the opportunity to find a publisher for some pamphlet he had written on the financial errors in the legislation of the day.

"Sherman, by this time, had acquired the faculty, rarer, perhaps, then than now, of expressing his thoughts in writing, in a fashion that was simple, clear, and straightforward. An artificial, overwrought, and overladen style of composition, if not the prevailing one, was certainly not uncommon among Americans during the middle of the eighteenth century. He wrote, as Franklin did, in the plain language of familiar conversation, with no straining after effect. I do not mean that he wrote as well as Franklin. There was a long, long interval between them; but they were of the same school. Both were men who thought more of what they had to say than of how they said it; of communicating facts or ideas, rather than of seeking to make them attractive by ornament.

"Sherman's reading was of a kind that both strengthened and disciplined the mind. The first President Dwight, in summing up his character, emphasized 'his attachment to books of real use,' adding that he 'was, what very few men unacquainted with the learned languages are, accurately skilled in the grammar of his own language.'†

"It is probable, however, that in paying this tribute to an old friend who had passed away, President Dwight had in mind Sherman's style of written composition, rather than his ordinary manner of speech. It is seldom that one born to poverty and denied the common advantages of education, escapes a certain rusticity, to say the least, not only in his choice of words in conversation, but in their arrangement and pronunciation.

"A franker, and I dare say juster, portrait of the man as he appeared in public discussions and debate is given in a series

* Boutell's Life of Roger Sherman, 32.
† Dwight's Travels, IV, 299.

of rough notes of the doings of the Convention of 1787 which framed our national Constitution, made by one of the Southern delegates, William Pierce of Georgia.

"'Mr. Sherman,' he writes, 'exhibits the oddest shaped character I ever remember to have met with. He is awkward, un-meaning, and unaccountably strange in his manner. But in his train of thinking there is something regular, deep, and comprehensive; yet the oddity of his address, the vulgarisms that accompany his public speaking, and that strange New England cant which runs through his public as well as his private speaking make everything that is connected with him grotesque and laughable;—and yet he deserves infinite praise, —no Man has a better Heart or a clearer Head. If he cannot embellish he can furnish thoughts that are wise and useful. He is an able politician, and extremely artful in accomplishing any particular object; it is remarked that he seldom fails. I am told he sits on the Bench in Connecticut, and is very correct in the discharge of his Judicial functions. In the early part of his life he was a Shoe-maker; but, despising the lowness of his condition, he turned Almanack maker, and so progressed upwards to a Judge. He has been several years a Member of Congress, and discharged the duties of his Office with honor and credit to himself, and advantage to the State he represented. He is about 60.'

"Silas Deane, his colleague in the Continental Congress, in a frank letter to his wife, thus paints Sherman, as he appeared at a New York dinner party:

"'Mr. Sherman is clever in private, but I will only say he is as badly calculated to appear in such a Company as a chestnut-burr is for an eye-stone. He occasioned some shrewd countenances among the company, and not a few oaths, by the odd questions he asked, and the very odd and countrified cadence with which he speaks; but he was, and did, as well as I expected.' *

"In the same letter Deane shows his vexation at Sherman's views regarding traveling on Sunday:

"'Mr. Sherman (would to Heaven he were well at New

---

* Collections, Connecticut Historical Society, II, 145.

Haven,) is against our sending our carriages over the ferry this evening, because it is Sunday; so we shall have a scorching sun to drive forty miles in, to-morrow. I wish I could send you his picture, and make it speak, and in the background paint the observations made on him here. But enough of this at present. I will have him drawn in Philadelphia, if it can be done at any reasonable rate.' *

"To judge these criticisms fairly we must remember that Deane was a man of fashion and of the world, while Sherman was neither. A plain country lad, a hardworking journeyman at his trade, a busy surveyor, a sagacious selectman, a shrewd store-keeper, a hard-headed lawyer, an industrious judge, he had qualities not of a kind that shine in polite society, but of a kind nevertheless that count in life, in every position which a man may be called to fill. He would have made a better figure with better manners. But a rusticity that would have ruined the advance of most men was everywhere tolerated in Sherman, because there was felt everywhere an admiration for his mind and heart,—his solid sense, wise forecast, and practical wisdom.

"While living in this town, Sherman was asked one day by a neighbor, the next time he went to the county seat, to retain counsel for him to bring a petition to court in a matter connected with the settlement of an estate. He noted down the facts which he thought it would be necessary to state in the papers prepared for such a proceeding, and the lawyer whom he consulted was so much impressed with the clearness and precision of the memorandum that he strongly advised him to adopt the legal profession.

"There were then no American, and, indeed, no English law schools. An education for the bar was commonly gained by studying the works of some of the English judges of former generations, under the advice of a local practitioner, but with little other assistance from him. The system of justice administered in Connecticut was rough and unhewn, and not a few of the judges of the highest courts had never followed the profession of the law.

"Sherman began to read law, in consequence of the inci-

* Collections, Connecticut Historical Society, II, 146.

dent to which I have alluded, when he was about thirty years of age, and was admitted to the bar in Litchfield County in 1754. There were then few lawyers in the colony who gained the whole of their livelihood from their profession. Many were also farmers. Sherman retained his interest in the New Milford store.

"Meanwhile he had been sent to the General Assembly, and made first a justice of the peace, and then a side judge of the County Court.

"The record of one of the early justice suits tried before him well illustrates the difference in political ideas between those times and ours. It shows the conviction and fine of one of his fellow-townsmen for a violation of the Colony statute in not attending public worship in any congregation allowed by law on January 29, 1758, nor on any Sunday in the month next preceding.

"'Squire' Sherman, as he was now called, brought to his new profession the strong common sense and good business judgment which had served to advance him in his previous employments, and which, if added to sound learning, will always assure success at the bar.

"The late President Porter, who, in early life, was settled as a minister at New Milford, once told me of a story which he heard here of some wise words uttered by Sherman at this period in his history. 'Squire Sherman,' said one of his neighbors to him, one day, 'tell me, are most controversies that come before Judges in lawsuits decided justly or unjustly?' 'Sir,' was the reply, 'it's not the point whether they are decided justly or unjustly: they are decided, and made an end of.' And in truth it is perhaps the best office of courts of justice that, however often they may err in their processes, they certainly bring every human controversy that is within their reach to a final stop. The conclusion may be right or wrong; but a conclusion it is.

"Sherman was a deacon of the New Milford Church, the clerk and treasurer of the society, and one of the school committee. At the age of forty, he removed to New Haven, and connected himself with the White Haven Church, one of the two original bodies out of which grew the United Society and the United Church. Here again the records show his faithful work on committees and as collector of the rates imposed by the society.

"Five years later he was appointed a Judge of the Superior Court, a position which he continued to hold for nearly a quarter of a century.

"The British legislation culminating in the Stamp Act had now begun to arouse the spirit of independence in the American colonies. Sherman was one of those who took the most advanced ground. He maintained that Parliament had no jurisdiction over them whatever.

"Connecticut sent him as one of her delegates to the first Continental Congress, in 1774, and there he maintained this doctrine with all his power. John Adams reports him as declaring upon the floor that there was no legislative power superior to the Colonial Assemblies, and that Americans had adopted the common law of England, not as the common law, but as the highest reason.

"It was his thorough-going republicanism, indeed, which had carried him into public life, and put him in a leading place among the legislators of his State. He had been first elected to the Governor's Council or upper house of the General Assembly in 1766. The Stamp Act had brought the 'Sons of Liberty' into existence. They had forced, under threat of death, Jared Ingersoll, who, under the advice of Franklin had accepted the position of stampmaster for Connecticut, to resign the office. Governor Fitch, though with reluctance, had taken the official oath which the obnoxious Act required. It cost him his place, William Pitkin being elected his successor a year later. With him went out of office four of his Council who sympathized with his deference to parliamentary authority; dropped by the people to make room for others who were regarded as more fully Americans in spirit and doctrine.

"No one was then eligible for a seat on the Council-board who had not been officially nominated in the previous year.

Twenty nominations were annually made for the twelve places, and the election was so managed that the twelve in office always headed the list and were voted on first. A majority was not required for an election. To be once nominated for the upper house was in this way a substantial assurance of an ultimate election, and to be once elected was a substantial assurance of an annual re-election for life.

"Sherman, in 1766, had been on the waiting list for five years. A political whirlwind, unexampled in our Colonial annals, then made five vacancies, and death a sixth. He went in with five other new men, and remained a member until after the close of the Revolution.

"Religion in those days, so far as form at least was concerned, was a part of politics. There was a religious establishment in Connecticut. It put the church beside the schoolhouse on the village green. It made Church and State largely one.

"Sherman was not wiser than his generation in regard to matters of religion. His reading had been mainly in English history and law; but the subject next most interesting to him was theology. He accepted Calvinism. He believed in the Puritans. He distrusted and feared the Church of England. It was the day when so tolerant and fair-minded a man as President Stiles could record as among the fourteen trials and difficulties of this life: 'Concern for the Congregational churches, & prevalence of Episcopacy & Wickedness.' *

"When, therefore, about the middle of the eighteenth century, the Episcopalians, who were especially strong in Connecticut, began to push for the appointment of one or more American bishops, it is not surprising that Sherman's voice was raised in opposition.

"A long letter on this subject, written in 1768, which, it is believed, came from his pen, is among the files of the New Haven East Association, to which his church belonged. In this it is urged that if Parliament provides for American bishops, they might bring here all the functions and authority

*Stiles, Literary Diary, I, 16, July 8, 1769.

of those of England, and hold ecclesiastical courts like those of Laud, from which our fathers fled into the wilderness.

"There was this piece of solid ground under Sherman's argument. Grant the power of Parliament to establish an American episcopate, and a new point was made in favor of the general right of Parliament to legislate as to all American affairs. This consideration, no doubt, greatly influenced his course; and it was sufficient to defeat the consecration of any bishop for America until that of Dr. Seabury, which followed closely after the Revolution.

"The Wyoming controversy between Connecticut and Pennsylvania was one in which Sherman took an active part.

"Our charter bounded us 'on the North by the line of the Massachusetts Plantation; and on the South by the Sea; and in Longitude as the Line of the Massachusetts Colony, running from East to West, *That is to say*, From the said Narragansett Bay on the East to the South Sea on the West part, with the Islands thereto Adjoining.' This gave us a paper title to a swath of North America sixty miles wide, at least, running from Rhode Island to the Pacific, and taking in what are now the sites of Wilkesbarre, Cleveland, Chicago, and Omaha. Our people, as early as 1762, began to make settlements in that part of it in western Pennsylvania known as the Wyoming Valley. The General Assembly made it a county in 1776, styling it Westmoreland County, and it furnished the Twenty-fourth Connecticut Regiment in the Continental Army.

"Sherman was one of a committee appointed by the legislature in 1774 to report upon measures to support the title of the Wyoming settlers, which Pennsylvania now disputed, under a later and conflicting grant from the Crown. Energetic measures were recommended and adopted, and, knowing the power of the newspapers, Sherman shortly afterwards followed up the report by a clear and full statement of the position of Connecticut, in a letter to the Connecticut *Journal* of New Haven. Public sentiment, here, was much divided. There were many who thought that such an 'expansion' threatened the safety of our liberties. Sherman proposed that the colony should secure a determination of its bounds from the King in Council. Such a law suit, said those who were for letting Wyoming go, would be slow and costly; and, even if we should win it, what then? A defeat, Mr. Ingersoll had declared in another newspaper article, 'would be very detrimental, but a victory must be absolute ruin.' 'But,' replied Sherman, ' he gives no reason for his opinion. And can his bare assertion make the people of this colony, who are a company of farmers, believe that to be quieted in their claim to a large tract of valuable land would ruin them?'

"The Revolution transferred the judicial decision of this controversy from the King in Council to the Congress of the United States. A Court of Commissioners was organized to try the issue, and, in 1782, judgment was rendered against us.

"The Commissioners had prudently determined, before hearing the case, to give no reasons for their decision, whatever it might be. That they were not of the strongest may be inferred from the fact that four years later Congress accepted from Connecticut a relinquishment of the rest of her Western title, with an express reservation of a large strip of northern Ohio. This is still known as the Western Reserve. We soon sold it, and the proceeds constituted our State School fund of $2,000,000.

"The services rendered by Sherman to the United States outshine those which he rendered to Connecticut; but it is only because the field was larger, and the circumstances more striking.

"Three are commemorated upon a mural tablet erected to his memory in the church of which he was a member in New Haven. This states that he was 'one of the committee which drew the Declaration of Independence, of that which reported the Articles of Confederation, of the Convention that framed the national Constitution, and a Signer of these three Charters of American liberty.'

"To no other man came the good fortune to set his hand to these three great State papers. One marked the birth of the nation. The next was its first attempt to agree on a constitution of government—a necessary compromise, and temporary as compromises always are. The last was what has made the United States the greatest, richest, freest country that the sun shines upon to-day; and it was in that, that the work of Sherman told most.

"He was among the leading members of the Convention from whose hands it came. Connecticut was wise enough to send to it her strongest men. Our delegates were William Samuel Johnson, Oliver Ellsworth, and Roger Sherman.

"Johnson was the representative in his generation of the family in the State most distinguished for public services and personal attainments. He had ably represented our interests abroad, in important matters, and twenty years before had received the degree of Doctor of Civil Law from Oxford University. The Convention made him head of the committee to put the measures which it adopted in proper form and style. Oliver Ellsworth, who had been the foremost lawyer at our bar, was then an associate of Sherman on the bench of the Supreme Court, and was soon to be Chief Justice of the United States. But Sherman had a truer sense than either of his colleagues of what must be the nature and soul of the new government. He felt that it must stand upon a double foundation, that of the States, acting each for itself, and that of the people of all the States, acting for all together.*

"He felt, too, that it must stand for human liberty.

"Our State was then a slave-holding State, but he was one of those who were determined that the word *slave* should not stain the pages of the Constitution of the United States. Later, when he was a member of the first Congress, one of the representatives from Virginia (for Virginia statesmen were then looking to the gradual abolition of slavery) proposed to put into the tariff act a duty of ten dollars on each slave imported. Sherman opposed it. He could not, he said, reconcile himself to the insertion of human beings as an article of duty, among goods, wares, and merchandise; and, when it was replied that the doctrine of the Declaration of Independence required the endeavor to wipe off the stigma of slavery from the American

* Elliot's Debates, 178.

government, his reply was that the principles of the motion and the principles of the bill were inconsistent: the principle of the bill was to raise revenue, and the principle of the motion was to correct a moral evil. These few and well put words illustrate that strong sense of proportion and relation which gave Sherman such weight in every deliberative assembly.

"In the Convention which framed the Constitution, he was the author of the compromise by which, in Congress, the Senate represents the States and the House, the people.

"Afterwards, when Congress was engaged in formulating the first ten amendments of the Constitution, which serve as a bill of rights for the people and for the States, it was he who gave the final shape to the last and most important.

"This (originally the Twelfth, for Congress proposed twelve of which ten only were ratified by the States), as reported by the committee, read thus: 'The powers not delegated to the United States by the Constitution, nor prohibited by it to the States, are reserved to the States respectively.' Sherman moved, and the House voted to add the words, 'or to the people.'

"He knew, as a lawyer, that when anything is reserved in a grant it is reserved by and for the maker of the grant. Who made this grant? From what authority did the Constitution proceed? Was it from the States, and were the powers reserved to be reserved to them and each of them? This was said, or implied, in the original draft of the amendment. Sherman's addition recognized the principle, afterwards affirmed by Chief Justice Marshall, that the people also had a share in ordaining this Constitution for themselves and their posterity.

"It is also worthy of remark, that he was careful to follow the phrase used in the preceding amendment (the Ninth) in which it is declared that the enumeration in the Constitution of certain rights shall not be construed to deny or disparage others retained by the people. What people is thus meant? Is it the people of each State, regarded state-wise, or the whole people of the United States regarded nation-wise? That was a question on which public opinion had been divided, and which it remained for the Civil War to settle by force of arms.

"Sherman did not seek to precipitate this issue. The framers of the Constitution of the Southern Confederacy met the same question and decided it. By the article of that document (the Sixth) which corresponds to the Tenth Amendment to the Constitution of the United States, the powers not delegated to the Confederate States were 'reserved to the States respectively, or to the people thereof.'* Here is the doctrine of States Rights, clear and unmistakable. It is not improbable that Sherman would have preferred the use of similar language by the First Congress, in drafting the Tenth Amendment. The interest of his State lay or seemed to lie in that direction. But he had been willing, as a political necessity, to build the Constitution on pillars of compromise, and this was one of them. He was content to use words of comprehension, which the adherents of each school of American politics could read in their own sense, and to leave it to another generation to determine which should prevail.

"Another service of importance rendered by Sherman in the First Congress was to bring the cent into actual use in the financial system of the United States.

"The revenue measure for the collection by the United States of customs duties on imported goods, which Congress had urged upon the States in 1783 as an amendment to the Articles of Confederation, had stated the proposed duties in dollars and nineties of a dollar. Thus, on rum of Jamaica proof, the rate fixed was four nineties of a dollar, and upon all other spirituous liquors three nineties.† This mode of reckoning fractions of a dollar continued to be that pursued in government accounts down to the close of the Confederation.‡ In 1786, Congress had, indeed, provided for the coinage of both cents and half-cents.¶ The next year a contract was made with James Jarvis of New Haven to strike off three

* Davis, The Rise and Fall of the Confederate Government, I, 672.
† Journ. of Congress, XIII, 155.
‡ Id., XIII, 122, 161, 162, 165.
¶ Id., XII, 179, 180, 252.

hundred tons of these coins.* This contract was fulfilled at least in part, and many of the cents struck under it are to be found in the cabinets of collectors. They bear the legend *Fugio*, and the date 1787. The work was done at New Haven; Connecticut being then the great copper-producing State.

"It is probable, however, that these New Haven cents had a very limited circulation. Hildreth says that but a few tons were issued, and it is certain that in New York the old plan of reckoning by ninetieths of dollars remained in use for several years more.

"In 1789 Madison reported a tariff bill to the First Congress under our present Constitution. The rates of duty were left blank. Sherman, who had been chairman of a committee appointed by the General Assembly of Connecticut to supervise the coinage of copper coins under State authority,† took an early opportunity to propose that in filling the blanks that Madison had left, they should begin with rum, and tax it fifteen cents a gallon. He preferred, he said, to use the term cent, for its convenience, as ten made a dime, and ten dimes, a dollar.‡ This explanation was evidently necessary to make the House understand what a cent was. They approved his suggestion, and the bill when passed stated all duties in dollars and cents. It was thus that the inconvenient and senseless division of the dollar into ninetieths never afterwards obtained recognition on the statute books of the United States.

"At the close of the Revolution Connecticut found herself a tributary State to her neighbors on each side. Her citizens were buying heavily from New York, Newport, and Boston importers, and thus paying duties for the benefit of New York, Rhode Island, and Massachusetts. Connecticut consumed, according to an estimate by Chief Justice Ellsworth, as late as 1787, about a third of all the goods entered at the New York custom house, and paid in that way for New York customs something like twenty thousand pounds a year¶—a vast sum for those early days.

* Journal of Congress, XII, 54.
† Papers of the New Haven Colony Historical Society, I, 177.
‡ Annals of Congress, I, 125.   ¶ Elliot's Debates, II, 189.

"It was thought that if New Haven were made a free port, and special encouragement offered to merchants to settle there in business, we might be able to import what we wanted for ourselves.

"Our first city charter was thereupon issued, and New Haven became a city in 1784, with all the privileges of a free port for seven years. Her city seal devised by President Stiles still bears the legend, *Mare liberum*.

"Roger Sherman was elected its first mayor. The charter made the term of office during good behavior, and he remained the mayor until his death.

"Sherman was fond of studying problems of controversial theology. The first President Dwight, in summing up his character, described him as a 'profound logician, statesman, lawyer, and theologian.' *

"Religion is the philosophy of life, and theology is, or ought to be, the philosophy of religion. No thoughtful man can avoid occasional reflection on these high themes. It is our good fortune to study them in the light of sciences unknown to him. Put any doctrinal discussion of the eighteenth century by the side of those of our day, directed and controlled as ours must be by the truths of biology, the discoveries of archæologists, and the principles of evolution, and the older statements seem unreal and unsubstantial.

"Sherman's thought, however, in theology, as in everything else, was clear and plain. In 1789, he published, in New Haven, a sermon of his own composition. A year later he exchanged several long letters with Rev. Dr. Samuel Hopkins of Newport, in which he attacked that divine's peculiar doctrine that a man ought to be willing to suffer eternal damnation, if need be, for the glory of God. Calvin was quoted as an authority for this, by the advocates of 'Hopkinsianism.' 'Calvinists,' replied Sherman, 'do not found their faith on the authority of his opinions: that would be to entertain an opinion contrary to his, viz., that the word of God is the only rule of faith in matters of religion.'

"In 1765 Sherman accepted the position of Treasurer of

* Travels, IV, 299.

Yale College, filling it until 1776, when the cause of American independence demanded all his energies. He came to this office during the last years of President Clap's administration, and held it through most of the long *interregnum* during which Professor Daggett was acting President. It was, as I have said, a dark time for the College; a day of small things. Daggett and Sherman were for some years the only permanent officers. The means of the institution were slender, and the utmost economy was necessary to secure its maintenance. Sherman's prudence and business judgment were here of substantial service, though the struggle of the College then was more to live than to grow.

"He was also in a position to befriend it, where it then much needed support, before the Legislature. There was a long and strong effort during the last half of the eighteenth century to bring it under State control. Here, writes President Stiles in his Literary Diary, he was 'ever a friend to its interests, and to its being and continuing in the hands of the clergy, whom he judged the most proper to have the superintendency of a *religious*, as well as a *scientific*, college.' *

"In 1792, while he was a Senator in Congress (to which position he had been elected the year before), that controversy came to a peaceful close. The General Assembly offered the College a grant of what was estimated to be worth about thirty thousand dollars, provided it would admit the Governor and Lieutenant Governor and the six senior assistants as, for all time, Fellows of the Corporation. This left the clergy still in full control, for they held twelve seats, and could dictate the election of the President to occupy another. Nevertheless, the clerical Fellows were divided in opinion, as to the policy of agreeing to this friendly overture. One of them, Rev. Nathaniel Taylor of this town, was especially reluctant to take this step. He consulted Sherman, whose pastor he had formerly been, and by his advice yielded to the rest, and so made the vote of acceptance an unanimous one.†

"This was almost Sherman's last service to Yale. In the

---
* Lit. Diary,I II,500.
† Stile's Diary, III, 460.

next year, under date of July 23, in Stiles' Diary, we find this entry:

"'About VII^h, or about sunsetting, a bright Luminary set in New Haven: the Hon. Roger Sherman, Esqr. died æt. 72¼, mayor of the city & Senator in Congress.' *

"He died at his residence on Chapel Street, which is still standing opposite Vanderbilt Hall, and, on July 25, his funeral was attended from the North (now the United) Church. President Stiles was one of the officiating clergyman, and the students and tutors of the college headed the procession to the grave.† His pastor, the Rev. Dr. Jonathan Edwards, preached the funeral sermon. Edwards was a metaphysical theologian. One of the audience wrote of this sermon, a few days later, to a friend in a neighboring town: 'To do the Doctor justice he preached better than I expected to hear him, and seemed to keep almost free from *moral obligation, cause and effect, etc.*'‡

"The discourse is in print, and a few of the personal touches in it may give a clearer idea of how Sherman appeared to his friends and fellow-townsmen at home.

"'I need not inform you,' said Dr. Edwards, 'that his person was tall, unusually erect and well proportioned, and his countenance agreeable and manly. . . . As he was a professor of religion, so he was not ashamed to befriend it, to appear openly on the Lord's side, or to avow and defend the peculiar doctrines of grace. . . . In private life, though he was naturally reserved and of few words, yet in conversation on matters of importance, he was free and communicative.'

"The theology of the day appeared in the concluding observations, in which the preacher referred to the loss they had sustained by this bereavement as a token of 'divine displeasure.'

"President Stiles, during the same week, records his estimate of Sherman in these terms:

"'He was formed for *Think^g* & *Acting, but Law & Politics* were peculiarly adapted to his Genius. He was an admirer

* Lit. Diary, III, 499.   † *Ibid.*, 500.   ‡ Boutell; Life, 283.

of Vattells Laws of Nature & Nations. . . . He was exemplary for Piety & serious Religion, was a good Divine; once printed a well & judiciously written Sermon of his own Composition, tho' never preached. He was far from all Enthusiasm. He was calm sedate & ever discerning & judicious. He went thro' all the Grades of public Life, & grew in them all & filled every Office with Propriety, Ability, & tho' not with showy Brilliancy, yet with that Dignity which arises from doing every Thing perfectly right. In no part of his Employments has he displayed his intrinsic Merit and acquired that Glory, so much as in Congress. He there became almost oracular for the deep Sagacity, Wisdom & Weight of his Counsels. Tho' of no Elocution, he was respected & listened to with great Attention; and was successful in carrying the Points he laboured. He was an extraord' Man—a venerable uncorrupted Patriot!' *

"Many years later Sherman's character was thus sketched by the discriminating hand of Professor James L. Kingsley:

"'No man in Connecticut ever enjoyed the confidence of the people of the State more entirely, or for a longer period, than Roger Sherman. Where he doubted, who ventured to be positive? Where he saw his way clear, who hesitated to follow? In the whole course of his public life Roger Sherman never failed to leave in those with whom he had intercourse an impression of deep sagacity, and stern integrity; and he bequeathed, as a public man, to those who should come after him, the character of a great, and what is much more rare, of an honest, politician.' †

"Sherman's English ancestors were of the yeoman class. He was born in the ranks of what, for want of a better name, is called the 'common people.' He knew their virtues, but he knew their failings, too. It may fairly be said that, when he came to be entrusted with high public station, the people had more confidence in Sherman than Sherman had in them.

"This, no doubt, was an esoteric doctrine to be wisely kept

* Literary Diary, III, 500. † Historical Discourse, 1838, 69.

for those who had ears to hear. He stated it without reserve in the Convention which framed the Constitution of the United States. Governor Randolph of Virginia had proposed—what is now urged by many as a needed constitutional change—that the senators from each State should be elected by popular vote. Sherman opposed it, 'insisting,' as Mr. Madison reports him, 'that it ought to be by the State legislatures. The people, he said, immediately, should have as little to do as may be about the government. They want information, and are constantly liable to be misled.'*

"His views prevailed, and, if we may judge from the experience thus far of his own State, he was probably right in believing that it was safer to confide in the wisdom of the General Assembly than in a popular vote. He was speaking as the representative of one of the smaller States, of territorial limits such as to make it reasonably certain that every leading man among her citizens would be known to most of the leading members of her Legislature. The inhabitants of our towns, again, are quite generally personally acquainted with those whom they send to represent them at Hartford; and if these men betray their trust, they are called to a prompt account at home, before the bar of public opinion.

"It is to be remembered, of course, that Sherman's unwillingness to trust the people with the election of a Senator by a direct vote was not inconsistent with his confidence in their judgment on general questions of public policy or moral right. That confidence he always maintained.

"Sherman was an effective speaker, but it was not because he had in him anything of an orator.† His power in debate lay in his habit of never taking the floor unless he had something new and important to suggest,‡ and in stopping as soon as he had said it. It lay also in what Cicero said was the first qualification of the successful orator—being a good man. People believed him, because they believed in him.

"Justice was his polar star. He believed that it was the true mainspring of all political action on the part of the mass

* V Elliot's Debates, 135.   † 3 Am. Hist. Review, 326.
‡ Sanderson's Lives of the Signers, III, 297.

of the people. 'Popular opinion,' he said on the floor of the First Congress, 'is founded in justice, and the only way to know if the popular opinion is in favor of a measure is to examine whether it is just and right in itself.'

"'The popularity that follows, not that which is run after,' was what he thought should be the wish of the legislator.

"So lived, and so, in a green old age, still in high public station and still useful in it, passed away the man to whose commemoration this hour has been devoted.

"The Church no longer thinks a peaceful end of a well-spent life is to be taken as a token of the divine displeasure. It no longer discusses the theological opinions that were of such absorbing interest in Sherman's age. He belonged to the eighteenth and we are drinking in the inspiration of the twentieth century.

"But Sherman's religion is still our religion. He stood for justice, and truth: he stood for duty, quietly, daily, untiringly done, in whatever station, high or low, God may see fit to place us. He was a good shoemaker, and he was a good Senator.

"His example will never die out of American memory, because it appeals to every man in every walk of life, and shows how character, perseverance, industry, joined to common sense, under our system of government, put within the reach of their possessor whatever the times may have to give of opportunity for doing public service and winning public esteem.

"There are five names in the history of the United States that seem to me to stand alone. In the view of most Americans, I think, Washington, Franklin, Jefferson, John Adams, and Hamilton were above all others the founders of the Republic.

"In his 'Studies in History and Jurisprudence,'* James Bryce marshals in order the leaders in American affairs at the time of the adoption of our Constitution. Five, he says, belong to the history of the world: Washington, Franklin, Hamilton, Jefferson, and Marshall; 'and in the second rank are to be named John Adams, Madison, Jay, Patrick Henry,

* P. 306.

HONORABLE DANIEL DAVENPORT
of Bridgeport, Conn.

EGBERT MARSH
Founder of the Memorial Library

Gouverneur Morris, Roger Sherman, James Wilson, and Albert Gallatin.'

"John Marshall seems to me not so much a founder as a re-founder of the Constitution, and I should be unwilling to agree with Mr. Bryce in giving him a place which appears with greater right to belong to the successor of Washington in the presidential chair. So, in arranging the statesmen of the second order, it may be doubted if Gallatin does not more properly belong to a later generation. But that in that class is Roger Sherman, rather than Trumbull, rather than Ellsworth, rather than Johnson, rather than any other son of Connecticut, or, after John Adams, of New England, few will question who have closely studied the Journals of the Continental Congress, and the debates in the Convention of 1787, out of which our Constitution sprang."

The last speaker, Hon. Daniel Davenport of Bridgeport, was introduced as a descendant of John Davenport, the leader of the first group of colonists to settle the New Haven Colony, and the first pastor of the first church in New Haven. Mr. Davenport spoke as follows:

"The settlement of New Milford began in 1707, exactly a century after that of Jamestown, Va. At that time, although Milford and Stratford at the mouth of the Housatonic had been settled almost seventy years, and the river afforded a convenient highway into the interior, for much of the distance, this place, only thirty miles from the north shore of Long Island Sound, was still beyond the extreme northwestern frontier of New England, and indeed of English North America.

"The inhabitants of Connecticut then numbered about fifteen thousand, settled in thirty towns, mostly along the shore of Long Island Sound, and upon the banks of the Connecticut and Thames rivers. During the thirty years next before, a few families from Norwalk had settled at Danbury, from Stratford at Woodbury, from Milford at Derby, and from Farmington at Waterbury. With these exceptions, hardly more than pin points upon the map, and a few settlements about Albany, N. Y., the whole of western and northwestern Connecticut and of western Massachusetts and northern New York was a savage wilderness, covered with dense forests, and affording almost perfect concealment for the operations of savage warfare.

"Though the northwestern portion of Connecticut was then a most formidable and inhospitable wilderness, strenuous efforts were already being put forth by the Colony to encourage its settlement. For, strange as it seems to us now, at that time, owing to imperfect modes of cultivation and the difficulty of subduing the wilderness, the settled portions of the Commonwealth had begun to feel overpopulated. Twenty-five years before, the Secretary of the Colony had reported to the Home Government, that 'in this mountainous, rocky, and swampy province' most of the arable land was taken up, and the remainder was hardly worth tillage.

"This need of more land, and the protection from invasion which the settlement of this section would afford the communities near the coast, and the innate love of adventure and desire to subdue the wilderness, which have characterized the American people from the beginning, were the impelling causes which led to the planting of New Milford.

"So pressing did this movement become that, though what is now Litchfield County was then as remote and inaccessible to the rest of the Colony as were Indiana and Illinois to our fathers in the middle of the last century, within forty-five years after the first settler had built his log cabin and lighted his fire here twelve towns had been settled and the county organized with a population of more than ten thousand.

"In order that we may appreciate, somewhat, the broader political conditions under which the first settlers took up their abode here, which largely engrossed their thoughts and vitally affected them and their children for two generations, it is necessary, before taking up the narrative of their actual settlement here, to advert briefly to the state of affairs at that time in England, and on the continent of Europe, and in the English, French, and Spanish Colonies of North America.

"By 1707 it had become apparent to the people of Connecticut that, soon or late, they must fight for the very existence of their chartered privileges and natural rights, not alone the British Crown, but the English people. The disposition of the people of England to reap where they had not sown had become very clear. In April, 1701, Connecticut was named in the bill then introduced in Parliament to abrogate all American charters. She resisted with all her might through her agent, but it passed the second reading, and would have become a law but for the breaking out of the French War. Its principle was supported by the mercantile interests and the great men of England. Then for the first time the people of Connecticut fully realized that their foes were to be, not the exiled house of Stuart, but the English people themselves, and that, though they changed their dynasties, they did not change their own nature.

"In 1707 the principal kingdoms of Europe and their colonies were ablaze with war. Anne was Queen of England. In that very year she attached her signature to that long projected and most important constitutional arrangement, the Act of Union between England and Scotland, which made them one kingdom, the crown of which, by the Act of Settlement passed a few years before, had been forever vested in the person and heirs of Sophia, the electress of Hanover, the present reigning dynasty. Anne's accession to the throne in 1702 had been followed by the acknowledgment, by Louis XIV., of the son of James II., the deposed and fugitive king of England and the determined foe of the rights of the Colonists, as the rightful king, although in the Treaty of Ryswick, in 1697, he had solemnly stipulated to the contrary. This act of perfidy roused the English to fury. The primary cause of the war, then raging, was the acceptance by Louis of the crown of Spain for his grandson Philip despite a previous formal renunciation. But the immediate occasion was his espousal of the cause of the son of James II. as pretender to the British throne, which enabled the English Government to form a great European alliance to wrest Spain from Philip and prevent Louis from becoming the absolute master of Europe.

The year before, 1706, had witnessed the humbling of the

pride and ambition of Louis by the defeat of his armies at Ramillies by the Duke of Marlborough, in Piedmont by Prince Eugene, and in Spain by Lord Galway. Charles XII. of Sweden had advanced to Dresden in Saxony, an English and Portuguese army had occupied Madrid, and an attack of the combined fleets of Spain and France upon Charleston, S. C., then claimed by Spain as a part of Florida, had been repulsed by the vigor and martial skill of the Colonial authorities.

"At that time the valley of the St. Lawrence was occupied by about fifty thousand French settlers, imbued with bitter hostility towards the settlers in New England and New York. Already the vast design of La Salle to acquire for the King of France the whole interior of the continent seemed to have been accomplished. While as yet the English were struggling to secure a foothold upon the Atlantic seaboard, the French had explored the Mississippi and its tributaries to its mouth; and the whole vast region drained by them, between the Alleghanies and the Rockies, had been taken possession of by the French under the name of Louisiana; and a chain of military and trading posts from New Orleans to the St. Lawrence, admirably chosen for the purpose, had been established to hold it; and another chain was already planned to extend southward along the west side of the Alleghanies, to forever keep out the English. The French had been for fifty years hounding on the numerous tribes of Canada and northern New England to attack and exterminate the settlers of New England. The conquest of Canada by the English was, therefore, an object of the greatest political importance, and necessary for the peace and safety of the Colonists, and their future growth, and it continued to engross the efforts and exhaust the means of the Colonists, until their purpose was finally accomplished in 1763.

"The people who settled here were entirely familiar with the hardships, dangers, and horrors of Indian warfare to which they were liable in taking up their abode on this frontier. The horrible incidents which attended the massacre of the inhabitants of Schenectady, in 1690, seventeen years before, during the previous war, and of the inhabitants of Deerfield, Mass., and other places in 1704, during the war still raging, were household words throughout Connecticut, and had left an abiding imprint in the minds of the people on the border. Though the Indians, right about them here, seem to have been few in number and comparatively harmless, they knew from their own and their fathers' experiences that their position was one of extreme danger, and that at all times their scanty and hard won possessions and their lives were liable to instant destruction from unheralded irruptions by the more distant Indian tribes of the North and Northwest, urged on by their French instigators and allies. For the experiences of the last seventy years, from the time of the Pequot War, and during the subsequent troubles with the tribes in southwestern Connecticut, and on Long Island, and during King Philip's War, had fully taught them the craft, treachery, and pitiless cruelty of the savages, as well as their capacity for extensive combination among the widely separated tribes.

"When Major de Rouville, in 1704, with his band of civilized and uncivilized savages, committed the atrocities at Deerfield, Mass., the suspicions of the Colonists that the French had instigated the former Indian outrages became a certainty, for in this instance they openly shared in them.

"Their object was, as I have said, to drive the English colonists from North America, and substitute in their place their own colonial system. For this purpose they fitted out hundreds of parties of savages to proceed to other portions of the English settlements, shoot down the settlers when at work at their crops, seize their wives and children, load them with packs of plunder from their own homes, and drive them before them into the wilderness. When no longer able to stagger under their burdens, they were murdered, and their scalps torn off and exhibited to their masters, and for such trophies bounties were paid. The French Government in Paris paid bounties for the scalps of women and children, as Connecticut did for those of wolves, and it not only fitted out other savage expeditions, but sent its own soldiers to assist in the murderous work. Detailed reports of each case were regularly made to the Government at

Paris by its agents in Canada, which can now be read. This is true of every French and Indian war until 1763, and the fact was as well known to the settlers here in 1707 as it is to the historical investigator of to-day.

"In the beginning of 1707 reports of an expedition by the French and Indians against some part of New England gave alarm to the Colony, and on the sixth of February of that year a council of war was convened at Hartford, consisting of the Governor, most of the Council, and many of the chief military officers of the Colony. Suspicions were entertained that the attack would fall upon Western Connecticut, and that the Indians in this vicinity intended to join the French and Indians. The Council of War determined that the then western frontier towns of Danbury, Woodbury, Waterbury, and Simsbury, should be fortified with the utmost expedition. They were directed to keep scouts of faithful men to range the forests to discover the designs of the enemy, and give intelligence should they make their appearance near the frontier. At the October session in 1708 it was enacted that garrisons should be kept at those towns, and so it continued until after the close of the war in 1713.

"It was in the midst of alarms and dangers such as these that the settlement of this town was begun. One of the first houses constructed here had palisades about it to serve as a fort, which lasted many years, and, in 1717, soldiers were stationed here for the protection of the inhabitants; and this was repeated several times afterwards. Every man here was a soldier. He was a soldier when he sat at his meals, a soldier when he stood at his door, a soldier when he went to the cornfield, a soldier by day and by night.

"At the time the first settlers arrived here there was a tract of cleared land on the west side of the river called the Indian Field. It extended from where the river runs in an easterly direction south to the mouth of the little brook which runs along Fort Hill. It was not included in the original purchase from the Indians, having been reserved by them in their deed. It was, however, purchased from them in 1705 by John Mitchell, and was conveyed by him to the inhabitants of the town in 1714. This was of the greatest advantage to the first settlers. It furnished them a space of cleared ground, where each planter could at once plant his corn and other crops without the delay of felling the trees.

"It is thought also that the ground where we now stand and Aspetuck Hill had been in a large measure cleared of trees by the Indians by burning, as was also Grassy Hill, two miles east of here. There appears also to have been some meadow land partially cleared at the mouth of the Aspetuck River.

"At that time the country about here presented no such appearance as it does now. The river then flowed with a fuller tide. With the exceptions I have noted, a continuous forest overspread the whole landscape. No thickets, however, choked up the ways through it, for the underbrush was swept away every year by fires built by the Indians for that purpose. Winding footpaths led here and there, which the Indians and wild beasts followed. The roots of the smaller grasses were destroyed by this annual burning over. A coarse, long grass grew along the low banks of the river and wherever the ground was not thickly shaded by trees. After the occupation of the country by the white settlers this annual burning was prohibited. In lieu thereof, the General Court early in its history enacted that every inhabitant, with a few exceptions, should devote a certain time yearly, in the several plantations, to the cutting of brush and small trees in the more open forests for the purpose of allowing grass to grow in such places, as during the summer the cattle ranged through the forests near the plantations subsisting on what grew there. It is said that in the early settlement of this town all meadow land was secured by clearing marshy or swampy ground and allowing it to grow up with grass from the roots and seeds already in the soil. It was one of the early difficulties in the colony to secure grass from want of seed.

"The forests about here abounded with bears, wolves, foxes, and catamounts, deer and moose, wild turkeys, pigeons, quail and partridges, and the waters with wild geese, ducks, herons, and cranes. The river itself was alive with fish, and every spring great quantities of shad and lamprey eels ascended it. Strawberries, blackberries, and huckleberries were extremely abundant in their season.

"The winters were usually of great severity. In 1687 the snow lay on the ground three feet deep all over New England from the third of November until the twenty-third of March, and on the twenty-third of April it snowed for several hours in Boston, the flakes being as large as shillings. The springs were very backward, the summers extremely hot and often dry.

"Upon the petition of the people of Milford, in May, 1702, the General Assembly granted them liberty to purchase from the Indians a township at Wyantonock, the Indian name of this place, and directed them to report their doings to the Assembly. The next March they made an extensive purchase of the natives, and a patent for the same was granted by the Assembly. In October, 1704, the Legislature enacted that the tract so purchased should be a township by the name of New Milford, and that it must be settled in five years,—the town plat to be fixed by a committee appointed by the General Assembly. In October, 1706, the Legislature annexed the tract to New Haven County. In April, 1706, the first meeting of the proprietors was held at Milford, and it was voted that the town plat and home lots should be speedily pitched and laid out by the committee appointed by the Legislature, according to its own best judgment, following certain rules laid down by the proprietors. During that year and according to those rules, the town plat was laid out.

"It was originally intended to lay out the settlement on the hill immediately east of the present village, from this circumstance called Town Hill to this day. In point of fact, it was laid out on Aspetuck Hill, and consisted of the town street and sixteen home lots. The street was twenty rods wide. It began at the south end of the brow of the hill, or at the lower end of what was then called the 'Plain on the Hill,' and extended northward. Eight lots were laid out on each side of this street, each lot being twenty-one rods wide and sixty deep.

"By the rules adopted by the proprietors, these lots were to be taken up successively in regular order by the settlers as they should arrive. John Noble took the first lot on the east side of the street at the lower end, he being the first settler to arrive. John Bostwick took the lot on the opposite side of the street, he being the next settler on the ground. This method was followed by the others until there were twelve settlers, with their families, numbering seventy souls, located on this street in 1712. Of these twelve families, four were from Northampton and Westfield, Mass., four were from Stratford, two from Farmington, and only two from Milford. In 1714 the town street was extended southward to the south end of the present public green.

"The first houses constructed here by the settlers were of the rudest description. They were built of logs fastened by notching at the corners. They were usually from fifteen to eighteen feet square, and about seven feet in height, or high enough for a tall man to enter. At first they had no floors. The fireplace was erected at one end by making a back of stones laid in mud, and not in mortar, and a hole was left in the bark or slab roof for the escape of the smoke. A chimney of sticks plastered with mud was afterwards erected in this opening. A space, of width suitable for a door, was cut in one side, and this was closed, at first, by hanging in it a blanket, and afterwards by a door made from split planks and hung on wooden hinges. This door was fastened by a wooden latch on the inside, which could be raised from the outside by a string. When the string was pulled in the door was effectually fastened. A hole was cut in each side of the house to let in light, and, as glass was difficult to obtain, greased paper was used to keep out the storms and cold of autumn and winter. Holes were bored at the proper height in the logs at one corner of the room, and into these the ends of poles were fitted, the opposite ends, where they crossed, being supported by a crotch or a block of the proper height. Across these poles others were laid, and these were covered by a thick mattress of hemlock boughs, over which blankets were spread. On such beds as these the first inhabitants of this town slept and their first children were born. For want of chairs, rude seats were made with ax and auger by boring holes and inserting legs in planks split from basswood logs, hewn smooth on one side. Tables were made in the same way, and, after a time, the floor, a bare space being left about the fireplace instead of a hearthstone.

"No sooner had the first settlers taken up their abode here than they were called upon to defend the title to their lands in the courts of the Colony. About thirty-seven years before, the General Court had granted permission to certain Stratford parties to buy land from the Indians and settle a plantation at this place, and they had bought over twenty-six thousand acres hereabouts. Apparently, however, no attempt was made towards a settlement of the same until after the purchase of the same tract from the Indians by the Milford parties in 1702, and the grant for a patent for the same to them by the General Court in 1703. Soon after the settlers first broke ground here, in 1707, a suit was begun against them by the Stratford people in the County Court at New Haven in May, 1708, and it was carried thence to the General Court. It was tried sixteen times. The first fifteen times the plaintiffs won on the strength of their Indian title. The sixteenth, the defendants won on the strength of their Indian title, the patent from the General Court, and occupation. This incident is particularly interesting, because one of the plaintiffs and the lawyer in this great case was the famous John Read, one of the ablest men and most remarkable characters which New England has produced. Some notice of him will not be inappropriate here, as he was one of the earliest inhabitants of this place.

"He was born at Fairfield, June 29, 1679, and was a brother-in-law of Governor Talcott. He graduated at Harvard in 1697, and became a minister, preached in Woodbury as a candidate, and in various towns in Hartford and Fairfield counties, and preached the first sermon ever delivered in this place. He studied law, and when, in 1708, the General Assembly first provided for the appointment of attorneys as officers of the court, he was one of the first admitted. He held the offices of

Colony Queen's Attorney, 1712-16; Deputy for Norwalk, 1715-17; Commissioner to settle the boundary with New York, 1719; and he was Connecticut's representative in the Inter-Colonial Commission in regard to Bills of Credit, in 1720. He removed to Boston in 1722 and became the Attorney General and a member of the Council of Massachusetts. He was by far the most eminent lawyer of New England, and was called ' The Pride of the Bar, Light of the Law, and Chief among the Wise, Witty, and Eloquent.' It was he who prepared the instructions to Lord Mansfield, the counsel for Connecticut in the great case of Clark vs. Tousey, in which was discussed the question whether the Common Law of England had any force in Connecticut other than as it was adopted by the people of Connecticut. His exposition of the principles involved was most masterly, and it was the great authority upon which in a later generation the people of Connecticut relied to sustain them in their opposition to the measures of the crown in 1775.

"In a centenary sermon delivered at Danbury in January, 1801, the Rev. Thomas Robbins had this to say of him:

"'One of the early inhabitants of Danbury was John Read, a man of great talents and thoroughly skilled in the knowledge and practice of the law. He possessed naturally many peculiarities and affected still more. He is known to this day through the country by many singular anecdotes and characteristics under the appellation of "John Read, the lawyer."'

"In 1712 the town was incorporated, which gave it the power to tax the inhabitants to support a minister, and the place became thereby an ecclesiastical society. In March, 1712, the Rev. Daniel Boardman was called to preach to the settlers. In May, 1715, the settlers petitioned the General Assembly that they might obtain liberty for the settlement of the worship and ordinances of God among them, and the Legislature granted them liberty to embody in church estate as soon as God in his providence should make way therefor. On November 21, 1716, Mr. Boardman was duly ordained as the pastor of the Church of Christ in New Milford, the total number of the inhabitants of the town then being one hundred and twenty-five. The first vote of the town to build a meeting-house was passed in 1716, but work was not commenced upon it until 1719, and it was not completed until 1731, after infinite struggling. It was forty feet long, thirty wide, and twenty feet in height between joints, and was provided with galleries, pews, and a pulpit. Long before completion, when it was first used for religious purposes, the congregation was accustomed to sit upon its outer sills, which were able to accommodate every man, woman, and child in the town with a little squeezing. In 1713, the town voted to build for the minister a dwelling house forty feet between joints. In 1726, thirteen years later, the house was still unfinished. The first Sabbath Day house was not built until 1745.

"In 1721, when there were but thirty-five families residing here, a public school was ordered by the town to be kept for four months the winter following, one-half of the expense to be borne by the town. The children were taught reading, spelling after a phonetic fashion, writing, and the first four rules of arithmetic. In 1725 it was voted to build a schoolhouse twenty feet long, sixteen feet wide, and seven feet in height between the joints.

"The first settlers crossed the Housatonic to their lands on the west side by fording it at a point near the mouth of Rocky River, about a mile above the settlement, or at Waunupee Island in times of very low water. In 1720 the town built a boat for the purpose, which was used until 1737, when the first bridge ever built across the Housatonic from its source to its mouth was constructed at what is now the foot of Bennett Street.

"The settlers for many years crushed their grain by hand in mortars or carried it to mill at Danbury, Woodbury, or Derby, and brought back the flour and meal. In 1717 John Griswold, under an arrangement with the town, built a grist and saw mill on Still River, at what is now Lanesville.

"It is said that in 1713 there was but one clothier in the colony. The most that he could do was to full the cloth which was made in the homes. A great proportion of it was worn without shearing or pressing. He lived at Woodbury, and thither the early inhabitants of this town resorted to have their cloth fulled. People, to a very large extent, wore clothing made from the skins of animals. They also wore wooden shoes and moccasins, or went barefoot, although leather boots and shoes were sometimes used.

"The implements which they used in subduing the wilderness, their axes, saws, plows, hoes, and scythes, were of the rudest description. Their horses, cattle, sheep, and swine, we should now regard as of very inferior quality. The same was true of the few vegetables they cultivated and of their fruits, especially their apples. Turnips, squashes, and beans were the principal vegetables. Potatoes were not as yet cultivated in New England, onions were not generally, and tomatoes were looked upon as poisonous. Some of them owned negro slaves, but worked the harder themselves to make them work.

"They had little or no currency, taxes and debts being paid in produce. What they ate, what they wore, what they coaxed from the reluctant soil of these hillsides, cost them infinite labor. As was to be expected, a stingy avarice was their besetting sin, which manifested itself in all the relations of life. They were without newspapers, none being published in the Colony until 1755. They had few books, the first printing press in the Colony not having been set up at New London until 1709. They suffered greatly from malaria and other forms of sickness, as did all the early settlers in the State. Medical treatment was poor and difficult to obtain. The women went to the limit in childbearing, and the burden of rearing their large families was awful. The art of cooking was little understood. They had no stoves nor table forks. The food was served in a very unsavory fashion, and was very indigestible. The people therefore had frightful dreams, and dyspepsia was very prevalent. No carpet was seen here for a hundred years after the settlement. Communication with the outer world was slow, difficult, and rare. On several occasions, owing to the failure of their crops and the difficulty in getting relief from distant places little better off, they nearly starved to death.

"Truly the task which they had undertaken to subdue this wilderness, to plant here the civil, religious, and educational institutions of Connecticut, and to prepare this beautiful heritage for their children and children's children, was no holiday pastime, no gainful speculation, no romantic adventure. It was grim, persistent, weary toil and danger, continued through many years, with the wolf at the door and the savage in the neighboring thicket.

"Besides the physical evils with which they were beset, they had spiritual troubles also. They fully believed in witchcraft, as did all their contemporaries, in a personal Devil who was busily plotting the ruin of their souls, in an everlasting hell of literal fire and brimstone, and in a divine election, by which most of them had been irrevocably doomed from before the creation of the world to eternal perdition, from which nothing which they could do, or were willing to do, could help to rescue them. The great object of life to them, therefore, was to try to find out what their future state would be. Said one of their preachers: 'It is tough work and a wonderful hard matter to be saved. 'Tis a thousand to one, if ever thou be one of that small number whom God hath picked out to escape this wrath to come.' That we may get a touch of reality from those far-off days, let me quote to you a few lines from the saintly Thomas Hooker, the founder of Connecticut and long the model for her preachers:

"'Suppose any soul here present were to behold the damned in hell, and if the Lord should give thee a peephole into hell, that thou didst see the horror of those damned souls, and thy heart begins to shake in consideration thereof; then propound this to thy own heart, what pains the damned in hell do endure for sin, and thy heart will shake and quake at it. The least sin that thou ever didst commit, though thou makest a light matter of it, is a greater evil than the pains of the damned in hell, setting aside their sins. All the torments in hell are not so great an evil as the least sin is; men begin to shrink at this, and loathe to go down to hell and be in endless torment.'

" The only test which they were taught to apply to ascertain whether they were predestined to suffer or escape this fearful doom was in their ability and willingness to conform their wills to the will of God as revealed in the Bible. According as they succeeded in this, they had a reasonable assurance as to their fate, though no wile of the Devil was more frequent than to falsely persuade men that their prospects were favorable. To study the Scriptures day and night to ascertain the will of God, and to struggle without ceasing to conform their wills to his as therein revealed, was therefore the great object of existence for them, not that they could thereby alter in the least their future state, but that they might, if possible, find out what it was likely to be.

" Should this recital of their beliefs provoke a smile, our amusement will soon be checked by the thought of the little progress which has been made in the last two hundred years towards solving the same problems. The origin of evil, the ineradicable tendency of the human heart to sin and do evil, the mournful spectacle of ruin and desolation in the moral world, and the future life are the same inscrutable mysteries to us as to them. If we have constructed or adopted a more comfortable theology, it is probably because we are less logical than they. It is perhaps because we have forgotten or refused to look at some things at which they did not blink.

" Then, too, the Lord was abroad in those days. Their thoughts were deeply tinged by the semi-pagan views with which the authors of both the Old and New Testaments were imbued. When the thunder crashed, it was the voice of an angry God that spoke. When the lightning flashed, it was the gleam of His angry eye. Benjamin Franklin was then but a year old, and electricity had not become the packhorse of the world. The smiles and frowns of nature in all her varying moods through all the days and seasons, which we ascribe to the operations of law, were to them the visible tokens of the wrath or favor of the Almighty. On December 11, 1719, for the first time in the history of the Colony, the northern lights were seen here. They shone with the greatest brilliancy. The consternation they caused was fearful. The people had never heard of such a phenomenon. They considered it the opening scene of the Day of Judgment. All amusement was given up, all business was forsaken, and sleep itself was interrupted for days. Again, on the twenty-ninth of October, 1727, a mighty earthquake occurred, which shook with tremendous violence the whole Atlantic seaboard. The people here believed that the Lord was about to swallow them up in His fierce anger. The women throughout New England immediately discontinued the wearing of hoop skirts, then recently come into fashion, believing that the earthquake was the sign of the Lord's displeasure at the sinful innovation.

"Hardly had the first settlers here begun to build permanent homes for the living when they were called upon to provide resting places for the dead. The first person to be buried in yonder burying ground was a child, a girl, Mary, the daughter of Benjamin Bostwick. The next was John Noble, the first settler and the first Town Clerk. He died August 17, 1714. The town formally laid out the burying ground in 1716. Within fifty years three hundred had gone to rest there.

"There were no religious exercises at the funerals, neither singing, praying, preaching, nor reading of the Scriptures. This was by way of revolt from former superstitious practices. The friends gathered, condoled with the afflicted ones, sat around a while, and then the corpse was taken to the burying ground. After that the party returned to the house of the deceased, where much eating and drinking was indulged in, and, if the weather permitted, outdoor games and horse races were in order. The next Sabbath an appropriate funeral sermon was preached. A bereaved husband or wife usually soon married again.

"The meeting-house was never heated, but the people, summoned by drum beat, attended it every Sabbath, morning and afternoon, even in the severest weather, although no Sabbath Day house was erected here until 1745.

"The sacramental bread often froze upon the communion plate, as did the ink in the minister's study. The people worked their minister very hard, as was the case in all early New England communities. They went to church not so much because they had to as because they wanted to. Church-going was their principal recreation. They demanded long prayers and two long sermons each Sabbath from their minister, usually on doctrinal points, which they acutely criticised. Services began at nine o'clock in the forenoon and continued until five in the afternoon, with an hour's intermission. Soldiers, fully armed, were always in attendance throughout the services ready to repel any attack upon the settlement. It should be added, however, that with all their strictness in Sabbath-keeping and catechising, in family and church discipline, there was great license in those days in speech and manner, much hard drinking, and rude merry-making, due to their rough form of living. They were not what they wanted to be, nor what a loyal posterity perhaps longs to believe them. They had red blood in their veins. They were among the most enterprising men of their generation. They were backwoodsmen, the vanguard of that wonderful race which in two hundred years pushed westward the frontier from this place to the Pacific, fighting with man and beast the whole way, and sowed the land with vigorous sons and daughters.

"The congregational singing in those days must have been an interesting performance. When the first settlers came to New England from the old country, they brought with them a few tunes, to which they sang all the psalms and hymns.

"The proper mode of rendering these was through the nose. With the lapse of time and the advent of a new generation, these tunes became jangled together in inextricable confusion. The practice was for a deacon as leader to read a line of the psalm or hymn, and the congregation then sang at it as best they could, each one using such tune as he chose, and often sliding from one tune to another in the same line or improvising as he went on. Finally, in 1721, the Rev. Thomas Walter of Roxbury, Mass., published a treatise upon the grounds or rules of music, or an introduction to the art of singing by rote, containing twenty-four tunes harmonized into three parts. The attempt to supersede the old Puritan tunes and restrict the liberty of the individual singers met with the greatest opposition and was long successfully resisted in all the churches in New England, so tenacious were they of the rights of the individual singer. It caused great dissension in the church at this place. Finally, in February, 1740, the church voted to halve the time for the next year, singing the old way one Sabbath and the new way the next, and in 1741, at a meeting specially called to settle the matter, it was voted thirty to sixteen to sing thereafter after the new way.

" No musical instruments were allowed in the meeting-house. They had never seen or heard a church organ. But they knew that their fathers likened its sound to the bellowing of a bull, the grunting of a pig, and the barking of a dog, and had resisted its use in religious services even to the shedding of blood. Nor were flowers allowed in the church.

" In those days in New England women were not thought to have minds worth educating, and they were brought up in extreme illiteracy. Nevertheless, their natural wit, brightness, and good sense made them very agreeable companions of the superior sex. And their influence over their husbands, sons, and brothers was quite as great as that of their more cultivated daughters of the present day. The refining, educating, stimulating influence of the women had much to do in withstanding that tendency back to barbarism which life in an isolated and new community led to. The debt which is owed to them is incalculable.

" As the descendants of these people assemble here to-day, after the lapse of two hundred years, to commemorate their work and rejoice in all the strength, beauty, and order, now smiling around us in peace and plenty, which have grown out of what they began, and as we look back upon their condition, trials, and experiences, we are apt to imagine that their lot, contrasted with our own, was an unhappy one. Nothing could be further from the truth. They were a brave, hardy, thrifty, frugal, industrious, and most capable people. Man for man, and woman for woman, they were probably superior to those here to-day in faculty, and in the capacity for healthy enjoyment. Their whole previous lives had inured them to their experiences. They were the sons and grandsons of the original pioneers of New England, and they had been born and reared in rude settlements. They never indulged the delusion that this region was a land flowing with milk and honey. Before they came they knew that they were to wrest their living from an uncongenial soil, to struggle with penury, and to conquer only by constant toil and by self-denying thrift. The forest would supply them with the materials for shelter and fuel and to some extent with food and clothing. All the rest must depend upon their own exertions. There was a pleasure in facing and overcoming the perils and difficulties which they encountered which those, more delicately reared, who live here now can never know. Their individual helplessness in the face of appalling obstacles to be met but bound them closer together in mutual helpfulness. Accordingly we find that their social faculties were highly developed. It may well be doubted whether the sum total of human pleasure among the whole five thousand inhabitants of the town to-day is any greater than it was among the few hundred who settled it. Probably our own superabundance of good things has actually lessened our capacity to enjoy, in comparison with theirs. Their simple tastes and homely joys amid their rude surroundings were probably more productive of positive pleasure and real happiness than all the refinement and culture of our twentieth century civilization.

"It would be a pleasing and instructive task to trace the progress of this old town from those rude beginnings to its present strength and wealth. But the limits of the time and subject allotted to me on this occasion forbid. It is the product of the labors of eight generations, who now sleep beneath its soil. They never could have foreseen the present. They never knew or thought of us. Each generation was busy with its own problems, tasks, and experiences.

"As we look back upon them our hearts are filled with

gratitude for the results of their work. A clean-blooded, land-loving, thrifty race, through their activities they escaped from the poverty of their beginnings and attained unto an almost ideal abundance of the primal needs of civilization. Their physical condition became probably as good as that of any other village community in the world. Their experiences stimulated their intellectual life into full activity, and they bore their full share in the wonderful work which Connecticut has done in the world. In all critical times in both State and nation, the sons of New Milford, both native and adopted, have been very active and influential, and one of them, Roger Sherman, performed a work which will last as long as this nation shall continue to be free and independent, or as long as the Constitution of the United States shall endure.

"We know that the past two hundred years are but the beginning of a long history of this town. We believe that as the years roll by, at the close of each century of its life, the events of this day will be repeated here. What will be the lot of those who shall stand here, one two, three, and four hundred years hence, to recall the origin and history of this town, we cannot conceive. Our hope is that it will be as peaceful, as prosperous, and as contented as our own.

"Whatever it shall be, we expect that their desire to know what can be known of that long-vanished world, in which both present and future have their roots, will lead them to examine the memorial of what is said and done here to-day. We are not more sure that the Housatonic will then be flowing than that they will share with us in affectionate interest in what has gone before."

The rendering of the "Star Spangled Banner" and several other selections by Prof. Clemence's Bi-Centennial Chorus was an inspiring feature of the Historical Meeting.

THE COLONIAL RECEPTION

Soon after the close of the Historical Meeting, the booming of cannon announced the arrival in New Milford of Governor Woodruff, his staff and a detail of the Governor's Foot Guard. They were met at the railroad station by a train of automobiles, in which they were taken, after a short ride about the village, to Ingleside School, where they dined in the company of a number of prominent citizens.

Promptly at 8:30 o'clock, the gubernatorial party arrived at Roger Sherman Hall, where it was arranged that they should meet the people of the town, and entered it by a side door. Before the main door was opened for the admission of the general public, seats were given upon the stage and on the floor of the hall in front of the wings on either side to the members of the Colonial Reception Committee and of the Invitation, Reception, and Entertainment Committee; also to the following persons, who had been requested by these committees to assist them in receiving:

Mr. and Mrs. John F. Addis, Mrs. F. E. Baldwin, Dr. and Mrs. J. C. Barker, Mr. and Mrs. A. G. Barnes, Miss Mary Barton, Miss Hattie Bassett, Mr. and Mrs. C. M. Beach, Mr. and Mrs. S. C. Beach, Miss Charlotte B. Bennett, Mr. and Mrs. W. F. Bennett, Mr. and Mrs. C. P. Bentley, Miss Helen M. Boardman, Miss Kate T. Boardman, Miss Ruth Booth, Miss Lena Botsford, Miss Bessie Brown, Miss Adaline Buck, Miss Alice Buck, Mr. and Mrs. H. S. Donnelly, Miss Susie C. Erwin, Miss Minnie A. Ferriss, Miss Jeannette Gaylord, Mr. and Mrs. Minot S. Giddings, W. G. Green, Mr. and Mrs. S. S. Green, Mr. and Mrs. C. N. Hall, Miss Elsie Hall, Mr. and Mrs. H. D. Hine, Mrs. J. S. Halpine, Mr. and Mrs. G. H. Jackson, Rev. and Mrs. F. A. Johnson, Dr. and Mrs. F. E. King, Mrs. W. F. Kinney, Mr. and Mrs. David Kyle, Miss

Carrie Marsh, Mr. and Mrs. Chauncey Marsh, A. H. McMahon, Miss Grace Merwin, Mr. Perry Green, Mr. C. H. Noble and sister, Miss Lizzie Noble, W. B. Pell, Mrs. Pettibone, Mrs. J. F. Plumb, Mr. and Mrs. H. L. Randall, Miss Juliette Rogers, Mrs. Wm. Schoverling, Miss Harriet V. Sherman, Mr. and Mrs. F. E. Starr, Miss Minnie Toussaint, F. M. Williams, Dr. and Mrs. G. H. Wright.

The New Milford Cadets (Captain Gifford Noble) were drawn up as guard of honor about the hall, forming an aisle around an open square, through which the people walked as they advanced to greet the Governor and passed out again after shaking his hand. The members of the staff, in full uniform, were in front of the stage and back of the Governor, while, to the right and left of them, the detail from the Foot Guard were stationed as a special guard. By the side of his Excellency stood W. Frank Kinney, the chairman of the Bi-Centennial Invitation, Reception and Entertainment Committee, who presented every one by name. There were many Colonial costumes, many gay uniforms, and many elaborate evening toilettes. In the exquisite setting provided by the pale blue, white and yellow colonial draperies and festoons with which the hall was most artistically decorated, the reception offered an exceptionally brilliant spectacle. In fact, it was probably the most striking affair of its kind New Milford has ever witnessed.

Dancing was begun, to the music of Gartland's Band, when the handshaking was over, and was kept up for two or three hours after the Governor and his party had retired.

Governor Woodruff was also entertained in the rooms of the Commercial Club; in Odd Fellows' and Masonic Hall, where he was formally welcomed by Henry O. Warner, Past Master of the New Milford Masonic lodge; and by the New Milford Fire Department, in their quarters, where he was welcomed by Chief John F. Addis, who presented him with an engrossed certificate of honorary membership in Water Witch Hose Company, No. 2.

GOVERNOR WOODRUFF, STAFF AND GUARD, IN FRONT OF ROGER SHERMAN HALL

GOVERNOR'S DAY

On Tuesday, the culminating day of the Bi-Centennial Celebration, New Milford possessed a population variously estimated at from ten to fifteen thousand—the largest, probably, of any moment in its history. The heat was intense, and some were so tactless as to prophesy showers. Others—and these were right—scoffed at such a possibility, basing their optimism on the fact that the new uniforms of the Governor's staff had never yet been wet and that New Milford was not going to be ungracious enough to be instrumental in wetting them.

The forenoon was devoted to the preparation of the Civic and Military Parade, which was scheduled to begin at noon. Only a few minutes after the time appointed, the column began to move in the following order:

FORMATION OF PARADE

CHIEF MARSHAL SAMUEL R. HILL IN CHARGE.

First Division

Platoon of Police, Capt. David Bradley of Danbury
Chief Marshal and Staff (Perry Green, Noble Booth, Charles Pomeroy, Madeline Dodd, Louise Beeman.)
Gartland's Tenth Regiment Band
Second Company, Governor's Foot Guards, Major Weed
Governor Rollin S. Woodruff and Staff
Bugle Corps
Company G, Third Infantry, C. N. G., Captain Ryder
Upton Post, G. A. R., John F. Williams
New Milford Cadets, Captain Gifford Noble
Official Guests in Carriages

Second Division

Marshal David E. Soule and Staff (Dr. C. B. Blackman, George Dean, Louis Wilton)
Second Regiment Band
Water Witch Hose Company, No. 2, of New Milford
Danbury Military Band
Litchfield Fire Department
American Brass Band of Waterbury
Fountain Hose Company, No. 1, of Ansonia
Holt's American Band of New Haven
Echo Hose, Hook and Ladder Company of Shelton
Ansonia Brass Band
Eagle Hose, Hook and Ladder Company, No. 6, of Ansonia
Bethel Drum Corps
Danbury Volunteer Fire Department

Third Division

Marshal George E. Ackley and Staff (Granville Breinig, W. M. Keeler, Clifford A. Trowbridge)
Boys of Center High School, Marching in Costume
School Children in Floats in District Order

Fourth Division

Marshal Henry O. Warner and Staff (James Marsh, W. C. Beeman, Clifford Marsh)
Wheeler & Wilson Band of Bridgeport (by courtesy of Roger Sherman Chapter, D. A. R.)
Colonial Features
Industrial Floats

There were more military organizations, fire companies, drum corps, and brass bands in line, probably, than had ever been seen at one time in New Milford, and they elicited by their brilliant uniforms, stirring music, and fine marching the admiration and the hearty applause of the crowds massed along the line of march; but the features which differentiated this parade from all previous ones, which lent it special distinction, and

SAMUEL R. HILL
Chief Marshal

SAMUEL RANDOLPH HILL, JR.
And Gun Used in Firing Salutes

which will make it memorable as long as the youngest persons who witnessed it shall survive, were the school floats, the Colonial floats, and industrial floats of the Third and Fourth divisions.

The school features were as follows:

Boys of the Center School costumed as Indians and farmers—the Indians emitting blood-curdling war-whoops from time to time.

Pony cart trimmed with pink and white containing members of " Miss Treat's class " representing butterflies.

Float of " Room 1 " (Center School), trimmed with white and yellow, carrying under a canopy twenty girls dressed in white. It was drawn by two sorrel horses also trimmed with white and yellow.

Another float of " Room 1 " trimmed with flags and bunting. It contained twenty-three girls and was drawn by four horses.

Flower girls dressed in pink and green—to represent the petals and sepals of flowers—on a " Cinderella " float provided with a pink canopy. It was drawn by a pair of black horses.

Float of " Rooms 5 and 6 " (Center School), trimmed mostly with green and white and carrying twenty-four girls. It was drawn by black horses which were decorated with flags.

Float of " Rooms 7 and 8 " (Center School), green and white—stars of green laurel against white bunting—carrying twenty children in white wearing white wreaths.

Float of " Rooms 3 and 4 " (Center School), yellow and white, carrying forty children under a canopy.

Park Lane Float, pink and white, carrying thirty-one children—the girls wearing white gowns with pink sashes. It was drawn by iron-gray horses wearing pink and white harnesses. David Rothe's dog, trimmed with white, blue, and pink, rode proudly on the driver's seat beside the driver.

Hill and Plain Float, decorated with evergreens, bunting, and flags.

Second Hill Float, representing an open trolley car, bearing the legends—" Second Hill Traction Co.," " Cross Town," and " Fireworks To-night "—and, in the advertising spaces, cards provided by the village merchants. The conductor amused the spectators greatly by the tireless energy he displaying in collecting and ringing up the fares. This float, which was trimmed with patriotic bunting, was drawn by three horses and carried thirty-five children, each holding a flag. It was designed by Mrs. Andrew Clark.

Upper Merryall Float, decorated with red, white and blue bunting. It was drawn by black horses and carried twenty-two children.

Chestnut Land Float, white and green—ground pine and laurel against white bunting—carrying forty children. It was drawn by four horses decorated with greenery.

Aspetuck Float, representing a sixteen-foot flower-bordered birch-bark canoe. It was trimmed with garnet and gold and was provided with a garnet banner. It carried sixteen children (gaily adorned "braves" and maidens) and the teacher.

Boardman Float, decorated with flags and patriotic bunting, bearing the device, "1707-1907" in green letters on a white ground. It carried twenty-eight children.

Lower Merryall Float, trimmed with Colonial yellow, white, and blue bunting and flying a big flag. The children, who were seated under a canopy, wore rosettes of the same colors. Four footmen in yellow walked beside it.

Gaylordsville and Waller Float, decorated with bunting and flags. The children, fifteen in number, sat on raised seats, one row above another, and held flags and baskets of flowers. It was drawn by four horses, whose driver was disguised as Uncle Sam.

Northville and Hunt Float, a "little red schoolhouse," trimmed with evergreens. It was drawn by two yoke of Nelson Kenney's steers. Children leaning out of the front windows held red, white, and blue ribbons, which were attached to the horns of the steers.

Long Mountain Float, decorated with white bunting, flags, and ground pine. It carried twenty-two children.

Still River Float, trimmed with flags, plumes, and bunting, and provided with a white canopy and a bell. It was drawn

MAIN STREET FROM THE NORTH

by four horses and carried thirty-five children (the girls in white dresses, the boys in shirt waists) wearing flag sashes. The teacher sat upon a throne.

The Colonial features of the parade were preceded by a man carrying a beautiful blue and gold banner of Roger Sherman Chapter, D. A. R., Charles G. Peck of Newtown in Colonial costume on his famous high-stepping horse, and the Wheeler & Wilson Band of Bridgeport—the first and last named, by courtesy of and at the expense of Roger Sherman Chapter, D. A. R.

Next came Mr. Williams and Mr. Lee of the Brookfield Drum Corps in Colonial costumes with drum and fife; and Joseph Cowan, Fred Kinbloe, and William Cogswell in Indian costume on horseback, the last named being a descendant of the Schaghticoke tribe of Indians.

Next, a float with a log cabin representing the one built by John Noble, the first white settler in New Milford. Chauncey B. Marsh and his little daughter, Esther Noble Marsh, seven years old, rode on this float, in the doorway of the cabin, impersonating John Noble and his little daughter. A watch-dog was chained beside the door, a musket hung over the door, and, during the early part of the parade, smoke issued from the cabin chimney. The float was drawn by oxen.

Back of this was started Jim Harris, better known as "Jim Pan," the last of the Pequots, and the only full-blooded Indian left in the Schaghticoke Reservation. Having filled up with firewater before the parade started, he soon left the Colonial section, marched most of the route with the fire companies, and ended up among the Governor's Foot Guards. He lost only his wig in the shuffle, the rest of his Indian suit begin securely strapped upon him.

Next came Mrs. R. S. Todd and her daughter, Parthenia, in an old-fashioned chaise, with a dignified colored footman on the rumble—all attired in Colonial costume, the ladies wearing sun-bonnets and dimity gowns.

Next, Andrew Humeston, on horseback, with his sister, Athalia, on a pillion, attired as a Quaker and Quakeress. Mr.

Humeston's real white fur Quaker hat, which he went far afield to get for this occasion, was a relic well worth seeing.

Next, Samuel Porter and Charles Donnelly, also on horseback, as a bride and groom of Colonial times. The saddle and pillion used by this happy pair were very interesting.

Next, a float with six young ladies in old-time costume operating different spinning and flax wheels. This float was decorated with dark green and bore the inscription, "HOMESPUN DAYS." The young ladies were Miss Florence Merwin, Miss Elsie Hall, Miss Julie Barker, Virginia Stevens (Miss Barker's little niece, three years old), Miss Flora Stilson, and Miss Minnie Toussaint. The float was drawn by oxen.

Dr. Griswold Bragaw, in Colonial costume, rode a horse following this float.

Next came a carriage, said to be one hundred years old, brought from Merryall and driven by two boys in Indian costume.

The last float represented the different styles of dress of periods fifty years apart in New Milford history. Mr. Frederick N. Fowler and Mrs. William Percy wore the costume of 1707; Willis Barton and Miss Hattie Bassett, that of 1757; Merrit Merwin and Miss Grace Merwin, that of 1807; Mr. and Mrs. Frederick E. Starr, that of 1857, and Arthur Brown and Miss Bessie Brown, that of 1907. This float was canopied with yellow and bore the inscription, "TIMES AND COSTUMES CHANGE."

Wm. W. Stilson impersonated the "Town Crier" and, ringing a huge bell, was typical in every way of that old-time character.

The yellow and dark green draperies which concealed the base of all these Colonial floats gave them a highly finished appearance.

The industrial features of the Parade were:

Float of the Bridgeport Wood Finishing Company, decorated with the national colors and displaying the signs, "Wheeler's Patent Wood Filler," "Paint That Lasts," etc. It carried boxes and cans of the company's products and pieces of silex in its natural state.

MAIN STREET FROM THE SOUTH

Float of G. B. Shiappacassee, the Bank Street fruit dealer, — a brand new wagon decorated with the national colors and carrying oranges, bananas and pineapples, arranged with a fine consideration for color and form.

Float of the New Milford Hat Company, decorated with the national colors and carrying a group of hat-makers, who gave a practical illustration, along the line of march, of the different processes of hat-making.

A tobacco float displaying the firm names—S. Rossin & Son, J. Lichtenstein, C. F. Schoverling & Co., Staubb & Mallett, J. Marquesee—and the legend, "NEW MILFORD SUPPLIES THE WORLD WITH TOBACCO," and carrying a large number of tobacco boxes.

Float of W. H. Coleman, a new milk wagon decorated with the national colors and bearing the inscription, "Conetia Farm Dairy."

Float of Chauncey B. Marsh, proprietor of a New Milford saw-mill, decorated with white and green and carrying wedge, ax, saw and chain, and an enormous artificial log, which two dummies sawed persistently with a cross-cut saw.

Float of the Aspetuck Valley Grange, decorated with green and white, roofed over with grain, and displaying the principal implements of husbandry and the principal products thereof.

Float of the ice dealer, Samuel J. Ferriss—a capital, white cotton imitation of a snow-bank between snow-laden "Christmas trees." Upon this float rode two small boys (S. Boynton and Charles J., sons of Mr. Ferriss), offering dippers of ice.

After passing through the principal streets of the village, the parading column was reviewed from the reviewing stand on the village "Green" by Governor Woodruff and his staff and other distinguished visitors. The paraders were then disbanded and provided by the Committee on Refreshments with abundant good cheer in a colossal dining tent back of the Knapp building.

After dinner, at two o'clock, the last formal exercises of the Bi-Centennial were held on "The Green," Charles M. Beach presiding. In introducing the first speaker, Rev. Timothy J. Lee, Mr. Beach said:

"There is much cause for regret that, on account of ill health, our President, Mr. Henry S. Mygatt, has been unable to be present or to take any part in the exercises of this Celebration. It was at his suggestion that the movement was inaugurated bringing about this event, and we all know that he worked most heartily and earnestly for its success. I am sure that there is a universal feeling of sympathy for him in the keen disappointment which is his. Because of his absence, the duty devolves on me to take charge of the exercises of the day.

"The first address will be words of greeting by the Rev. T. J. Lee, a former pastor of the Congregational Church. Mr. Lee comes to us as a representative of two of the oldest families in New Milford, Mrs. Lee being a lineal descendant of the Rev. Daniel Boardman, who was the first pastor of the old Congregational Church, and also of the Rev. Nathaniel Taylor, who was inaugurated its second pastor in the year 1748, and continued the pastorate for a period of fifty years.

Among other things, Mr. Lee said:

"The other day I met one of our recently adopted sons whose home is in the great West. In the course of our conversation I referred to this Bi-Centenary; but he pushed the subject aside as trivial, and began to boast of his own great State. 'Why,' said he, 'you can put twenty-two Connecticuts into our Nebraska.' Then he added that the time has come in the history of our country when we can cut out New England and not feel it. Cut New England out from the great life of this nation! Yes, you may, when you can cut out a thread of gold woven in and out in a beautiful fabric without ruining the entire piece. Cut New England out! Yes, you may, when you can cut out from the loaf the leaven that has made it sweet and light. Cut New England out! Yes, you may, when, without disfigurement, you can cut out the features of a mother from the face of her child. There may come a time in some far-off age when this great American people may become so afflicted with some strange, new form of insanity as to desire to cut out from its vast domain that sharp northeastern angle which was alike its birthplace and its cradle and the seminary of the best elements of its greatness. If that time ever comes, New England, true to her ancestral pride (I speak as one who knows and loves his mother), New England will say to you: 'I am ready to go; I desire to stay no longer where I am no longer wanted. But first—first, in all justice and fairness, give me back some of the contributions I have made to your greatness. Give me back the free, forceful words which from my pulpit, my press, and my platform have kindled the fires of religion and of patriotism, and quickened the intellectual life of generations. Give me back my millions of capital that have stretched across the broad land the iron bands of travel and of trade, changed the Western wilderness into a smiling garden, the desert into a fruitful field. Give me back some of the descendants of those loyal sons and daughters of mine, who, under the canvas covers of those old emigrant wagons, carried with them not merely their humble household goods, but the very principles of their nurture—give me back these, I say, and then, if you do not feel so utterly impoverished, so stripped of everything that can make a nation great and strong and enduring as to repent of your rashness and folly, I will go.'

" It is true that henceforth New England's influence in the nation will not be that of numbers, nor of territorial greatness, but she will still rule by the force of ideas and convictions, by the sovereignty of principles that can never be discrowned.

Mr. Beach next presented Governor Woodruff in these words:

" During my business experience, it has been my privilege to make many congenial acquaintances, one of which stands out most prominently to-day. A number of years ago, a young man called upon us representing a firm with which we had established relations. He has risen step by step in his business career, until he now occupies a position at the head of the firm which he then represented. A few years ago his name became mentioned in political circles, and he has risen so rapidly in this sphere that he comes to us to-day as the Chief Executive of the State.

"For integrity of character, for honesty of purpose, for having the courage of his convictions, he is a Governor whom the people of the State of Connecticut will do well to honor. Roosevelt at Washington, Hughes at Albany, Woodruff at Hartford, are the type of public officials which the people want.

"It is my very great pleasure, as well as honor, to present not only to the people of New Milford, but also to the guests whom we are entertaining to-day, his Excellency, Rollin S. Woodruff, of New Haven, Governor of Connecticut.

Governor Woodruff said:

"My friends, I am very glad to join with you in celebrating the two hundredth birthday of the settlement of New Milford. This commemoration will become an interesting experience in your lives, and your children will never forget the history that is taught them by this event. They will learn of the early struggles of those who laid the solid foundation of Connecticut, in the establishment of her towns, in the making of her laws, and building of a great commonwealth out of the materials of industry, education, and patriotism.

"It was no easy task your forefathers set out to perform, when they determined to have a government as nearly democratic in its intention as it was possible to conceive. The scheme of the founders of our State was to insure happiness for all by making all the people independent and free to govern themselves, and to advance themselves in a way that had never before been dreamed of by any race of men. The wisdom of those early settlers in organizing society upon a liberal plane seems to us almost marvelous. What they hoped for has been realized.

"The people who founded New Milford and the other Connecticut towns were unselfish. They planned not only for themselves and their time, but they planned for those that were to come after them. They saw through the years what might be

HONORABLE ROLLIN S. WOODRUFF
Governor of Connecticut

ours, if their plans prevailed. They saw the human race rising to its highest perfection in an atmosphere of liberty and of opportunity. Yet their most daring fancy could not have pictured this surprising scene of to-day. They were rough and rude men two hundred years ago. And they were determined men, and their lives were the serious lives of hardship and peril. What they wanted was freedom and a government that would keep them free. They wanted to do what was right—justice to all men was the motive that inspired them. They had faith in themselves and believed that the real government was that which came from the people; and they made their laws to last for all time, trusting to the people the responsibility of taking care of themselves. They were the fathers of freedom in its truest sense, and intended to leave their children a house that was built upon a rock.

"In all this, they gave evidence of the very noblest patriotism, and they have set for us an example which we have followed for two hundred years—an example which must continue to guide us in our government, if this grand development of Connecticut is to go forward to its highest possibilities. We must keep our foundations solid and build for the future. We must grow better as we grow older. Our lawmakers must be sincere and serious men. They must be representative in the deepest meaning of the word, for the whole happiness of our people depends upon the making and the administration of laws that are enacted in the interest of all the people of our State, and our representatives should be held responsible for their acts at the polls. The rights of the people are sacred and must be kept inviolate, and no law should be placed upon the statute book that will be a burden to the people, or that takes from the people any right that belongs to them all. Let there be no hasty, inconsiderate, or careless legislation that robs them of their own. Great privileges should never be given away to private interests, and every man's property should be protected throughout the State. We frequently learn what we have lost, when it is too late. I do not mean to alarm you, but I do mean to warn you that you may keep guard over your right against oppression, which is sure to come when the people lose interest in their own affairs.

"What an advancement you have made in two hundred years! The country towns of to-day share with the large cities all modern advantages. Your children have matchless chances for education, and your commercial conditions offer every opportunity for success in life. The farmer of to-day is a prince among farmers and lives in the surroundings of comfort and luxury: with vast systems of water supply; a high sanitary arrangement protecting health; gas and electricity for light, heat, and power; the telegraph in every village, and the telephone in every home where it is required; the best facilities for travel at your doors—a prosperity in business never known in the history of mankind. All men are educated by the affairs of the hour, and all men think. You are better equipped to govern yourselves than any people in the world. Contrast all these comforts with the inconveniences of your ancestors, and tell me have we not reason to rejoice at this Bi-Centennial of New Milford?

"In my position as Governor of this State I have kept steadily in view the general prosperity of all the people, and I have always believed in an educated public sentiment as the safeguard of law and order in our Commonwealth. I believe in the people of Connecticut and in the future of the State; and I believe that the more interest you take in public matters the better your government will become. I want to congratulate you upon the growth of New Milford, and thank you sincerely for the privilege of joining in this triumphant Celebration."

Mr. Beach next presented Rev. Watson L. Phillips, D. D., saying:

"At this time it is in my power to speak a word of welcome to my comrades of the Foot Guard. They have been connected with the history of Connecticut since 1775, when the Company marched out to Lexington and Concord. It has not been my privilege to be as close to the armory as I should have liked, but I am proud to belong to that old organization which has done so much for the honor of Connecticut, and I will simply ask the Chaplain of the Company to speak to you more fluently than I can."

Chaplain Phillips delivered an eloquent eulogy of the Foot Guard. Among other things, he said:

"The Second Company of Governor's Foot Guards was born in that strenuous time when ideas were crystallizing, opinions taking shape, men beginning to realize something of the struggle that was before them; something of the real significance of the Mayflower, of the Colonial forms of government, and of those acts of protest by which the colonies had lifted their voices against the usurpations of the mother country. In 1775, when the clouds were beginning to gather, when men's hearts were beginning to tremble within them for fear, this company was born. On the first roster, you will find the names of the leading citizens of old New Haven town. The first men of the town were its sponsors. Back of them was a patriotic and humane purpose, and, having that purpose in view, I am able to declare that we are the oldest military organization of the sort in the State.

"The First Company in Hartford antedates us by a few months, but the First Company was what its name implies, the Governor's Guard. The Second Company came at the call of the danger to liberty and its first act was to make response to the call of Lexington and Concord. Under the man, then a magnificent patriot, Benedict Arnold, the company marched to the defense of their endangered brethren in Massachusetts.

"And these men, before they left, listened to a sermon by Jonathan Edwards, the benediction of which went with them throughout their march. They marched to the powder house— they asked for ammunition; the selectmen of the town denied their request. Arnold drew up his men before the door, and said: 'We will give you five minutes to comply with our request; if the ammunition is not then forthcoming we will break down the doors and help ourselves.'

"That was the spirit with which they started on their march to Cambridge, and that spirit has animated the command through all these years. It has been our privilege to have been represented in every war the country has waged from 1775 to the present day, beginning with the attack upon West Haven, to repel which the company marched as a body under the command of Captain Hezekiah Sabin. Down through all the wars and in the most conspicuous battles, representatives of this Governor's Guard have been found, shoulder to shoulder with the patriots of other States and other towns, contending for our liberties."

The next speaker, Hon. Ebenezer J. Hill, was presented as one who needs no introduction to New Milford. Congressman Hill said:

"One year ago I united with some of your citizens in celebrating the fiftieth birthday of New Milford's offspring, the town of Bridgewater.

"To-day I congratulate you that the parent has reached the hale and hearty age of two hundred years.

"While New Milford has had many trials and sore experiences, the old town shows no wrinkles, or scars, but is fresh and blooming and ready to enter upon the third century of its career with a courageous heart and unfaltering purpose to maintain in the future, as in the past, the splendid character of our New England civilization.

"There is no higher standard in the world than that, for it was established in the beginning of our history by men who feared none but God. Our fathers built upon the granite hills of New England communities and States, which, though small in area, have been mighty in influence, molding and shaping the destiny of the nation, and through it giving to the whole world an example of self-government, based on the sanctity of the home, the common school, freedom of religion, and the New England town meeting. With these maintained, the prosperity of the future is assured, for, while old age with all its weaknesses comes to *men* with the passing years, the lapse of time, if rightly used, should make a community or a nation stronger and more enduring.

"Temporary success may come from many causes, but, in

the long run, it is character which counts, not only in the individual, but in the nation as well.

"A few weeks ago I visited the site of old Panama, a city on the Isthmus to which it gave its name. It was founded in conquest and plunder, a century before the Pilgrims landed at Plymouth Rock. A hundred and fifty years later, in conquest and plunder, Morgan and his pirate crews swept it from the earth; and now, nothing but an old church and tower, almost hidden in the tropical jungle, mark the spot where this once flourishing and populous city stood.

"A few years ago I walked from the ruined palaces of the Cæsars down the slope of the Palatine Hill into the Roman Forum. The way was paved with stones which were put there twenty-six hundred years ago by the shepherds and farmers as the stones with which their streets were paved, and their descendants, imitating those virtues, ruled the world for a thousand years. But at last, licentiousness, extravagance, and lust from the Alban Hills. Their virtues were as strong and rugged for wealth came in and rotted the moral fiber of the Empire, until the very men who had sworn to guard the nation sold the positions of honor and trust, and even the Empire itself, at public auction at the city gates, as cattle and sheep were sold in the open market; and Rome fell from its high estate never to rise again. It was a literal exemplification of the proverb which was old even then, that ' righteousness exalteth a nation, but sin is a reproach to any people.'

"But why multiply illustrations? The history of the world is full of them, and, on the other side, none more marked than is shown in our own land in the marvelous progress which the New South has made since the curse of human slavery was lifted from her in the desolation and horror of the Civil War.

"This town, this State, this nation is just exactly what you and I, as individuals, are making it to-day. The past is unchangeable, the future is in the hands of God. Only the present is ours. We have come in our own experience to times of great unrest and discontent with existing conditions. I am glad of it. It shows that the world is growing better and that we are not satisfied to-day with the solution of the problems of yesterday, but it does not follow that the new problems of to-day are unsolvable. It simply proves that there is still room in the world for a large amount of civic righteousness and that it is for the individual citizen to prove that the supply has not been exhausted.

"There is an old hymn which we sing in our churches,

> "'We are building, building every day,
> A temple which the world may not see,
> We are building, building every day,
> Building for eternity.'

So far as the immortal and divine in us is concerned, the hymn is all right, but so far as this work-a-day world is affected by our actions I would paraphrase it thus,

> "'We are building, building every day,
> A temple which the world can see,
> We are building, building every day,
> Building for humanity.'

"A few days ago I read a story in a newspaper of a man who advertised that he wanted to buy a horse. In a day or two men came with all sorts and kinds, young and old, blind and lame and halt. They told him of the splendid records of the old hacks, and the great possibilities of the young colts, till he finally sent them all away, saying, 'I don't care anything about your "has beens" or your "to be's," what I want now, is an "is-er."'

"The men of New England are the heirs to-day of more than two centuries of growth, and progress, and education, and we owe it to ourselves and to our children to add something in our lives to the sum total of human happiness and the public welfare; for there is a mighty difference between always trying to get the better of the community in which we live, and giving *to* the community the best that there is in *us*.

"From the very beginning of our State, till now, there have

never been lacking men, who, by their strength of character and devotion to the public welfare, have made an impress on their day and generation, until at length Connecticut is known among her sister States as "The Land of Steady Habits." I can only refer now to two of them, Colonel Abraham Davenport of Stamford, and Hon. Roger Sherman of New Milford. Of the first, Timothy Dwight, in his book entitled 'Travels in New England and New York,' tells us that he was a judge in Danbury and a member of the Governor's Council in Hartford, and cites this incident concerning him:

"'The 19th of May, 1780, was a remarkably dark day. Candles were lighted in many houses, the birds were silent and disappeared, and the fowls retired to roost. The Legislature of Connecticut was then in session at Hartford. A very general opinion prevailed that the Day of Judgment was at hand. The House of Representatives, being unable to transact their business, adjourned. A proposal to adjourn the Council was under consideration. When the opinion of Colonel Davenport was asked, he answered, "I am against an adjournment. The day of judgment is either approaching, or it is not. If it is not, there is no cause for an adjournment; if it is, I choose to be found doing my duty. I wish, therefore, that candles may be brought."'"

"Such a man would be a success at any period of the nation's history.

"Of Roger Sherman, for many years a citizen of New Milford, time would fail me to properly speak of the long and distinguished public services which he rendered, not only to the community in which he lived, but to the nation at large.

"Some years ago, in studying his life and character, I collected from the Colonial Records of Connecticut every mention of his name, and will present the record* to the New Milford *Gazette* for publication; for, of such a citizen, New Milford may well be proud.

"The lives which these men lived, and countless others in the early days, should be an inspiration to us all.

* The chronology here referred to is to be found in Part I. of this volume, pages 115-118.

"Opportunity does not come alike to all, but these men simply did their duty honestly, faithfully, and well; and all of us can do the same to-day, in full confidence that the motto of our dear old State — '*Qui transtulit, sustinet*' — has not yet lost its meaning or its power."

After a witty speech by Rev. Marmaduke Hare, who spoke as an Englishman who is an American in the making, Mr. Beach terminated the exercises with these words:

"One brief thought in closing. As the sun sinks behind the hills of our western horizon to-night, we close the second century of the history of New Milford; but let us not linger too long in contemplation of the setting sun. Rather, let us turn our faces eastward and greet the rising sun, which will usher in the third century. Yes, it will be our privilege to enter the portals of another century, but certain it is that not one present will reach its exit. Let us press forward, doing faithfully each duty as it presents itself, placing our confidence 'in the God of our fathers, from out whose hand the centuries fall like grains of sand.'"

Tuesday evening was devoted to a magnificent display of fireworks in Riverside Park on the west bank of the Housatonic, and thus, in a blaze of glory, Governor's Day, the last of the New Milford Bi-Centennial, came to an end.

THE AFTERMATH

THE great event is over, and New Milford has excelled all records and exceeded all anticipations. This might sound egotistical, were it not a fact that it is only the plain truth, and corroborated by the speech of everyone who witnessed the Celebration. Our town stands higher to-day in public estimation than it ever stood before. As we look back, it is not possible to name an event which should have been omitted or a feature which should have been added. A four-days' celebration has been held, covering every point which such a celebration should cover; dignified and formal, where dignity and formality were appropriate, informal, happy and homelike at all other times.

A celebration very carefully planned, ably financed, and splendidly conducted; with every contingency provided for and the most minute details planned in advance. Our townspeople have shown that they can accomplish great enterprises, for it is the universal verdict of our guests, especially of those who have traveled much and participated in such events, that this was a great enterprise, never equaled in some respects, and never excelled in the matter of perfect appointment. Our townspeople have found, too, that in oratory, music, and literature they have men and women of whom any community may well be proud.

Some special points should be noted regarding the celebration. Perfect order was maintained throughout; during the four days, some sixteen thousand different people have occupied our streets, but, during all that time, there has been no disturbance, no violence or theft, no accident of any kind, and a very noticeable absence of drunkenness. That such admirable order prevailed is a great credit to our town and its visitors, and this community owes a debt of gratitude to the Committee of Public Safety and the selectmen of the town.

Perfect system prevailed, so that every event occurred on time and exactly as planned, with no break or delay at any point. This fact appealed very strongly to our official guests, who had attended other similar events, and knew that delays and unforeseen contingencies almost always arise at such times.

The decorations, public and private, were beautiful and appropriate, and brought the warmest commendation from visitors.

The literary, religious, and historical exercises were of a very high class. Every address and sermon being most appropriate to the occasion and excellent of its kind.

The musical programme was splendidly conceived and carried out, and high praise is due the committee, the chorus, and, especially, Professor Edwin G. Clemence.

The pleasure and success of the Celebration were very largely added to by the presence of Gartland's Tenth Regiment Band of Albany during the entire four days. Such splendid band and orchestral music was never heard here before.

The Loan Exhibit was a great success; admirably managed and very greatly admired.

The spectacular features were beyond any criticism. Both parades were perfect in appearance and in management, and the fireworks received the highest praise. The Civic and Military Parade was a surprise to everyone; newspaper men and guests, who had seen the world's greatest parades, declared that the School Division had never been equaled in originality and attractiveness. Our prominent visitors stated that, while a great city undoubtedly could do as well, no great city ever had done as well.

New Milford has won a high place in the estimation of thousands, and has gained vastly in civic pride and public spirit; may these, and the good feeling engendered by the Celebration, last for the next two hundred years.—*New Milford Gazette.*

The day after the close of the Bi-Centennial Celebration, the President of the Bi-Centennial Committee received the following letter:

"EXECUTIVE DEPARTMENT, STATE OF CONNECTICUT,
"HARTFORD, June 19.
"HON. H. S. MYGATT, New Milford, Conn.

"MY DEAR MR. MYGATT: Upon my return to Hartford, I want to say just a few words to you in appreciation of the scope of the celebration prepared by you and your fellow committeemen on the occasion of the Bi-Centennial of the town of New Milford. It was a success in every particular, and reflects great credit upon your community, and upon the men who planned and carried it out.

"For myself, personally, and the members of my staff, let me say we enjoyed every minute of our visit, and appreciate to the fullest extent the hearty welcome and the unfailing courtesy of your people.

"It was a source of regret to me, and I learned from others that it grieved them, too, that you were ill and unable to see the fruit of your thought and labor. I hope it will be a gratification to you to know that what you wrought was so well carried out by those who took up the work and followed your plans. You have reason to feel very proud of the whole affair, and I trust that you will soon be restored to health and strength, and be able to return to your delightful home town.

"With best wishes, I am sincerely yours,
"ROLLIN S. WOODRUFF."

The same day, the following letter came to Charles M. Beach:

"EXECUTIVE DEPARTMENT, STATE OF CONNECTICUT,
"HARTFORD, June 19.
"MR. CHARLES M. BEACH, New Milford, Ct.

"MY DEAR MR. BEACH: Upon my return to Hartford I want to congratulate you and your fellow committeemen, and, in fact, the entire town, upon the magnificent celebration of New Milford's Bi-Centennial. I wish also to thank you for your unfailing courtesy and your thoughtfulness for the comfort of myself and staff during our delightful stay there.

"I enjoyed it myself very much, and I am proud that Connecticut holds New Milford as one of her communities. The enterprise of your citizens, and the scope of their celebration, is equal to what much larger places might have attempted, but few of New Milford's size. We shall remember our visit there with much satisfaction.

"Sincerely yours,
"ROLLIN S. WOODRUFF."

Another letter of similar purport came to H. LeRoy Randall (Chairman of the Bi-Centennial Finance Committee) a few days later:

"DANBURY, June 22, 1907.
"H. LeROY RANDALL, Esq., New Milford, Conn.

"MY DEAR SIR: New Milford has reason to feel proud over the success of the Bi-Centennial. The Governor said he had the time of his life, and so say we all of us.

"Yours very truly,
"J. MOSS IVES,
"Of the Governor's Staff."

THE FINANCES OF THE CELEBRATION

The work of the Finance Committee and Treasurer was not only of the most vital importance to the success of the Bi-Centennial, but was so remarkable in many ways as to deserve a chapter to itself.

When the first estimates of cost were made, about $4000 was, in round figures, the amount asked for. To many this seemed a large sum to raise by subscription, but the Finance Committee stated without hesitation that the amount would be raised, and more if needed; and the promise was made good by a total subscription of about $5000, secured in an almost incredibly short time. This was accomplished without any noise or public display, and was the result of careful planning and perfect system. The funds were paid out by the Treasurer to the several committees, on approval of the Executive Committee, and a most accurate and detailed account of all expenditures was kept by the Treasurer, and may be inspected by subscribers at any time. There remained a substantial balance on hand after all bills were paid, and while this will probably be devoted to publishing the Book of the Bi-Centennial, the sales of the volume—when published—should return to the treasury the amount expended, and more. No appropriation was asked for from the town treasury, and the only items of expense met by the town were the necessary ones of decorating its own buildings and furnishing the police force during the Celebration. It is safe to state that no enterprise of this nature was ever more ably and successfully financed than was the New Milford Bi-Centennial of 1907.

INDEX

NOTE. Names given in lists, such as soldiers in the wars, members of committees and contributors to the loan exhibit, may be found by reference to the pages under "Soldiers," "Committees," "Loan Exhibit," etc.

Adams, John, 16
Addis, John F., 276
Addresses
  Charles M. Beach, 283, 285, 288
  Simeon E. Baldwin, 232
  Rev. George S. Bennitt, 171, 208, 215
  Daniel Davenport, 255
  Charles N. Hall, 137
  Samuel Hart, 228
  Ebenezer J. Hill, 290
  Rev. John T. Huntington, 171
  W. Frank Kinney, 170
  Rev. Timothy J. Lee, 284
  Edwin W. Marsh, 171
  Timothy Dwight Merwin, 171
  Rev. Watson L. Phillips, 288
  Rev. Charles J. Ryder, 202, 208
  Henry C. Sanford, 171
  Frederic W. Williams, 228, 232
  Rollin S. Woodruff, 286
  Boardman Wright, 171
  Frederick A. Wright, 202
Adelphi Institute, 92, 112
Agriculture, 84
Allen, Ethan, 42
Andrews, Governor, 76
Anthony, George W., 87
Aunty Thatcher, 79
Automobile Parade, 226
Averill, J. K., 93, 112

Baldwin, Albert N., 112
  Ashel, 32
  Hezekiah, 32, 33
  Israel, 32, 33, 104, 107
  Jared, 42
  John, 42, 226
  Jonas, 42
  Jonathan, 98
  Josiah, 33
  Judthon, 40
  Simeon, 105, 106, 107
  Simeon E., 232
  Theodore, 42
  Theophilus, 102

Band, 94, 137, 296
Banks, 94, 95, 112, 113
Barnes, Andrew G., 86
Bartlett, Isaiah, 3, 98
Barton, Edward, 88
Bassett, Abigail, 26, 27, 28, 29
  Alice Canfield, 26
  Josiah, 26, 28, 79
Battles
  Danbury Alarm, 39, 40
  Germantown, 42
  Heights of Abraham, 34
  Kipps Bay, 35
  Monmouth, 42
  Mud Forts, 42
  Princeton, 39, 42
  Saratoga, 42
  Siege of Boston, 35
  Stony Point, 42
  Ticonderoga, 42
  Trenton, 39
  White Plains, 35
Beach, Charles M., 297, 283, 285, 288
  Rev. Mr., 12
Beard, Samuel, 100
Beebe, Samuel, 99
Beecher, Eleazer, 110
Beeman, Hannah, 14
Bennett, Caleb, 104
  James, 33
Bennitt, Rev. George S., 171, 208, 215
Benson, Henry, 110
Bentley, Charles P., 139
Black, Mrs. William D., 9, 90, 93
  William D., 19, 90
Blaisdell, Roger, 36, 38, 39
Blatchford, Elnathan, 32
Blizzard, 113
Board of Trade, 13, 97
Boardman, Daniel, 4, 8, 9, 14, 101, 108, 109
  Rev. Daniel, 99, 100
  David S., 20, 111
  Homer, 109
  Rev. Mr., 34
  Sherman, 14, 104, 105, 107

Bolles, Joshua A., 93, 94
Booth, Charles H., 95
　Henry W., 95
　Reuben, 104, 106
Booth's Assembly Room, 17
Bostwick, Amos, 41
　Benjamin, 41, 98
　Bushnell, 104, 109
　Daniel, 98
　Ebenezer, 41
　Elisha, 41, 109
　Elijah, 41
　Henry S., 87
　Mrs. Henry, 11
　Isaac, 35, 36, 39, 40, 41, 43, 103
　Israel, 41
　Joel, 41
　John, 98, 99, 101, 102
　John, Jr., 98, 99
　Joseph, 102
　Nathan, 108
　Nathaniel, 101
　Oliver, 41
　Ruben, 32, 106, 107
　Robert, 107
　Samuel, 13, 104
　Solomon, 41
　Solomon E., 112
　Walter B., 87
　Zadock, 32
Botsford, Nathan, 13
Bounty for Continental Service, 105
Breinig, David E., 91
Bridges, 8, 90, 101, 102, 103, 108, 109, 110, 111, 112, 113
Bridgewater, 84, 86, 93, 112, 171
Bridgewater Society, 86, 93
Bristol, Mrs. Andrew, 92, 113
　Mrs. Isaac, 226, 227
　Isaac B., 87, 95
Brooks, Thomas, 103, 107
Brookfield, 84, 107
Bronson, John, 32
Brownson, Benjamin, 105, 106, 107
　Roger, 98
　Samuel, 98, 99, 100
　Thomas, 104
Buck, Barrall, 32
　David, 32
　Ephraim, 107, 108
Buckingham, Earl, 94, 112
Buell, David, 33, 36, 38, 39, 40, 42, 43
Burying Ground, 100, 101, 103, 107
Buttonmaking, 87, 113

Cablegram, 173
Calhoun, George B., 91
　Newell, 97

Callahan, Francis, 86
Camp, Abram, 104, 107
　Israel, 107, 108
Canfield, Alanson, 77
　Amos, 41
　Ezra, 41
　Herman, 108
　Jeremiah, 33, 104, 106
　John, 42
　Joseph, 33, 103
　Josiah, 33, 42
　Moses, 42
　Nathaniel, 42
　Samuel, 15, 34, 42, 101, 102, 104, 106, 108, 109
Carr, Mrs. Helen, 15, 16
Chittenden, Frederick G., 94
　Stephen, Jr., 108
Church organized, 100
Church singing, 13
Churches, 4, 9, 10, 93, 109
　Advent, 12
　Baptist, 108, 110, 111
　Congregational, 10, 12, 102, 111, 114
　Episcopal, 12, 102, 108, 109, 113
　Methodist, 12, 110
　Methodist Episcopal, 110, 112
　Quaker Meetinghouse, 101, 108
　Roman Catholic, 12, 112
　Union, 110, 114
Civic and Military Parade, formation of, 277 to 283
Clark, James S., 110
Clarke, George, 98
　Samuel, 100
　Thomas, 98
Clemence, Edwin G., 136, 274, 296
Cogswell, William, 104
Collings, David, 32
Colonial Reception, 275
Commercial Club, 97, 276
Committee on Colonial Features, 128, 134
　Colonial Reception, 123, 130, 134, 275; Assistants, 275
　On Decoration, 123, 129, 133
　District, 131, 132, 133
　Executive, 123, 128, 130
　On Exercises, 123, 128, 131
　Finance, 123, 128, 130, 299
　General Arrangements, 122, 123 to 128
　On Historical Research and Permanent Publication, 123, 130, 133
　Of Inspection and Correspondence, 104, 105
　Of Inspection on Provisions, 107

INDEX 303

Committee—*Continued*
  Of Invitation, Reception and Entertainment, 123, 129, 133, 170, 275, 276
  Loan Exhibit, 123, 130, 134
  Nominating, 122
  On Public Health and Comfort, 134
  On Public Safety, 123, 130, 133
  On Publicity, 123, 129, 133
  On Refreshments, 123, 129
  On Religious Observances, 123, 131, 133
  On Vocal Music, 123, 130, 134
Comstock, John, 104
  Samuel, 102, 104
Confederacy, articles of, voted on, 105
Couch, Ebenezer, 34, 35, 39, 44, 103, 105
Crossing the Delaware, 39
Curtis, Lewis F., 90
Cushman's Tavern, 43

Daton, Daniel, 32
Daughters of the American Revolution, Roger Sherman Chapter, 114
Davenport, Daniel, 255
Dayton, Abraham, 106, 107
  Nathan, 106
DeForest, Isaac, 106
Delegates in Congress, 105
Delevan, Marcus L., 93
Douglas, Dominie, 32
Drinkwater, Thomas, 34
  William, 33, 39, 40
Dunlap, Robert, 226, 227

Earliest settlers, 3, 4, 98
Ecclesiastical Society, 15
Electric light, 90, 114
Ellis, Rev. Elisha J., 196
Emmons, Edwin J., 95
Erwin, Robert, 93
  Silas, 95
Everett, Daniel, 16, 104, 106, 107

Fairchild, Jesse, 32
Ferriss, Joseph, 101
  Sarah, 98
  Zachariah, 3, 32, 98, 99
Fires, 21, 96, 112, 114
Fire Company, 95, 96, 111
Fire Department, 276
Fireworks, 294
Fisher, Beatrice, 226
  Moses, 32
Flag, 139
  Pole, 133, 139

Garlicks, Henry, 89
Gas, 90
Gaylord, Benjamin, 104, 105, 107
  Deacon, 42
  Ebenezer, 107
  Homer, 89
  Nathan, 106
  Peter, 89, 109
  William, 99, 100, 101, 102
Gaylordsville, 84, 89
Giddings, Franklyn Henry, 93
  Levi P., 3, 8, 90
  Minot S., 7
Gillett, William, 101
Grand List, 101
" Green," The, 11, 18, 19, 21
Green, General, 40
  Seymour S., 86, 95
  William G., 86, 121
Griffin, Charles E., 90
Grist Mill, 88, 89, 90, 100, 106, 109, 113
Griswold, John, 100
  Rev. Stanley, 108
Good Shepard's Lodge, 113
Gould, William, 32
Governor's Day, 277

Hall, Charles N., 137, 173
  David, 32
  Elijah, 85, 89, 109
  Perry, 85
Hanke, E. W., 87
Hare, Rev. Marmaduke, 208
  Rev. Samuel, 181
Hart, Samuel, 228
Hats manufactured, 86, 110
Hartwell, Joseph, 107
Hawley, Benjamin, 32
  Joseph R., 94
  Nehemiah, 107
Hayes, Abraham, 108
Heacock, Rev. Stephen, 202
Highways, 100, 112
Hill, Albert S., 88, 112
  Merritt W., 87
  Samuel R., 139
  Samuel R. Jr., 139
Hine, Abel, 104, 106
  Anan, 110
  Edward S., 226
  Frank, 173
  Henry D., 226, 227
  James, 11, 95, 108
  Noble, 107
  Walter C., 134
Hinman, Colonel, 33
Historical Meeting, 228
Hitchcock, Isaac, 32
  Samuel, 99

304 INDEX

Hoar, George F., 94
"Home," by Mary Murdoch Mason, 172
Hotchkiss, Ebenezer, 104, 105, 106, 107
Housatonic Agricultural Society, 112
Housatonic Institute, 92, 112
Hungerford, J. Edwin, 97
Huntington, Rev. John T., 171
Indian Deed, 98

Industries
  Agricultural, 84
  Buttonmaking, 87, 113
  Electric light, 90, 114
  Gas, 90
  Grist Mill, 88, 89, 90, 100, 106, 109, 113
  Hatmaking, 86, 110
  Iron Works, 89, 102
  Lime Works, 90, 114
  Lounges, 87
  Machinery, 88, 111
  Paper, 88, 112
  Pottery, 91
  Plows, 89, 109
  Saw Mill, 88, 89, 106, 109
  Tobacco, 85
  Wood Finishing, 91, 114
  Wool and Linen, 89
Ingersoll, Briggs, 108
Ingleside School, 9, 93
Iron Works, 89, 102
Isbell, Robert H., 87
Ives, J. Moss, 298

Jacklin, Phil, 80
Jackson, George H., 97
  Uri, 107
Jones, Joseph, 32
  Mayor, 15, 16
Johnson, Rev. Frank A., 137, 195, 203
  J. R., 93
  Moses, 32
Jumel Mansion, 36

Kent, 4
Kindergarten, 113
Kinney, W. Frank, 170, 276
  Mrs. Sara T., 94
Knapp, Frederick, 131
  Levi S., 108
  Residence, 3, 10

Lafayette, General, 15, 105
Lake, H., 226
Landon, William P., 88
Lane, Jared, 103
Law, Jonathan, 99

Lazarus, Dandy, 79
Leach, Ray W., 95
Leavitt, Rufus, 87
Lee, Rev. Timothy J., 283
  Letter, 173, 297, 298
Lewis, Thomas, 107
Lime Works, 90, 114
Lines, C. W., 226
Loan Exhibition, 140
  List of Exhibits, 141 to 169
Lombardy Poplar, 103
Lonetown, 4
Long, C. F., 226
Longevity, 76, 81 to 83
Lounges manufactured, 87
Lynes, Joseph, 32

Machinery, 88, 111
Mail delivery, 18
Marsh Chauncey B., 89
  Daniel, 95, 111
  Edwin W., 171
  Egbert, 93
Mason, Mary Murdoch, 171
Masonic Hall, 276
Masters, Nicholas, 16
  Nicholas S., 108
McAllister, 85
McDougall, General, 105
McMahon, Albert H., 95
  George, 85
Meetinghouse, first, 10
Memorial Hall and Library, 95, 114
Memorial Tablet, 114
Merwin, Samuel, 107
  Samuel, Jr., 106
  Sylvanus, 110
  Timothy Dwight, 171
Miles, Justus, 88
  Tavern, 88
Milford Company, 3
Morgan, 42
Mosher, Lewis W., 139
Murphy, J. E., 226
  Robert E., 95
Mygatt, Andrew B., 95
  Eli, 95
  Henry S., 91, 95, 173, 297
  Roland F., 95

Neck, The, 84
Newbury Society, 84, 102, 107
New Milford Cadets, 139, 276
New Milford, became a town, 8
  Original extent of, 84
  Owners of, 22, 23
  Plantation, 8, 98
New Preston Society, 84
Newspapers, 93, 112, 113

INDEX

Nicholson, Angus, 89
Noble, Asahel, 106, 107
  Charles H., 95, 96
  David, 100
  George B., 226
  Gifford, 139, 276
  John, 3, 8, 9, 14, 31, 98, 99, 100
  John, Jr., 3, 98 101
  Lyman, 39
  Russell B., 96
  Stephen, 31, 99, 101, 102
  William, 40
  Zadock, 104
  Purchase, 100
Northrop, Amos, 104, 106
  David, 88
  Jasper A., 88, 111
  Joseph, 102
  Roswell, 88, 111
  Sheldon, 88, 111

Odd Fellows' Hall, 276
Old Sugar House Prison, 37
"Our Forefathers," by Charles N. Hall, 175
Oviatt, Thomas, 32
Owners of New Milford, 22, 23

Palmer, Rev. Solomon, 12, 102
Paper Mill, 88, 112
Parade, Automobile, 226
  Civic and Military, 277 to 283
  Marshals, aides for, 184
"Patent" granted, 98
Payment for Army Service, 105, 106, 107, 112, 113
Payne, Ezekiel, 102
Peck, Joseph, 98
Pendleton, Daniel, 40
Pepper, De Watt, 87
Peterson, Peter, 226, 227
Phillips, Chester, 40
  Ruben, 40
  Rev. Watson L., 288
Plantation of New Milford, 98
Platt, Daniel, 20
Plow Foundry established, 89, 109
Plumb, Rev. J. F., 202
Population, 97
Porter, Edward E., 91
  John, 106
Pottery, 91
Power Company, 114
Prindle, Samuel, 3, 98
Prudden, Peter, 30
Public Library and Memorial Hall, 93, 114

Quaker Meetinghouse, 101, 108
Quakers, 12, 102, 108

Railroad, 111
Randall, Charles, 95
  H. L., 226
  H. LeRoy, 95, 298
Read, John, 3, 4, 9
  Colonel John, 4
Redding, 4
Reed, John, 100
Reynolds, Isaac, 86
Richmond, Seeley, 85
Rivers, 84
Roads, 110, 111
Robburds, Mary, 20
Roberts, Gerardus, 20
  Mary, 103
  William, 89, 110
Robertson, James S., 226
Rochambeau, General, 15
Roger Sherman Hall, 3, 94, 113
Rogers, Ambrose S., 92, 112
Roosevelt, Theodore, 114
Ruggles, Joseph, 101, 104, 107
  Lazarus, 102
Ryan, Rev. Joseph, 200
Ryder, Rev. Charles J., 202, 208

Sabbath Day House, 4
Sabbath work fines, 109
Sabins, Charles, 20
Sanford, David C., 12
  Glover, 86, 110, 113
  Harry S., 95
  Henry C., 171
  Joseph, 86
  Zachariah, 104
Sawmill, 88, 89, 106, 109
Schools, 4, 14, 92, 103, 108
Schoverling, William, 87, 88
  Mrs. William, 88
Seelye, Benjamin, 106
Separatists, 12, 103
Sermons
  Rev. Elisha J. Ellis, 196
  Rev. Marmaduke Hare, 208
  Rev. Samuel Hare, 181
  Rev. Frank A. Johnson, 175
  Rev. Joseph Ryan, 200
  Rev. Harris K. Smith, 189
  Rev. Orville Van Keuren, 193
  Rev. S. D. Woods, 187
Settlement, 3
Silliman, Rev. C., 110
Singing School, 14
"Sitting Down" Place, 75
Shanty Town, 21, 97
Sherman, Roger, 6, 94, 101, 102, 115 to 118, 232
  Addresses on, 232 to 255
  William, 94, 102
Slavery, 20

Slaves liberated, 20, 103, 107
Smith, David, 106
  George, 104, 107
  Rev. H. K., 87, 202
  Joseph, 32
  Perry, 109
  Reuben, 106
Starr, Eli, 110, 114
  Joseph, 103
  Josiah, 106, 109
  William J., 18, 34, 80
Staub, Nicholas, 90
  Verton P., 95
Stebbins, Benoni, 99
Sterling, Vincent B., 85
Stilson, Cyrene, 14
Stoddard, Gideon, 33
Stone, Benjamin A., 92
  B. J., 112
  Mrs. B. J., 112
  Ithiel, 104, 105, 107
  Lyman B., 86
  Mary A., 92
Strong, Nehemiah, 108
Sturges, Everett J., 95
Social Life, 17
Societies
  Agricultural, 95
  Daughters of American Revolution, 94
  New Milford Washingtonian Temperance Benevolence, 111
Soldiers, lists of, 32, 33, 34
  In Civil War, 54 to 66
  In Colonial Wars, 45 to 49
  In Mexican War, 53
  In Revolution, 49 to 53
  In Spanish-American War, 66
  In War of 1812, 53
Soule, David E., 86
  George T., 226
  Tourney, 88, 95
  Winifred, 94
South Farm, 100
Sunday School, 113, 114

Talcott, John, 4
Taylor, George, 110, 112
  Rev. Nathaniel, 15, 17, 99, 108
  Rev. Nathaniel, Jr., 15
  Mrs. Nathaniel, 17
  Tamar, 15, 16
  William, 108, 109
Terrell, Terrill; [see Turrill]
Thatcher, Partridge, 20, 103, 107
Thayer, Augustine, 20
Tithing man, 11
Tobacco Raising, 85
Todd, Jonah, 104
Toll bridge, 111, 112

Tomlinson, Henry, 3
Topeka Hall, 75
Tornado, 108
Town Court, 97, 114
"Town Plot," 8
Township granted, 4, 99
Train band, 31
Transportation, 18
Treat, Gideon, 20
  John, 107
  Joseph, 98
  Robert, 98
Trott, A. N., 226, 227
Turrell, [see Turrill]
Turrill, (Terrell, Terrill, Turrell),
  Ashel, 33, 41
  Caleb, 26, 27, 28, 29, 33, 41
  Daniel, 26, 28
  Ebenezer, 32, 41
  Enoch, 33, 41
  Isaac, 33, 41
  James, 104, 106
  Joel, 41
  John, 33, 36, 39, 40, 41, 43
  John S., 95
  Major, 26
  Nathan, 33, 41
  Stephen, 34, 41, 44
  William, 109
  Zorvia Canfield, 26

Ufford, Abigail, 30
"Underground Railroad," 20
Union Circulating Library established, 108
Upton Post, G. A. R. organized, 113

Van Keuren, Rev. Orville, 193
Village Improvement Society, 18

Wallis, Benjamin, 32
Watson, E. M., 226
Wallace, Mrs., 226
Wanzer, Nicholas, 108
Ward, Andrew, 34, 104
Warner, Colonel, 42
  Elizur, 106, 107
  Henry O., 34, 95, 276
  John, 100, 110
  Lemuel, 107
  Martin, 32, 107
  Oliver, 104
  Reuben, 107, 109
  Samuel, 104, 105
Washington, General, 35, 36, 39, 84, 105
Water Company, 95, 113
Water Witch Engine Company, 113
Water Witch Hose Conpany, 276
Wayne, Anthony, 42

Webb, Charles, 35, 103
Weller, John, 98, 99
  Thomas, 98
Wells, Edwin S., 88, 112
  Mary C., 92, 113
  Philip, 94, 112
  William W., 88, 112
Whiting, Captain, 32
  Colonel Nathan, 32, 33
Whittlesey, George W., 94
Williams, Frederick W., 228, 232
  Jehiel, 19

Wilkinson, Jemima, 107
Wilson, Fred, 79
Wood finishing, 91, 114
Woodruff, Rollin S., 275, 276, 277, 283, 285, 286, 297, 298
Woods, Rev. S. D., 187, 202
Wool and linen manufactured, 89
Wooster, David, 32, 33, 103
Wright, Boardman, 171
  Frederick, A., 202

Yates, Paul, 106, 107

THE END

www.ingramcontent.com/pod-product-compliance
Lightning Source LLC
Chambersburg PA
CBHW031702230426
43668CB00006B/79